# Open-Book Management

# OPEN-BOOK MANAGEMENT

# MANAGEMENT

*The Coming
Business Revolution*

# John Case

📖 HarperBusiness
*A Division of HarperCollinsPublishers*

*Designed by Irving Perkins Associates*

The Library of Congress has catalogued the hardcover edition as follows:

Case, John, 1944–
    Open-book management : the coming business revolution / by John Case.
  — 1st edition.
      p.  cm.
    Includes bibliographical references and index.
    ISBN 0-88730-708-6
    1. Industrial management—Employee participation.  I. Title.
  HD5650.C345   1995
    658.3'152—dc20                              95-14603

ISBN 0-88730-802-3 (pbk.)

96 97 98 99 00 ❖/RRD 10 9 8 7 6 5 4 3 2 1

*For my father, Everett Needham Case*

# Contents

*Foreword: An Idea That Works*  xi

*Introduction: A Different Way of Thinking*  xv

**PART ONE:**

**WHY CHANGE? RUNNING A BUSINESS IN THE NEW ECONOMY**

1 THE DEMANDS OF THE MARKETPLACE  3

*Competition*  3

*The New Workplace*  10

*What It All Means*  14

2 EVOLUTION OF AN IDEA  18

*The Origin of Old-Style Management*  18

*Old Management Meets New Economy*  24

*The Birth of Open-Book Management*  29

3 OPEN-BOOK MANAGEMENT  37

*The Basics*  37

*The Turnaround at Pace Industries*  38

*The Homely Truths of Open-Book Management*  43

*Why It Works*  45

*The Power of Metaphor*  51

**PART TWO:**

**IMPLEMENTING OPEN-BOOK MANAGEMENT**

*Introduction: Changing a Company*  57

4 FIRST PRINCIPLE: INFORMATION, PLEASE!  61

*The Power of Information*  63

*What's the Right Information?*  66

*How to Do It*  68

*Confronting the Great Fear*  70

5  SECOND PRINCIPLE: BUSINESS LITERACY                              73

   *The Power of Business Literacy*                                  75
   *How to Do It*                                                    78

6  THIRD PRINCIPLE: EMPOWERMENT (WITH BRAINS)                       85

   *The Trend That Never Happened*                                   86
   *Empowerment with Brains*                                         87
   *How to Do It*                                                    90
   *Some Final Advice*                                               95

7  FOURTH PRINCIPLE: A STAKE IN SUCCESS                             97

   *The Pitfalls of Profit Sharing (and Bonuses)*                   97
   *The Open-Book Approach*                                         101
   *What about Stock Ownership?*                                    108

8  TEN WAYS TO GET STARTED                                         111

9  ONE COMPANY'S EXPERIENCE: A *FORTUNE* 500 MANUFACTURER          123

   *The Background*                                                 123
   *How It Works*                                                   124
   *The Payoffs*                                                    127

10 ONE COMPANY'S EXPERIENCE:  A SMALL SERVICE BUSINESS             130

   *The Background*                                                 130
   *How It Works*                                                   131
   *The Payoffs*                                                    135

11 ONE COMPANY'S EXPERIENCE:  A FAST-GROWTH "STAR"                 137

   *The Background*                                                 137
   *How It Works*                                                   139
   *The Payoffs*                                                    143

12 ONE COMPANY'S EXPERIENCE:  "THE BIGGEST BANK IN TOWN"          145

   *The Background*                                                 145
   *How It Works*                                                   147
   *The Payoffs*                                                    151

13 ONE COMPANY'S EXPERIENCE: A TELECOMMUNICATIONS GIANT           154

   *The Background*                                                 154
   *How It Works*                                                   155
   *The Payoffs*                                                    159

14  OBJECTIONS, COSTS, CHALLENGES                    162

15  A COMPANY OF BUSINESSPEOPLE                      175

    *Next Steps*                                     181
    *References*                                     183
    *Acknowledgments*                                187
    *Index*                                          191

# Foreword
# An Idea That Works

This book is about a new idea—a new way of running a business. It's called open-book management.

After you read the book, I hope you think the idea is a good one. But the real test of a new idea, in business as in any other endeavor, isn't how it looks on paper. It's whether the idea works in practice.

Open-book management works.

Don't take my word for it; listen to the people who are using it, every day, in their companies.

*"When employees understand the economics of business, they feel, think, and act like owners."*

—JIM SCHREIBER, VICE PRESIDENT FOR
CUSTOMER ASSURANCE AND
CORPORATE CONTROLLER, HERMAN MILLER

*"Our commitment to open-book management is unwavering. It's the key to our competitive advantage in the market."*

—LESLIE FISHBEIN, PRESIDENT,
KACEY FINE FURNITURE

*"It allowed us to involve all our associates in the (previously) mystical world of financials. Now our people know what's at stake—and how they can make a real impact on the numbers."*

—JOHN D. CALLAHAN, PRESIDENT,
ALLSTATE BUSINESS INSURANCE

*"After years of being a skeptic, I would never manage any other way again."*

—ERIC PAULSEN, PRESIDENT, ENGINES PLUS

*"The fundamental result of open-book management is this: Our people have become financial managers who understand how their day-to-day decisions affect the bottom line."*

—DAVID ZAPATKA, PRESIDENT, Z-TECH COMPANIES

*"By sharing our financial condition as well as our stock, we've greatly increased the bond between line workers and top management. The result: measurably increased owners' equity."*

—ED ZIMMER, PRESIDENT,
ECCO (ELECTRONIC CONTROLS CO.)

*"If business is truly a game, how can you expect to win when only a handful of players know the rules?"*

—DAVID R. DWINELL,
DWINELL'S VISUAL SYSTEMS

*"Before, problems were the responsibility of me or my management team. Now, the responsibility is spread out over our entire organization."*

—BILL PALMER, PRESIDENT,
COMMERCIAL CASEWORK

*"Employees are more apt to concentrate on the numbers that will produce a small victory for them—and that will improve the likelihood of a big victory for everyone."*

—ROBERT WOBLESKY, PRODUCTION DEPARTMENT,
COMMERCIAL CASEWORK

*"By opening the books and sharing financial information—both the good and the bad—we found that employees spend less time worrying about job security and more time helping the company grow and be profitable."*

—EMMA LOU BRENT, PRESIDENT AND
EMPLOYEE-OWNER, PHELPS COUNTY BANK

*"Open-book management has eliminated our company's self-imposed limitations."*

—SAMUEL H. SMITH, PRESIDENT,
SMITH & COMPANY, ENGINEERS

*"We are looking at the future here. Ten years from now the majority of successful businesses will be using some form of open-book management."*

—JOE E. JENKINS, CO-OWNER,
JENKINS DIESEL POWER

*"Open-book management and all of its implications have provided the opportunity for our corporation to transform the health, the wealth, the lives of our people."*

—CHUCK MAYHEW,
PRESIDENT, FOLDCRAFT

*"Our company was, is, and will continue to be open-book. Why? Trust—a two-way street for employees and employers."*

—PATRICK C. KELLY, PRESIDENT,
PHYSICIAN SALES AND SERVICE

*"Sports are a good example of open-book management—and you can put the same energy, drive, feedback, and reward systems that make a great sports team into your business. It has made all the difference in the world to us."*

—TOM CORBO, PRESIDENT, MANCO

*"Keeping a daily scorecard that shows each employee the financial results of the company is one of the most powerful management tools we use."*

—TED CASTLE, PRESIDENT, RHINO FOODS

*"Open-book management has made our people 'owners' in the best sense of the word. They celebrate when things go well, and they worry and try to help when things don't."*

—TERRY FULWILER, PRESIDENT,
WISCONSIN LABEL GROUP

*"Open-book management has built trust among our employees, empowered them to make smart decisions, and allowed them to see the bottom-line impact of those decisions."*

—RICHARD BOHNET, PRESIDENT, ACUMEN INTERNATIONAL

*"We're talking about a revolution in culture and dynamics within the organization—and believe me, your organization will change. We can no longer operate with the 'boss knows all' attitude."*

—NEIL SCHMID, PRESIDENT, VIKING GLASS

*"Open-book management has eliminated a significant amount of unnecessary stress throughout the company. Our people enjoy coming to work! Absenteeism is about 33 percent of what it was."*

—STEVE WILSON, PRESIDENT,
MID-STATES TECHNICAL STAFFING SERVICES

*"A high-growth company has so many uncertainties that people must deal with—the ONLY way is to share the numbers. Open everything."*

—CRAIG TAYLOR, PRESIDENT, VECTRA

*"There's a genuine desire within every level of the organization to learn about the business and to participate in planning and decision making. Today, more timely and better-informed decisions are being made."*

—MARY HANSEN, MANAGER, SPRINT GOVERNMENT SYSTEMS DIVISION

Chris Lee is managing editor of *Training,* a magazine for corporate human-resources professionals. Not long ago Lee visited several open-book companies and came away dazzled by what she saw. She wrote: "Companies that practice open-book management seem to have captured some sort of lightning in a bottle."

So there you are. If you want to know what all the shouting is about, this is the book that will tell you.

It explains what open-book management is and why it's essential in today's business world. It tells, in nitty-gritty detail, how to implement it. This is a book that you will not only read but use, and that you'll want everyone in your company to read and use as well.

The ideas in it can transform a business. They already have transformed a lot of businesses. They can transform yours, too.

# Introduction

# A Different Way of Thinking

Bob Frey was trying to change his company, and there were times when he got the uncomfortable feeling that he was making no progress. None. Zero. It was at these times that he'd go berserk.

Maybe he'd be discussing a production run with line workers.

"How can we cut the waste on this run?" he'd ask. Or, "How are we going to allocate the overtime on this order?"

The workers would give him the time-honored Employee's Reply, used by employees from all walks of life. "That's not my job."

He'd ask them why it wasn't their job. They'd say it just wasn't.

He'd remind them he wanted a workplace in which everyone was involved. He'd ask them how he could have involvement unless people helped make decisions.

"I don't know," they'd answer. "Because that's not my job either. That's your job."

That's when Frey would blow his cork. Rant and rave. Yell and holler.

Like most losses of temper, these had a history.

Frey's company is called Cin-Made. It manufactures mailing tubes and other containers. When he and a partner bought it in 1984, it seemed to have every problem in the book. Its product line was too broad. Its machinery was antiquated. The unionized workforce was pugnacious.

Frey, new to running a company, didn't always help matters. He liked to go out on the floor with a stopwatch and time people as they did their jobs. One morning he remarked that running the machines looked like work a moron could do. "By noon, the whole workforce had heard that I thought they were mentally retarded."

Cin-Made's previous owner had signed an impossibly generous

union contract shortly before Frey bought the company. It called for three straight years of across-the-board raises, 9 percent a year, even though orders and profits were on the decline. When the contract expired, Frey said he'd have to have hefty wage cuts. The workers went out on strike.

Frey and his partner tried to keep the factory going—which caused no end of mirth on the picket line. "Now there really was a moron running the machines."

But Frey wouldn't budge, because Cin-Made's situation wouldn't allow it. It was hold the line or go broke. Faced with such bullheadedness, the union got scared and came back to work.

Frey had won the battle. But the war, alas, was still raging. Workers "stuck to their job descriptions like glue." They filed grievances at the drop of a hat. Peeved, Frey quit buying dinner for those working overtime, reversing a long tradition. Morale plunged.

Finally, after a little while of this guerrilla skirmishing, Frey says he wised up.

It wasn't a sudden epiphany, it was several small ones.

If things didn't change, the business would never succeed.

Life is too short to spend fighting.

So one day he announced that the adversarial era was over and that employees would now be expected to involve themselves in running the business.

He began holding monthly gatherings—"state-of-the-business meetings"—to show everyone the company's financials.

In place of raises, he instituted a generous profit-sharing program. The employees could make more money—a lot more money—so long as they, and the company, earned it.

Frey attacked on other fronts as well. He got costs in line. He developed a strategic plan for product development and marketing.

And he started to go berserk whenever he heard the words "It's not my job."

At first the outbursts were real. Later he started faking them a bit. "Sometimes," he confesses, "I didn't know myself if I was really mad or simply playacting. But people had to understand that those were words they weren't allowed to utter."

Over time, at any rate, the outbursts grew less frequent, and finally disappeared. The reason was that things were beginning to change.

Employees did get involved. They learned quality-control techniques. They began tracking scrap rates and efficiency. An employee committee took over scheduling. At the meetings, Frey and the workers would discuss year-to-date sales and operating efficiencies and profit projections. People began to solve problems on their own.

A new spirit began to permeate the place. "I couldn't see how we were going to protect ourselves and keep our jobs if the company went under," reflected Ocelia Williams, a shop steward for the United Paperworkers. "And I couldn't see how the company could work unless we all took our share of responsibility."

Today, says Frey, productivity is up 30 percent. Grievances amount to one or two a year. The workers don't get traditional cost-of-living raises; instead, a skill-based pay system (administered by employees) grants increases to people who demonstrate proficiency in new jobs. Profit sharing adds about 33 percent to everyone's base pay.

Best of all, profits are healthy. The company is prospering. The future is secure. You don't hear the phrase "It's not my job" anymore.

The workers at Cin-Made, thinking quite differently than they used to, understand their job very well. Their job is to make money.

This is what open-book management is about: creating companies in which everybody understands that they are competing in a marketplace, trying to make money.

In open-book companies, people learn to follow the numbers and help make decisions. They learn to think and act like owners, like business-people, and not like hired hands.

Strip a business down to its essentials, after all, and what is it? It's just an organization that provides products or services and that hopes to make a profit in doing so.

The business's success in this endeavor determines whether the owners will get a return on their investment, and how much that return will be. It determines whether employees' economic prospects are bright or dim. Over the long haul, only profitable companies can provide job security, chances for advancement, and a rising standard of living.

*Since the economic future of every blessed individual on a company's payroll depends on whether the company succeeds in the marketplace, everyone who works there is "in business" all the time, whether they know it or not.*

So let's think about this a moment.

Everyone is in business.

But in most companies just a handful of people, the owners or the top executives, are the *only ones* charged explicitly with worrying about whether the business as a whole is making money.

In a store, the responsibility for profit or loss belongs to the manager, not to the sales clerks. In a machine shop it lies with the owner, not the machinists. In a corporate division it falls to the appropriate vice president or regional chief, not to the minions toiling below. "P&L responsibility" is the bureaucratic phrase.

Wow. This is like a school in which only the principal cares how good an education the kids are getting. Or a football team in which only the coach and the quarterback care who wins. Or an army in which—well, you get the idea.

I guess we should be grateful that somebody, somewhere has P&L responsibility.

If you have P&L responsibility, you think like a businessperson. You try to understand the big picture. You make decisions, and you know you'll be held accountable for them, by the marketplace if by no one else. On the job, you do whatever has to be done. Even if you're not the owner, you act like an owner. Like Harry Truman, you know that the buck stops with you.

Businesses need this kind of thinking. At Cin-Made, it was good that Bob Frey thought like this. It's a lot better now that everyone else is, too.

This way of thinking pays off for individuals as well. It's what makes business fun.

That's right: Running a business is fun. It's rewarding. Satisfying. You match wits with the marketplace every day. You're a player in the most important game around. If you win—if you do well—you can make some real money.

But what if, like 99 percent of the employees in America, you *don't* have P&L responsibility?

Well, then you think like a hired hand. You worry about your job, not the business. You run the department, serve the customers, operate the machines, distribute the mail. Think? "We don't pay you to think" was the classic rejoinder to the employee who came up with an idea about how to save some money or bring in some extra revenue. Managers today know it's bad form to be so blunt. But not many really want their underlings to meddle in managerial matters. And not many employees think they're supposed to understand the big picture.

As for fun, well, a few workplaces are fun. Most are drab, humdrum, routine. Instead of the excitement of being in business, employees have the thrill of putting in their time and picking up their paycheck. As my kids used to say when asked to clean up their rooms, some fun.

Note that this bizarre division of labor isn't limited to factories and fast-food shops. It permeates the business world.

I have a friend—call her Carole—who works for a big health mainte-nance organization (HMO). She's a highly trained mental-health clinician with an advanced degree and all kinds of certificates and licenses. So are the six or eight colleagues who work with her in her department. Her employer operates in a brutally competitive marketplace, and so has been relentlessly scrutinizing its costs. Carole's department is one of many that has come under sharp pressure to cut its expenses.

So, does the department manager publicize the budget and teach the clinicians to understand it, thereby engaging these highly educated minds in figuring out how to protect their livelihoods?

Hah. Of course not. "It's my job to protect you from budget pres-sures," the boss likes to say, as if he could. Neither Carole nor any of the other clinicians has any idea how much the department spends, let alone any responsibility for it. When the HMO does well in the marketplace, the bonus she gets might as well be pennies from heaven. When it does poorly, the threat of a layoff is a bolt from the blue.

It's hardly surprising, of course, that managers cling to their authority and that employees rarely think of themselves as businesspeople. That's the way we do things in this country.

But Americans' ideas about how to run a company evolved in a very different kind of economy. Today's new economy—fast-moving, entre-preneurial, fiercely competitive—demands another kind of approach entirely. Chapter 1 in this book describes what has changed in the mar-ketplace and why it matters for the way businesses are run.

Chapter 2 then traces the evolution of American managerial ideas, starting with the old style of rigid, bureaucratic, chain-of-command man-agement and going right on through to the invention of something quite different. We'll consider a few of the way stations on the journey to open-book management. (Think of phrases like *employee empowerment, involvement, teams,* and all the other buzzwords that trip off the manage-ment consultant's tongue.) We'll also see how the open-book idea emerged from the experience of a handful of extraordinarily successful companies such as Springfield ReManufacturing Corp.

If you're already sold on the idea of open-book management and just want to know how to do it, I'll confess the truth: You can skip the first two chapters. The how-to stuff begins in chapter 3 and goes right on through to the end.

But if you're new to the concept, those first two chapters are essential. The reason: Open-book management wasn't born in a vacuum. It has evolved precisely because it helps companies compete in this mercurial new economy of ours. There's a close fit between how companies need to act if they're going to succeed in the new marketplace and how they organize themselves internally. Today, I firmly believe that the open-book approach is the only way to go. But it isn't because I or anyone else says so. It's because, in the Darwinian world of the new economy, companies need open-book principles to survive.

## What Open-Book Management Is—and Is Not

Open-book management, you'll note, has two components. Open books. And management.

Open the books! Yes—you need to teach employees to understand the budgets and the income statements and the cash-flow analyses and the balance sheet. That's the first step in helping them to think and act like businesspeople rather than like hired hands.

Company owners and executives, the people who are supposed to watch out for the company as a whole, take it for granted that they'll have access to all those financial tabulations (and more) whenever they need them. The financials are their fundamental business tools. They measure success or failure. They help identify problems. They're useful in scoping out opportunities.

Opening the books means a whole lot more than just announcing quarterly results the way publicly traded companies do. It means communicating *all* the relevant information, monthly or weekly or daily, to people in every plant or department or store or unit within a company. No executive in his or her right mind would wait until the books are closed at the end of a quarter to gauge a unit's performance. And no employee who wants to act like a businessperson should have to make do with old data, either.

Sure, people who don't have CPA or MBA after their names—which is to say nearly everyone on the payroll—will need some instruction in using these tools. But as we'll see in chapter 5, that needn't be so difficult. (And yes, publicly traded companies must take care not to run afoul of the SEC's insider rules. We'll take that up, too.)

What we're talking about here, however, isn't just open books. It's open-book *management*.

Business management, whatever else it may mean, means trying to reach certain objectives. And the point of getting the data out there is so that people can work together in pursuit of those objectives.

They'll need a reason to do so. A stake in the company's success, like Frey's profit sharing. That's what makes it exciting and worthwhile.

And they'll need systems and procedures for making decisions. You can't empower people in a vacuum.

But when you give people those things, stand back.

Open-book management cuts through all the interpersonal garbage, the divisiveness and buck-passing and mistrust, that hamstring most companies' attempts to get things done. You may catch a whiff of this muck now and then in your own company. What happens when sales goals aren't met? The sales department blames marketing, and vice versa. If customer complaints mount, customer service blames the operations people. Operations blames the engineers who designed the product in the first place.

Meanwhile, line employees (who figure such troubles aren't their concern anyway) decide management is a bunch of idiots who don't know what they're doing. They may be right.

But when the books are open, everyone can see what's going on. It's harder for managers to fall back on excuses or to point the finger at someone else. Open-book management gets people involved and helps them take responsibility rather than shirk it. It's a way by which everyone in the business can hold each other accountable.

Chapter 3 describes and explains the basic ideas. Chapters 4 through 7 spell out the principles—what you need to implement open-book management. Chapters 8 through 14 get into nitty-gritty real-world experiences of companies in a wide variety of industries.

But before we plunge in, it may be a good idea to understand what open-book management is not. I don't want to get hauled into court for false advertising.

### Open-book management is not a panacea.

To succeed in today's marketplace, companies need an effective strategy. They need—as their industry and situation may require—smart marketing, timely innovation, astute use of financial resources, the ability to deliver a combination of price and value that's better than the competition.

Open-book management isn't a substitute for any of this. It *is* a way of unlocking the power of people. Once a company's leaders have determined the company's strategic direction, open-book management gets everyone pulling together in that direction.

### Open-book management isn't a substitute for TQM or reengineering or any other operational overhaul.

If your company needs to boost quality levels or reinvent its business processes, read the right books and hire the right consultants and go to it.

Contrary to what the consultants tell us, not every business needs these overhauls. But some do.

Don't be surprised, however, if your efforts run into a wall of skepticism—not to say cynicism—on the part of the very people who are supposed to begin doing things differently. Frontline employees generally mistrust management's motives. Many may figure they'll just hunker down until this latest fad goes away.

But it's different if the books are open. Seeing the numbers—and understanding them—helps people understand why TQM or reengineering might be important. It helps dispel the doubts. If you need to implement one of these programs, open-book management will give it a power boost.

### And open-book management is not a single system.

There is no manual for implementing the idea because there is no cookbook way of doing it.

The companies that you'll read about in this book have learned a lot from each other. They've emulated pioneers such as Springfield ReManufacturing Corp. But though every open-book company shares certain values and principles, each operates differently. "It's more of a philosophy than a how-to-do-it, step-by-step program," says Ronnie Miller, a senior manufacturing engineer at Pace Industries' Cast-Tech Division. That's OK with Miller, and indeed with most open-book practitioners. "Anybody in business over ten years realizes there is no perfect management system that fits every business."

One other note—an important one—about this book.

Most business books draw their case studies from the ranks of the *Fortune* 500. They tell stories of IBM and Xerox and BankAmerica. This one tells stories of Phelps County Bank and Mid-States Technical Staffing Services and Acumen International.

Granted, there are some names in this book that you'll recognize. Sprint. Intel. The Body Shop. Chesapeake Corp., number 388 on the 1994 *Fortune* 500. But most of the companies that are pioneering open-book management are small and midsized companies, entrepreneurial upstarts, turnarounds.

If you're tempted to discount their experience because they're small and your company isn't, don't. It will be the biggest mistake of your business life unless you happen to have invested your grandmother's savings in S&Ls, in which case it will be the second biggest mistake.

For one thing, these are the companies of the New Economy.

These are the companies that are reshaping industries, introducing innovations, exploring new business niches. They're the companies that are creating most of the new jobs. Many, incidentally, aren't staying any too small. In 1980, Springfield ReManufacturing Corp. was a small, struggling division of International Harvester (now Navistar). Manco, the consumer-goods distributor profiled in chapter 11, was a modest-sized marketer of duct tape. Today, both are $100 million companies and are growing like gangbusters.

Frankly, it's among these companies that the best new ideas are evolving. Remember what Justice Brandeis said about the states and the federal government? The states were "laboratories of democracy." They could try out a variety of policies and programs. Washington could pick up on whatever worked best. Entrepreneurial companies are like the states. The most ambitious among them are literally reshaping—re-creating—our nation's ideas about how business should be run. Big companies need to pick up on these ideas, now, before they find themselves left behind.

It may scarcely matter how big your company is, anyway. Ultimately, every big company is made up of a lot of small companies. Each K mart store has to operate in the black. Each General Motors plant better be making a profit. Every department at IBM needs to make its numbers and stick to its budget.

That's the level at which open-book management operates. It isn't a grand corporate strategy designed to please Wall Street. It's a shop-floor, office-level, business-unit reinvention of the way people in a company work together. Reinventing a big company in this way is harder than reinventing a small company. But it may be the only way a big company can compete in today's treacherous economy.


I began this introduction with a story, and I'll end it with one. It's a story told by Jack Stack.

You'll run into Stack a lot in this book. Remember I said that Springfield ReManufacturing Corp. (SRC) is one of the pioneers of open-book management? Well, Stack is chief executive and guiding light of that company and the prime creator of its system, known as the Great Game of Business. He has even written a book by that name. When you're finished with this book you should read that one. If you haven't already.

Anyway, Stack goes around giving speeches and doing a little consulting about open-book management on the side, and one day he finds himself talking to a guy who manages a Holiday Inn. The Holiday Inn manager is griping because his occupancy rate is averaging only 67 percent. That's below breakeven, and he is losing money.

"I ask him," says Stack, "'Who else knows that's the critical number?'" And he says he's the only one.

"And I say, 'Right, and what's the maid's job? To clean so many rooms and turn the beds down and put the mints on the pillow?' And he says, 'That's about it.'

"I say, 'What if we put everybody, maids included, on an incentive program to increase the occupancy rate? And what if we communicate that number every single day?' I ask him what he needs to do to make money, and he says if he ran over 72 percent it'd be great. So I propose that, for anything over that, the employees get a bonus."

Stack pauses for effect. "At the end of eighteen months they were up to 85 percent. The funny thing was, they now had people running out, carrying bags, greeting customers, being personable."

Only one thing, Stack says, he can't understand. "For all that time before, what kept the manager from thinking that all the employees could understand that critical number—and could respond to it?"

As I say, a different way of thinking. Happy reading, and happy experimenting. In a few years, I hope, there will be a new edition of this book, complete with new experiences to recount. Maybe your company's will be among them.

Part One

# WHY CHANGE? RUNNING A BUSINESS IN THE NEW ECONOMY

## CHAPTER 1

# The Demands of the Marketplace

## Why companies can't be managed the same old way

It's no secret: The business world is changing rapidly.

Despite this only-too-obvious fact, many companies are managed the same way they always were. You might wonder about that. I certainly do, particularly when I run into a printer, say, who thinks two weeks is a pretty good delivery time on a job, when I can get a two-*day* turnaround down the street. But management is another matter, which we'll get to in a little while. The economy has to come first, because a new approach to running a company is just so much idle chatter unless it fits the new economic environment.

So peer out into the marketplace, into that cacophony of customers and suppliers and moneymaking that you—and every other businessperson—must operate in. What you will see is a new economy, different in two major respects from the world in which most of us grew up.

## Competition

IN THE NEW ECONOMY, THE MARKETPLACE IS MORE COMPETITIVE—SOMETIMES BY ORDERS OF MAGNITUDE—THAN IT USED TO BE.

OK, I'm sure that if you went back forty years, you could attend a chamber of commerce luncheon and hear a speaker declaim on how the world of 1955 was more fiercely competitive than ever before. Maybe it was. But the marketplace of the 1990s has surely ratcheted the competition meter up a few notches, and it's not going to subside anytime soon.

The reason: This time around, at the end of the twentieth century, the increase in competition is being fueled by three historic trends. I don't use the word "historic" lightly: These are biggies. They weren't there in the 1950s, or in the 1960s, not at anything like the same level as now. Nor are they short-term, easily reversible phenomena—as, for example, the rising energy costs of the 1970s turned out to be. Indeed, none of the three has as yet shown any sign of slowing down or reversing itself.

### Trend #1: Globalization.

You've heard this before. The world is becoming ever more integrated. Markets are crowded with entrants from many countries. If you can't compete with _____ (Thailand? China? Germany? Fill in the blank), well, then, you're history.

Now this is a trend that's easy to overstate. My dentist isn't worried that I'll fly to Taiwan for a root canal. And Fidelity Investments isn't losing any sleep over Brazilian mutual-fund houses. Because the case is so often overstated, it has recently become fashionable to debunk the extent and impact of globalization. Exports were only about 10 percent of U.S. gross domestic product (GDP) in 1991, points out economist Paul Krugman, and imports only 11 percent. Small potatoes, he sniffs. In the middle of the nineteenth century, Great Britain was exporting something like one-third of its GDP. *That* was a real global economy.

Grant Krugman his point, however—he knows more about this stuff than most people do—and you can still argue that globalization is one of the central defining characteristics of the new economy.

For one thing, exports as a share of total economic activity may be small compared with what they were in 1850s-vintage Britain, but they're a good deal bigger than they were in the United States only a few decades ago. In 1960 (as Krugman acknowledges), exports and imports were each only 4 percent of GDP. So our international business is well on its way to tripling—even though we're measuring it against our constantly expanding output. There aren't many manufacturers who don't have a wary eye on Japan or Taiwan or Italy.

Then, too, globalization has business effects that aren't counted on the import-export ledger. Look at Granite Rock Co., for example, in Watsonville, California, just a little south of Santa Cruz. Granite Rock is a family-owned, middle-sized producer of gravel, concrete, and asphalt for highways and construction. Until the early 1980s all its competitors were similar family-owned businesses. One by one, they were bought out—mostly by big overseas construction interests. Suddenly Granite Rock found itself competing with companies whose pockets were so deep that they looked like banks.

The fact is, globalization alters the terms of competition in ways that will never show up on an economist's computer screen but that every businessperson is acutely, sometimes painfully, aware of. When the Japanese auto companies began selling cheap, high-quality cars in the United States, Detroit realized it simply couldn't compete very well— and that it would have to learn new techniques, both in manufacturing and in managing. But the Japanese automakers didn't just run their own factories differently; they expected their suppliers to run differently as well. OK, said Detroit, we'll do that, too. Pretty soon small, second- or third-tier auto-parts manufacturers in midwestern towns were being expected to learn cellular manufacturing, just-in-time inventory techniques, statistical process control, and all the other trappings of 1990s-style management. If they didn't learn all that, they could expect to be off the supplier list. So some—the survivors—learned it.

But once Acme Parts Inc. learns all this stuff, what happens? Acme suddenly realizes it doesn't have to put up with the cruddy service it has been getting from its steel supplier, its printer, its accountants, its landlord, and every other vendor on its own supplier list. Like the auto companies it becomes a demanding customer. Like the auto companies it threatens to take its business elsewhere if the vendors don't shape up. The vendors, in turn, find themselves thinking about topics like Total Quality Management and facing demands from their customers they never heard before. Maybe they didn't believe they were even in the global marketplace. But they're having to respond to it, as surely as if they were selling their wares on the streets of Tokyo.

In short, globalization raises the bar of competition. If one country can produce higher-quality or lower-priced goods, consumers at every level of the economic food chain soon come to expect that level of quality or price everywhere. Someone, somewhere, learns to do it—and now everyone has to do it if they want to stay in business.

### Trend #2: The Information Revolution

Or whatever else you choose to call the intertwined advance of computers and communications that is reshaping the way we deal with data and each other. This one is no surprise, either.

You can characterize this revolution in any of a hundred ways. Th are those always startling little statistics about the cost of compu

(*Fortune* magazine: "A greeting card that plays 'Happy Birthday' holds more computing power than existed on earth before 1950.") There are all the new industries that have come into being—from big, mainstream businesses such as PC manufacturing to niche businesses such as retrofitting highway toll booths for electronic toll collection, with a thousand others in between. Every year, *Inc.* magazine compiles a list of the five hundred fastest-growing small, private companies in the United States. Along with all the computer makers and software developers are companies such as MacTemps Inc., which provides Macintosh-skilled temporary personnel, and STATS Inc., which electronically compiles and distributes enough sports statistics to satisfy even the most obsessive fanatic. New industries, all.

But where everyday companies are concerned, what's important about the rapid spread of information technology is how quickly it spurs competition. Thanks to technology, entrepreneurs can set up new companies even in the stodgiest of old-line industries and rapidly outstrip entrenched adversaries. Thanks to technology, Company A can suddenly leave Company B in the dust—even though the two have spent their corporate lives in gentlemanly jousting for a point or two of market share. You doubt these statements? You should meet an ebullient, heavyset entrepreneur by the name of Jerry Kohl, who runs one of the faster-growing manufacturing companies in the Los Angeles area. Kohl's industry: leather belts. It was a mature business when he first got into it in the 1970s. It was a mature business in the late 1980s, when his company, Leegin Creative Leather Products Inc., was trundling along with annual revenues, year after year, of about $10 million.

It was also a mature business when Leegin began its rocketlike trajectory from $10 million to $65 million (and still growing).

Kohl's secret: information technology. As early as 1990, his field salespeople were carrying laptop computers as they visited the specialty stores that were Kohl's prime customers. Back then, the average belt manufacturer scarcely knew that laptops existed. Firing up their computers, Leegin's salespeople sat down with store owners and produced up-to-the-minute reports about what was selling in that store, what wasn't, what was hot in similar stores in Chicago or Miami. Meanwhile, Kohl had installed state-of-the-art hardware and software back in the office. Customer-service reps had information about shipments and billings and inventory levels at their fingertips. The information—which few competitors had so readily available—could be updated regularly and instantly. Customers found they could count on a level of service from Leegin that they couldn't get elsewhere. "I can call and place an order and they ship it right out, even if it's just one belt," said one. "Another company we deal with, their orders get messed up all the time and I'm constantly returning stuff."

Need it be said? There are a lot of Jerry Kohls out there, in large companies as well as small ones. The Information Revolution's rate of change is not tapering off. Neither is its effect on business.

## Trend #3: Entrepreneurialization

"Entrepreneurialization" is an ugly, cumbersome word. I use it only because we English speakers never did come up with our own word for "entrepreneur" and so had to borrow one from the French. (The Brits used to employ the term *undertaker* for a person we now would describe as an entrepreneur, but "undertaker" was soon appropriated for another use.) Awkward though the term may be, though, the fact is undeniable. The marketplace is being carved up, redefined, reconstructed every day, at a level unprecedented in recent memory, by people who go into business for themselves and do things just enough differently from everybody else in the industry to carve out a niche or swipe a little market share.

The innovations these entrepreneurs introduce come in any number of varieties. One is, "Why didn't I think of that?"

Staples and the other new office-supply chains took the big-store, low-price formula that had worked in other industries (toys, building supplies) and transferred it to a business still dominated by stationery stores and catalog-supply houses. Of course! Why didn't I think of that? A guy named Tom Baer went to build his daughter a wooden playground set and was appalled at the prices of kits on the market. So he designed a kit that could be built with off-the-shelf, standard-size lumber for a fraction of the cost. Baer now has a $50 million company.

A second category: "If they can do it, so can I."

When Fritz Maytag of Anchor Steam beer set out to establish the first premium-beer microbrewery, people figured it was a good thing his family (yes, it's that Maytag) was rich. Everybody knew that the beer industry was consolidating and that small breweries had no way of competing with giants such as Anheuser-Busch. Today, there are hundreds of microbreweries around the country—and the giant brewers, though not exactly starving, are wondering how to tap into all that growth. If your best friend wanted to establish one, your only fear would be that the market has become too crowded.

A third category: "Um, yeah, I, uh, think I see what you're doing. Could you explain it just once more?"

I found myself in this ego-deflating position when I was visiting a trucking company called OTR Express, headquartered not far from Kansas City. OTRX, as it styles itself, is a young company that competes in the so-called truckload segment of the industry, picking up trailer-at-a-time loads from big shippers and hauling them long distances. Most companies in this segment like to line up regular customers. That cuts down on marketing costs, gives their revenues some predictability, and allows them to lock in business by (for example) always having trailers stationed at the customer's loading dock.

OTRX, by contrast, figured it would go after the irregular ("spot") market. Its customers: shippers who couldn't guarantee so many truckloads a week. Shippers who suddenly needed a little extra hauling capacity. These shippers could always call some local hauler, but OTRX's founders figured they could deliver better service at lower cost if they could keep their trucks busy with profitable shipments. The trick: Write a computer program to calculate the profitability of any given load based partly on expectations about what the truck could pick up at its *destination* city. This "next load" analysis is complex; you have to factor in not only different rates paid in different cities but a certain level of uncertainty about whether loads will be available at all. And you have to make sure that, just because San Francisco looks good on a given day, you don't suddenly send two hundred trucks to San Francisco. OTRX's founders wrote some one hundred thousand lines of computer code to make sure all these calculations came out right.

Hearing the explanation, I was glad I could write down a few words about the company and go home. OTRX's competitors don't have that luxury.

The funny thing about all this entrepreneurial restructuring of industries, of course, is that it feeds on itself. New companies enter a market. They offer new combinations of goods and services. Maybe they drive down prices. Old companies feel the pinch, begin to cut costs, and lay off people—who then wonder if they can't go out on their own. Meanwhile, the whole concept of starting a business gains a certain currency. We read not only about the Bill Gateses of the world but about Jerry Kohl of Leegin, and Bill and Kathy Ward and Dick Walpole of OTRX, and we think, jeez, I could do that. So it is that the number of businesses has proliferated, wildly. In 1980 the IRS received about nine million tax returns from sole proprietorships, which is to say unincorporated businesses. By 1990 the figure was nearly fifteen million. The number of corporate tax returns, meanwhile, rose 37 percent to 3.7 million—even though the population grew only about 10 percent.

The lesson: The competitors you have today may or may not be around tomorrow. But as sure as death and taxes you'll have new ones.

Every now and then some pundit comes up with what he or she hopes will be the perfect symbol of how much more competitive the American economy has become. Maybe it's the telecommunications industry. Upended by deregulation and technical innovation, it went from One Big Company to a zillion. Or maybe it's steel, a business so transformed by global competition and entrepreneurial upstarts that U.S. Steel figured it had better masquerade as USX.

Myself, I choose the drugstore.

Remember the corner drug? I do, because the small town I grew up in actually had one, literally on the corner, complete with soda fountain. There was another drugstore in town, too, but only grown-ups went there. No soda fountain, no kids.

Over time, a lot of these mom-and-pop operations were pushed out of business by chains. Ten and twenty years ago, the chains versus the independents was the biggest battle in retailing.

But the skirmishes between chains and independents were like games of capture the flag compared to the take-no-prisoners competition in the industry today. Consider:

• Nationally, new pharmaceutical-benefits companies such as Medco Containment Services and PCS Health Systems handle prescriptions for huge groups of consumers. Many sell direct by mail order, cutting into pharmacies' market share. Powerful computers and 800 numbers let these companies offer customers the same level of personal service—or at least the illusion of it—they once got at the corner drug. (Oh, yes, Mrs. Jones, and aren't you due for a refill soon on your arthritis medication?)

(Both Medco and PCS, incidentally, are owned by drug manufacturers, which raises the possibility of all kinds of sweetheart deals. This possibility wasn't lost on chain pharmacies, which filed a variety of lawsuits in 1994 against the manufacturers.)

• Locally, health maintenance organizations and other managed-care plans seem to cut new deals with drug retailers every day. The deals guarantee a certain amount of volume but eat into profits. One industry consultant points out that prescription-drug margins have dropped for six consecutive years.

• Mass merchandisers such as Wal-Mart operate big drugstores of their own. So do supermarkets. On the high end, new specialty retailers such as The Body Shop (which originated in the United Kingdom) have entered the cosmetics business, luring trendy young customers away from the local pharmacy's skin-and-hair-care counter.

You see what has happened? There used to be this niche called a drugstore. Chain or independent, everyone knew what business drugstores were in. Druggists sold prescription drugs and what the industry calls HBA, health and beauty aids. If you had a good location and were at least minimally competent, you'd probably survive. Today, drugstore operators must compete with retailers of a dozen different varieties. They must decide whether to offer one-hour photo developing, a drive-up pharmacy window, or (like several chains) packaging and mailing services. They must figure out whether and when to install scanning technologies. They must assess the costs and benefits of discount prescription plans.

So that's why it's a symbol. Here's an industry that isn't new, isn't high tech, isn't directly involved in international competition—an industry that, you would have to say, seems as mundane and mature as they come. But sometime in the last ten or fifteen years even drugstores became a challenging, tumultuous, even treacherous business. Is there any industry that didn't?

# The New Workplace

WHILE THE COMPETITION WAS STIFFENING, SOMETHING ELSE WAS HAPPENING IN THE NEW ECONOMY: THE VERY NATURE OF WORK AND THE WORKPLACE WERE CHANGING DRAMATICALLY.

Here, too, you could look back in history and ask the skeptic's question: So when weren't work and the workplace changing? The skeptic's point is well taken, but today's mix of long-term trends and more recent ones has sped up the rate of change.

*The biggest long-term trend is the gradual emergence of the service economy.*

I hate to do it, but there's no way around it. You gotta look at the numbers. They tell a lot.

Start by adding up the number of people employed in the various sectors of the economy, and look how it has changed over the years.

In 1900, about 40 percent of working Americans earned their living on a farm. About half of nonfarm employees worked in some form of service industry, including government. (Note that what we're counting here is who works where, not what they actually do. An accountant who works for a manufacturing company, for example, counts as a manufacturing employee.)

By 1950, only 12 percent of Americans worked on farms. Three-fifths of the rest were in the service sector.

By 1990, the allocation of workers in the economy would have been virtually unrecognizable to a time traveler from the beginning of the century. Not even 3 percent of the nation's workforce was in farming. The service sector employed three-quarters of the rest.

A second way of counting—looking at individual occupations rather than the sector that people work in—tells much the same story, so I'll mention only a few numbers.

White-collar workers as a share of the total labor force: In 1900, 18 percent. In 1990, a whopping 57 percent. That figure includes professionals, managers, engineers, clerical employees, and salespeople.

Manual workers, figured the same way: In 1900, 36 percent. In 1990, only 15 percent.

What's interesting about the growth of the service sector is that it continues apace. Look at what happened between 1980 and 1992, which is the last year I have statistics for. In those twelve years, the American economy added some eighteen million new jobs. Yet farming, mining, construction, and manufacturing as a group actually employed *fewer* people in 1992 than in 1980. So *all* the new jobs—and then some—were in service-producing industries.

This is the service economy: today, nearly three-quarters of us work in some form of service business. Many more of us work at service *jobs* (accountant, janitor) in manufacturing businesses.

And this is what service-sector work is: working mostly with information (processing catalog orders or insurance claims, say) or working mostly with people (retail sales clerk, nurse), or working with both at once (mortgage banker, airline reservation agent). There are exceptions, like janitors. But not many.

Which means, of course, that fewer and fewer people do work that involves *labor* in the old sense of plowing a field or building a house or manufacturing an automobile. For a long time now, more and more of our jobs have involved processing data and exchanging information and tending to the needs or wishes of our fellow human beings.

*But the shift in the nature of work doesn't stop there. In the last ten years or so, even traditional manual jobs have expanded to include a healthy component of what Peter Drucker calls "knowledge work."*

Farmers, for example, routinely use computers for planning and cost accounting. The gravel-pit workers at Granite Rock Co. learn statistical process control and the other techniques of Total Quality Management.

The change is most dramatic in factories.

Remember what factory work used to be? If not, I recommend a little book called *All the Livelong Day,* published in 1975 and recently reissued. It was written by a wonderful journalist named Barbara Garson (author of the play *MacBird!,* for all you 1960s trivia buffs), and it describes, among other workplaces, the Herbescence Eau de Parfume Spray Mist production line at a Helena Rubenstein plant. "The lead lady takes the filled bottles of spray mist out of cartons and places each one on a black dot marked on the moving belt. The next two women put little silver tags around the bottle necks. Each one tags every other bottle. The next nine women each fold a protective corrugated cardboard, unfold a silver box, pick up every ninth spray-mist bottle, slip it into the corrugation, insert a leaflet, put the whole thing into the box and close the top. The next seven ladies wrap the silver Herbescence boxes in colored tissue paper. . . ."

At one point Garson is distracted by a minor altercation at another line and overhears the exchange.

"I asked you, 'What are you stopping the machine for?'" said a supervisor. The gray-haired grade three at the filling machine made no answer. (The women who work the machines are one of two grades above the grade ones, who do the hand operations.)

"What are you stopping it for?" he repeated.

"When I see the work coming down the line, I'll start my machine," the thin gray-haired lady answered icily.

A fellow employee advises the gray-haired lady to call the shop steward if the supervisor gives her any trouble. "He's not gonna give me any trouble," she replies. Later Garson gets a chance to speak with her privately.

"These new supervisors," she practically spit. "They've been here all of two months and they act like you're the one that's new. They can't respect your manner of doing a job. It's always the new ones."

The woman had been at Rubenstein's for twenty-two years.

So there was factory work in a more or less typical situation, c. 1975. It was routine, stultifying—and closely, intensely supervised. Through their union, the women doing handwork on the Rubenstein lines had won the right to rotate jobs every couple of hours. But they still had to wait for a relief worker before they could go to the bathroom.

Factory jobs like this haven't disappeared. But if you walk into a factory today you're likely to find an altogether different environment.

Instead of assembly lines under some supervisor's tight control, for example, you might find manufacturing cells or small, U-shaped lines in which teams assemble product from start to finish, regulating their own pace.

Instead of purely manual work, you see machine tenders pausing to fill out statistical process control charts—or to reprogram the computer that controls their machine.

Instead of supervisors breathing down the necks of underlings, you see line workers doing their jobs with little or no supervision.

And instead of workers feeling like no more than cogs in a machine, many feel more or less in charge of their own work area.

I don't want to sound like Pollyanna. Factory work is hard, often boring, sometimes dirty, occasionally dangerous. Factories can still be contentious places. But people who haven't recently set foot in a plant (not to mention those whose picture of industrial labor comes only from Charlie Chaplin's *Modern Times* or books such as Garson's) rarely know how much the industrial world has changed. For example:

• Ford's Walton Hills metal stamping plant near Cleveland has been enlisting employees to come up with labor-saving and cost-cutting ideas since 1985 and now "does as much work with 2,000 employees as it did in the 1970s with more than 3,000," according to *The Wall Street Journal*.

• At Eaton Corp.'s Kearney, Nebraska, engine-valve plant, frontline workers sit on dozens of teams designed to unplug production bottlenecks or solve other problems.

• At a company called XEL Communications Inc., near Denver, an hourly employee named Teri Mantooth runs the wave-solder machine, used in the production of circuit boards. Mantooth used to work under the supervision of an industrial engineer. He made the decisions, she carried them out. Then the engineer quit, and XEL didn't replace him. Instead, Mantooth learned what she needed to know and began making decisions about the machine herself.

I'm not trying to persuade you that today's factory managers are somehow more virtuous or nicer than yesterday's meanies. The changes have come about for any number of reasons, none of them related to the moral character of businesspeople. Technological advances—computers again—made it possible for plants to automate a lot of routine jobs.

Cost pressures—competitiveness again—encouraged executives to eliminate as many layers of management as possible. ("Our customers don't
want to pay for supervisors" is one plant manager's blunt explanation.)
Finally, Americans learned, as the Japanese had already learned, that
people work harder and smarter when they're given a little responsibility. This is a subject we'll come back to. It bears on open-book management.

By itself, the expansion of manual work is neither good nor bad. Some
employees want more to do; it expands their horizons and makes their
jobs more interesting. Others want no more to do, figuring they have too
much already. But the point isn't whether job expansion is good or bad;
the point is that it's happening. Willy-nilly, for good or ill, companies are
getting by with fewer people than before. Each of those people is learning to do more—and different—tasks.

## What It All Means

ALL THESE HISTORIC CHANGES, THESE LONG-TERM AND SEEMINGLY INEX-
ORABLE TRENDS IN THE ECONOMY, HAVE PROFOUND IMPLICATIONS FOR COM-
PANIES AND THOSE WHO MANAGE THEM.

Time was, you could figure on running a business tomorrow the same
way you were running it today and had run it yesterday. Sure, you always
had competition. But competition was mostly of the low-key, gentlemanly variety. Procter & Gamble might mount a new marketing campaign, hoping to get another point or two of market share from the likes
of Colgate-Palmolive. The two drugstores on the same block might compete by advertising special sales. But everyone knew what business they
were in, and knew that competitors faced similar costs and constraints.
Brutal, cutthroat competition, in which upstart companies essentially
change the whole game, was rare.

Today, it's as different as can be. We saw what happened to the drugstores. But even giants such as Procter & Gamble aren't immune to the
new kinds of competition. In disposable diapers, for example—a category that accounts for a significant fraction of P&G's revenues—the
Cincinnati behemoth must face not only fellow behemoth Kimberly-
Clark but intruders such as Drypers Corp. Drypers, the Houston-based
brainchild of a couple of thirtysomething entrepreneurs, sells brand-name
disposables in direct competition with the big boys—and zipped from

start-up to $140 million in sales in exactly five years. When P&G suddenly announced it was scrambling to slim down and get more entrepreneurial, no one who was watching the paper-diaper industry had to ask why.

So what do companies have to do to compete in this new economy? Boil it all down and you come up with two tasks.

First task: Develop a clear, sensible plan for the business, meaning a mission (or a set of objectives) and a strategy.

Southwest Airlines, for example, has about the clearest mission and strategy imaginable: to offer no-frills flights at rock-bottom prices. The mission and strategy inform everything the company does. To keep training and maintenance costs low, it buys only one kind of aircraft. To keep those planes in the air and making money, it expects employees to get them emptied and reloaded faster than any other airline. It eliminates travel agents' commissions by selling tickets directly rather than through agents. It offers no reserved seats or in-flight meals.

This book, however, isn't really about mission and strategy. There are already a lot of good books out there on these topics—not to mention seminars, conferences, magazine articles, videos, and speeches, along with an army of consultants ready and willing to impart their strategic thoughts in private rather than in public.

The subject of this book is how—indeed, whether—the strategy can be executed.

For my money, this area of management is every bit as important as the strategic stuff. Maybe more. Execution is where the rubber meets the road. Generals, football coaches, and the harried managers of Subway sandwich franchises know the truth: No matter how brilliant the plans, no matter how smart the strategy, nothing gets accomplished unless people execute. In business, execution is what happens (or doesn't happen) every day in offices and shops and warehouses and factories, in the management meetings and on the sales calls and on the front lines. It's about what people do on the job every day. It's what they think about and how they work together.

So the second task for a company that hopes to compete in the new economy is all-important. Execute. Get people working together productively, creatively, toward common purposes, without too much lost effort. All the big-picture stuff, the mission and the strategy and everything else, is critically dependent on getting individuals working together.

Here is an account from *The Wall Street Journal* of what happens when a Southwest Airlines plane arrives at an airport:

PHOENIX, Ariz.—Wally Mills is watching the clock.

At 3:15 P.M., Southwest Airlines Flight 944 from San Diego lands, on time, at Sky Harbor International Airport here. By 3:30, Mr. Mills, a rotund crew leader, and six other Southwest ramp agents must have this plane turned around and on its way to El Paso, Texas. "I think of this as a game," says Mr. Mills. "I like to play against the [gate agents] up there working with the people to see if we can beat them."

With Indy pit-stop precision, workers attach the push-back gear to the Boeing 737, unload the Phoenix bags, load the ones for El Paso, restock the galleys, and pump aboard 4,600 pounds of fuel. A last-minute bag costs the ramp crew the race with the gate agents, who have boarded 49 passengers. Then Mr. Mills puts on a headset and prepares to direct the jet away from the gate. It is 3:29.

Mr. Mills and his team have done in less than 15 minutes what other airlines, on average, need triple the time to do. That kind of hustle isn't a fluke at Southwest: 80% of its 1,300 flights a day get into the air as quickly as Flight 944.

Fast turnaround is an essential ingredient of Southwest's low-price strategy. It works because the airline's employees want it to work. Gate agents help clean the plane when necessary. Even pilots have been known to help out with the bags. If the employees didn't care—if, for example, they were more concerned with union-protected job descriptions and work rules—the low-price strategy would be so much empty posturing.

It's the same anywhere. In the hotel business, if you want world-class service, the desk clerks and bellhops and room-service attendants better buy into that mission. If they don't—if there's just a hint of aggravation in their voices, if they "forget" how to solve an irritated customer's problem—your "world-class" service will suddenly be low-class. Or suppose you run a software company. Your long-term success depends on coming out with a constant stream of new products. But no matter how much you spend on R&D, you aren't going to get the work you need if your product developers don't care whether the company succeeds. All businesses are dependent on the willing cooperation of their workers.

All the changes in jobs and the nature of work that I described under the "new workplace" heading make this task harder than ever. You need to get people working together efficiently, but knowing whether they're doing so can be difficult.

When "work" consisted mostly of manual labor, after all, it was pretty easy for a boss to see if an employee was slacking off or screwing up. The sandpile didn't get shoveled. The bolts didn't get tightened. When "work" consists mostly of delivering services, however, supervision is less effective. Health-center managers may not pick up the fact that a doctor's manner with patients is so brusque as to make them feel uncomfortable. A restaurant supervisor may not notice that the new waiter spends too much time chatting and not enough time keeping an eye on his tables. Things aren't much different even in factories. The "work" is producing goods— but producing goods involves tending several machines, tracking output variances, reprogramming the computer when necessary, and helping untangle a work-in-process bottleneck. If workers aren't willing and eager to do all these jobs right, it's tough for a supervisor to make them.

Maybe you've heard businesspeople complain about employees. Maybe you've even complained a little yourself. They aren't well educated or well trained. They don't have a good work ethic. They don't pay attention to the little things. You know the line.

But it's unlikely that most workers are less well trained or less motivated than twenty-five or fifty years ago. *What has changed is the work.* In the past, employees with average or low skills and desire could be stuck in a job where, frankly, they couldn't do too much damage. If they screwed up badly enough they could be fired. If they did just enough to get by, well, the company would survive.

There aren't many of those jobs left. Today, employers are asking the same people to perform more demanding tasks—and are staking their businesses' future on the employees' ability to carry them out. No wonder businesspeople like to complain. They're just complaining about the wrong thing.

The overarching lesson of the new economy for management? It's this. Yes, a company needs a mission, a strategy. But more than anything else it needs eager, willing employees, people who have a reason to care about their employer's prosperity and who know how to help it succeed.

## CHAPTER 2

# Evolution of an Idea

## Where open-book management came from

American companies, alas, plunged into this demanding new market-place with ideas about management forged a hundred years ago. Like a modern-day army equipped with muskets, they didn't do real well.

## The Origin of Old-Style Management

Go back in time a century or so and you see an economic world that felt as chaotic and fast-changing as today's. New technology? In one forty-year period we got electric power and lights, telephones, cars and trucks, farm machinery, radio, movies, and the earliest airplanes, not to mention such modern indispensables as breakfast cereal. And new markets! The spread of railroads and highways opened up vast stretches of a growing nation to commerce. New manufacturing technology boosted productivity to unprecedented levels.

The business landscape, too, was changing every day, mostly because entrepreneurs and investors were creating enterprises of unheard-of size.

In 1870, for instance, the McCormick reaper plant in Chicago was one of the biggest in the nation. It had all of 500 employees. Thirty years later, some seventy factories counted more than 2,000 employees apiece. A dozen or so were up in the 6,000-to-10,000 range. By 1915 mass-production manufacturing had taken off. The United States Steel complex in Homestead, Pennsylvania, employed 9,000. Ford's Highland Park, Michigan, plant employed 16,000.

If you were managing a company back then, your first job would have been to maintain enough people on the payroll to keep your factories humming. This was no small task.

For one thing, your labor force was new to the industrial world. Maybe you had enticed them off the farms of New England or the Midwest or the South. Maybe you had hired them right off the boat from Italy or Poland or Ireland. Wherever they came from, they were rural men and women with no inkling of what life in a factory might be like.

Then, too, what you were offering was not exactly a picnic.

Workdays were long—no surprise there, especially to anyone brought up on a farm. But the market was subject to dramatic booms and busts, so layoffs were frequent. (About a quarter of the workforce was out of a job for some time every year.) Since wages were often determined by some form of piece rate, the pace was intense. When new technology or procedures led to an increase in output, most companies just cut the pay rate.

As for working conditions, let's just say that the whole concept of industrial health and safety had yet to be invented. Cotton mills were heated with live steam to maintain high humidity all year long. The floor of a typical meat-packing plant, according to a contemporary account, had "slime and grease . . . so thick that a foothold was hardly possible." At the Homestead steel works, between fifteen and twenty-five people died in accidents in a typical year.

Strangers in a dangerous land, the workers grumbled and protested and walked off the job.

Between 1880 and 1900, for example, there were nearly twenty-three thousand strikes. That, as the historian Stuart D. Brandes points out, amounted to "an average of three new strikes a day for twenty years." Quit rates and absenteeism were astronomical. The Amoskeag textile mills in New Hampshire had to hire 24,000 in one year to maintain a labor force of 13,700. Ford's Highland Park plant had to hire 54,000 over twelve months to maintain 13,000 employees. At Highland Park, between 1,300 and 1,400 workers were "missing from their stations" every single day—some because of illness or walkouts, others because they had simply decided not to show up.

So plants were adding or replacing people all the time. The managerial conclusion was inescapable: Most of a company's employees better be essentially interchangeable. Someone quits? See who's standing at the gate. Training or skill development? Forget it—the new employee had to get up to speed in a matter of hours, even minutes. Skilled workers were a liability, not an asset. If they left, they were hard to replace.

That need for interchangeable employees must have created an indelible impression in the minds of businesspeople, because it left us with two assumptions about work and workers that survived nearly a century.

### One: A job must be defined as narrowly as possible.

The simpler the task, the easier it was to replace people.

New production technology, developed around the turn of the century, hurried this specialization along. Before, handworkers and craftspeople had produced goods with general-purpose tools or machinery (sewing machines, lathes). Now factory workers used special-purpose machinery, often arranged into rudimentary assembly lines, to turn out the goods. This was the system that Henry Ford refined and improved upon when he created the first full-scale automobile assembly line. Company owners and plant managers liked the system. Not only was it more productive, it also reduced required skill levels. That allowed them to replace workers more easily.

### Two: Workers need close, direct supervision.

Daniel Nelson, a historian at the University of Akron, refers to the turn-of-the-century factory as "the foreman's empire."

Foremen hired workers, assigned them to jobs, and showed them what to do. They set pay rates. They handed out discipline, which in those days included everything from fines to physical abuse. The typical foreman's style of management was known as driving—a combination, says Nelson, of "authoritarian rule and physical compulsion." Driving had a certain realistic logic. Given the conditions, what besides a foreman's wrath or beneficence would induce workers to work? This was not the age of the loyal employee—or of the loyal employer.


As the industrial economy matured, American companies created a *paradigm* of management.

They institutionalized and routinized their management methods. They developed practices and procedures that came to be taken for granted in the business world. It took maybe half a century for all the pieces to fall into place. But those two ideas—that jobs must be specialized and that employees need close supervision—were always at the heart of the system.

Looking back, you can see three key steps in the development of the old management paradigm.

### Step 1: the rise of engineering, and of the engineering-inspired movement known as scientific management.

Engineering was a fast-growing profession back then, and the engineers who worked in industry fancied themselves the management consultants of the day. The new companies surely needed help. They had grown so fast that they were plagued with bottlenecks, shortages, and cost over-runs. Their reliance on foremen meant that top management had little control over who was hired, how hard the employees worked, how they were deployed, even what any individual was paid.

So engineers began gathering up detailed cost data and developing standard forms to track orders or work in process. They recommended that foremen's duties be parceled out to an army of low-level white-collar workers—timekeepers, cost clerks, stockroom clerks, and so on.

No engineer was as influential as Frederick W. Taylor (1856–1915), originator of the term "scientific management." Taylor turned workplace reorganization into a kind of national movement.

Most of Taylor's ideas were pretty useful in the new factories, though both he and his followers (like at least a few of their modern-day counterparts) regularly exaggerated their benefits. Analyze every step of the production process, they preached. Scrutinize every worker's every motion, calculating time and output with a stopwatch. Break jobs down into their smallest components. Then set up a central department to standardize production methods, job descriptions, and pay rates. "All possible brainwork," Taylor wrote, "should be removed from the shop and centered in the planning or laying-out department."

Though Taylor was in effect curbing foremen's authority—it was now the planning department, not the foreman, that would determine how the work got done—he had no thought of abolishing close supervision. Indeed, he believed that more foremen than ever were needed to make sure that workers did exactly what the planners prescribed.

The scientific-management movement hastened the specialization of work. "An entry in the 1915 diary of Will Poyfair, Jr., a worker in Buick's Flint works, says simply, 'Stopwatched today,' " writes historian David Montgomery. "One week later, the work of [Poyfair's] four-man drip-pan gang was divided into separate tasks for each man, each with its own quota and piece rate." Scientific management also spawned a growing number of white-collar and supervisory employees. "Managers discouraged workers from hunting up their own materials or devising their own tools and fixtures. These were to be delivered and accounted for by clerks." Between 1910 and 1920, the ranks of supervisory employees grew nearly two and a half times as fast as the ranks of wage earners.

**Step 2: the professionalization of management—the creation, in effect, of a separate managerial class.**

It's astonishing how little management, in the modern sense, some early companies got by on.

The Amoskeag mills—a huge enterprise for nineteenth-century America—were owned by Boston-based investors and were run on the owners' behalf by the treasurer of the corporation, who was also based in Boston. A salaried employee called an agent was the on-site boss in New Hampshire. Foremen, known as overseers, ran the mill operations. Accounting was handled in the Boston office. If Amoskeag had been an army, it would have had thousands of privates, a handful of sergeants, and only two or three officers.

But that seat-of-the-pants approach to management didn't survive the growth of huge, national, multiproduct corporations.

Influenced by Taylorism, the rapidly expanding corporations added line-and-staff management structures, division heads, and rank after rank of a species no one had heard of before, the middle manager. An organizational chart of Armour & Co., from 1907, is reprinted in Alfred D. Chandler, Jr.'s, classic work, *The Visible Hand.* Portraying a company that had more in common with today's Pentagon than with Amoskeag, the chart shows dozens of different units and departments, each peppered with branch managers, district superintendents, assistant superintendents, sales managers, credit-and-accounting managers, and plant superintendents. In companies such as Armour, functions that had once been performed by foremen or plant bosses were given to specialists. Personnel offices took over hiring, firing, and record keeping. Cost accountants took over the gathering and analysis of cost data.

Gradually, these white-collar jobs came to be defined as professional careers requiring formal training and accreditation. Engineers, accountants, even marketing managers formed their own associations and sponsored their own professional journals. General managers formed organizations as well. (The American Management Association was born in 1925.) Business education moved from secondary schools to colleges and then to new graduate schools, such as Harvard's Graduate School of Business Administration and the University of Pennsylvania's Wharton School.

Thus was born the corporate bureaucracy, in which ranks of professionally trained managers supervise other managers and specialists, all the way down to the lowly hourly worker. Each individual had his or her slot in the organizational chart. Each had a superior and a set of subordinates.

Thus too was born the central social schism of nearly every company in twentieth-century America: the division between the "office" and the "shop." Blue-collar workers were paid by the hour, worked with their hands, and were expected to do as they were told. White-collar workers had technical or supervisory responsibility, were paid a salary, and were expected to work for the good of the company. Eventually the distinction was written into law: exempt and nonexempt employees. Eventually, too, it led to all the differences of perks and privilege that characterized most American companies not so long ago: different benefit packages, different time restrictions, even different lunchrooms, all depending on the color of your collar.

## Step 3: the rise of the adversarial union.

Unions in America, like unions everywhere, were born in bloodshed.

Not many of the businessmen building the new industrial economy were willing to countenance a union on their premises. They fought unions not just with firings and blacklistings but with goons and Pinkerton guards. It wasn't until 1935 that unions got legal protection, so the hardball tactics were usually successful. When the modern corporation was being created, in short, workers rarely had any organized voice.

That didn't stop them from protesting innovations like scientific management, which they feared would curtail what little autonomy they had. Workers at the Watertown, Massachusetts, arsenal, for instance, walked off the job in 1911 at the very appearance of a Taylor disciple with a stopwatch. But employee protests had little impact on the development of managerial practice.

The National Labor Relations Act, or Wagner Act, passed in 1935, gave union organizing the protection of law. Even so, some die-hard employers refused to give in. The so-called Little Steel strike, in 1937, was bitterly opposed by the steel companies' management. It led to outbreaks of violence in nearly every steelmaking community. Managers of the Bethlehem Steel plant in Johnstown, Pennsylvania, stockpiled tear gas and munitions. A picketing worker was killed in Youngstown, Ohio, and Governor Martin L. Davey called out the troops.

So by the time unions had established themselves in major industries—after World War II—a couple of assumptions about labor relations were widely shared by both sides.

One—drummed into everybody's head by decades of enmity—was that *labor and management were adversaries, not partners.*

Union contracts were drawn up only after head-to-head confrontation or antagonistic negotiations. Union work rules and grievance procedures were designed to protect workers from exploitation and abuse by management. Strict job-bidding procedures curbed the power of foremen to reward docile workers and punish recalcitrant ones.

Detailed job descriptions spelled out exactly what workers could be asked to do. Consider, for instance, the specifications in U.S. Steel's 1946 contract with the United Steel Workers of America. A sand shoveler was expected to shovel 12.5 fifteen-pound shovelfuls of river sand (moisture content approximately 5.5 percent) per minute. No more, no less. At times, the adversarial culture created an aggressive, let's-see-what-we-can-win mentality. That led to well-publicized abuses such as featherbedding and impossibly restrictive work rules.

Behind this assumption of adversarialism was another one, which is that *it's management's job to run the business*.

Those same work rules and grievance procedures took it for granted that workers would be told what to do. The limits on job descriptions assumed that no worker would ever want to do more than the contract called for. Union employees who went beyond their assigned responsibilities could find themselves in violation of the contract—not to mention the object of other workers' hostility.

And unions as organizations explicitly disavowed any interest in how a company was run. Paragraph eight of a typical contract between the United Auto Workers and General Motors read: "The products to be manufactured, the location of plants, the schedules of production, the methods, processes, and means of manufacturing are solely and exclusively the responsibility of the corporation."

## Old Management Meets New Economy

I once met a guy named Charlie, who worked for the big B.F. Goodrich tire factory in Akron, Ohio, back when Akron was Rubber Capital of the World. Charlie belonged to the United Rubber Workers, and he told me about one of the perks of union membership.

"Guys would come into work, work half a day, and go home. The company knew about it, but the union would make some excuse and get 'em back in again."

Akron, of course, no longer has any big tire plants.

Then there's the story told by John Hoerr, for many years a labor reporter at *Business Week* and the author of a fine book on the steel industry called *And the Wolf Finally Came*. As a kid Hoerr had worked in the steel mills. His job, in those salad days, involved about ten minutes' worth of calculation every few hours. The rest of the time he read and slept. A friend of Hoerr's, nearby, had a difficult job stacking heavy lengths of pipe. But both company and union rules prevented Hoerr from helping him.

Those mills in Pittsburgh are closed now.

Even in nonunion situations, employees in old-management companies tended to figure that screwups and problems were management's concern, not theirs.

There was the guy in the appliance factory who put a huge dent in a refrigerator by dropping it off a forklift. Undaunted, the guy crayoned "compact model" on the carton and sent it out to shipping.

And there was the insurance clerk who OK'd a store owner's policy calling for $5,000 protection against fire and $165,000 against vandalism—exactly the reverse of what she figured the right numbers were. "I was about to show it to [the supervisor]," the clerk admitted, "when I figured, Wait a minute! I'm not supposed to read these forms. I'm just supposed to check one column against another. And they do check. So it couldn't be counted as my error."

It wasn't just the bad blood between managers and workers that hamstrung American companies as they blundered into the new economy; it was the whole bureaucratized, overspecialized, sclerotic division of labor within the corporation. Over time, companies had added layer upon layer of management. U.S. Steel in Hoerr's day had four layers in headquarters and six more in each mill. Requests and orders had to go up and down the hierarchy. Departments didn't talk to one another. Tasks became more and more specialized, procedures more and more cumbersome—a phenomenon that in some companies has persisted until quite recently.

Michael Hammer and James Champy, in their book *Reengineering the Corporation,* tell how IBM Credit Corp. used to handle a "request for financing"—in other words a sale, since IBM Credit's business was financing customers' purchase of computers:

Step 1: Whoever takes the call logs the request and ships it to the credit
  department.

Step 2: The credit department enters the information into its computer and
  checks the buyer's credit.

Step 3: The "business practices" department reviews the request and modifies it if necessary.

Step 4: The request goes to a pricer, who determines the rate and delivers it
  to a clerical group.

Step 5: An administrator in this group turns the information into a quote
  letter "that could be delivered to the field sales representative by Federal
  Express."

And to think we wondered how IBM got itself into so much trouble.

The fact is, no business could hope to compete in the fast-moving, viciously competitive new economy with the attitudes and structures of the old.

Companies needed eager, willing employees and managers at all levels—people who saw some reason for going the extra mile, doing what needed to be done, looking at the big picture rather than the tiny one that was directly in front of them. What they had instead was specialized automatons.

Companies needed to work as a unit, to focus on beating the competition. What they had instead was a maze of conflicting dukedoms and factions—including one big one, labor, that saw management as its sworn enemy.

As the 1980s wore on, more and more companies realized the sad truth. The old way just wasn't working. The evidence was everywhere. They were losing sales, market share, money.

But businesspeople aren't stupid. They can't afford to be. If they stay stupid too long they don't get to keep on being businesspeople. So when they saw the old ways weren't working, they began groping for new ones.

That, of course, is what has led to the astonishing proliferation of new-management methods—not to mention managerial fads, fancies, and fetishes—in the last decade and a half. You can trace them by the books and catchphrases that helped to define them.

First came *In Search of Excellence,* published in 1982, a book that taught a startled publishing industry just how eager businesspeople were for new ideas. *Excellence*'s initial press run was fifteen thousand. It ended up selling more than four million copies in the first ten years.

Tom Peters and Robert Waterman offered all sorts of good advice for managers in the book, but they came down especially hard on the need to redefine how people in a company work together. ("Treat people as adults. Treat them as partners; treat them with dignity; treat them with respect.") Peters followed up *Excellence* with a series of best-selling books, each one hammering home (among many other points) the theme of changing this aspect of corporate life. "Achieving Flexibility by Empowering People" was one heading in *Thriving on Chaos.* "Eliminate Bureaucratic Rules and Humiliating Conditions" was another.

(By the time *Liberation Management* was published in 1992, the visionary Peters was onto some of the key ideas of open-book management. We'll come back to him later.)

Next came the quality movement, embodied in any number of books, seminars, speeches, training programs, consulting projects, and awards. It culminated in what is now known as Total Quality Management. What's interesting about TQM is that it might have been just a technical fix. The experts could have taught statistical process control and their other techniques only to engineers and managers, and then relied on them to establish and enforce the procedures that are supposed to ensure quality.

But the gurus, to their credit, understood that quality systems don't work unless frontline employees are taught (and constantly retaught) to understand their importance. Philip Crosby, who did as much as anyone to popularize the ideas and practices of quality (his Winter Park, Florida, Quality College has trained something like 150,000 managers), observed as much in an early book. "People are not interested in doing something just because they have been told to do it," wrote Crosby. He added, "It isn't enough to design a whizbang assembly operation; you have to help people want to participate in running it."

It was much the same with reengineering, which became the third great wave of management-reform thinking for the new economy.

Reengineering, like quality, has become a widely used term, but the thinkers who had the greatest impact were Hammer and Champy of *Reengineering the Corporation,* another runaway best-seller. Reengineering, they explained, meant starting over. "It involves going back to the beginning and inventing a better way of doing work." Again, reengineering could have been a purely technical fix. But these authors, at least, understood that it inevitably changed the old-management paradigm:

> Companies that undertake reengineering not only compress processes horizontally by having case workers or case teams perform multiple, sequential tasks but vertically as well. *Vertical compression means that at the points in a process where workers used to have to go up the managerial hierarchy for an answer, they now make their own decisions.* Instead of separating decision making from real work, decision making becomes *part* of the work. *Workers themselves now do that portion of a job that, formerly, managers performed.* [emphasis added]

Along with these three tidal waves of reform-minded thinking, of course, came any number of others. Serious theorists of organization such as Harvard's Rosabeth Moss Kanter weighed in with books and articles examining the need to change the way people work together.

(Companies that fail to make themselves "more people-sensitive and less bureaucratic . . . more cooperative and less hierarchical," Kanter wrote, will find themselves in trouble.) The consulting business boomed and kept on booming, partly because it fed on itself. "Consultants beget more consulting as they fuel the marketplace with new ideas and management fads," observed *Business Week*'s John A. Byrne.

Change has been in the air, in other words, for a good fifteen years now. And businesses have begun reshaping themselves accordingly.

Some have plunged into Total Quality Management, or into reengineering.

Most have tried dozens of other ways to cut costs—some effective, some not so effective.

And many, many companies have begun to restructure the way people work together in the business. (A *Wall Street Journal* headline from 1992: "Trying to Increase Worker Productivity, More Employers Alter Management Style.")

Instead of ever greater specialization they are broadening workers' jobs, as described in the previous chapter. Instead of ever tighter supervision they talk of "involvement" and "empowerment." (*Empowerment*— also known as *participatory management*—is an interesting concept with a history of its own, which we'll take up later in the book.)

Even the very words "employee" and "manager" are out of fashion. Progressive companies now call their workers "associates," their managers "coaches."

And in place of the usual bureaucratic hierarchy, companies have set up teams. Quality teams. Corrective-action teams. Problem-solving teams. Cross-functional teams. Self-managing teams. So many teams, a wag once remarked, that some companies could be mistaken for bowling leagues.

The one thing that everyone seems to be searching for—or trying to create—is just what we saw that companies in the new economy need: employees who care about the company's success and whose efforts on its behalf will therefore show up on the bottom line. Sometimes companies' attempts to change have seemed to work by this measure, other times not.

Quality efforts, for example, often improve quality. They don't always improve the business. The Wallace Co., a Houston oil-supply company, won the Malcolm Baldrige National Quality Award in 1990 and entered Chapter 11 shortly thereafter. An ambitious McDonnell Douglas quality program wound up "in tatters," according to one report, because "the program's advocates had not anticipated massive layoffs that poisoned labor-management relations." The accounting firm Ernst & Young, in a

1992 survey of quality practices, found that companies experienced "mixed results."

Reengineering often helps companies cut costs enormously. On occasion it crashes and burns. A 1994 study of the phenomenon by CSC/Index, the company headed by Champy, was generally favorable. But it acknowledged that some reengineering efforts failed completely. Worse, reengineering can become identified in employees' minds with downsizing. According to a survey by Pitney-Bowes Management Services, employees in 70 percent of reengineered companies felt that reengineering was simply "an excuse for layoffs." Champy himself acknowledged in a recent book that "reengineering is in trouble."

Finally, reengineering doesn't do much good for new businesses or for companies that are struggling for reasons other than sclerotic organizational structures.

As for teamwork, its effect is hard to gauge. Companies with successful team structures can experience big boosts in productivity. But team building is hard work, and teams are often introduced with a lot of fanfare only to die out later on. "We used to do a lot with teams," one small-company CEO told me sheepishly. "We should probably get back to that." A *Fortune* article in 1994—"The Trouble with Teams"—advised readers to mistrust the hype over teams. "Listen carefully and you'll sense a growing unease, a worry that these things are more hassle than their fans let on—that they might even turn around and bite you."

Meanwhile, astute observers couldn't help feeling there was something lacking after a decade and a half of experimentation. A basic theme. A central organizing idea.

Most of the new managerial ideas are "responses to the inadequacies of Taylor's original model," wrote David H. Freedman in *Harvard Business Review.* But despite the proliferation of techniques, he added, "the fundamental principles of a new managerial paradigm are far from clear."

Rosabeth Moss Kanter agreed. Each of "the popular management buzzwords and fads of the last decade," she said, seems like "a way station" on the road to more comprehensive rethinking of the business organization.

# The Birth of Open-Book Management

Amidst all the groping, the experimentation, the fads and fancies of new-economy management, you could, if you were looking in the right places, spot a handful of companies that were heading toward the development of that elusive new paradigm. They didn't always share the same language or use the same techniques. But they operated—do operate—according to remarkably similar principles. I think of them as the pioneers of open-book management.

First, *people should see themselves as partners in the business,* the pioneers figure, not on opposite sides of some labor-management fence.

When the company does well, everyone should do well. And when things are tough, everyone should know it. Conclusion: A noticeable portion of everybody's pay should come in the form of profit sharing or stock distribution.

Second, *people should be empowered*—not just to ensure quality, not necessarily as part of a team, just as part of their regular daily job.

Managers in the pioneering companies are responsible for setting directions, as in any business. But employees voice ideas, take part in decisions that affect them, and help run their workplace. The idea of specialized work—do your job and nothing but your job—goes out the window.

And then, the most important innovation: If people are going to see themselves as partners in a business, if they're empowered to help run things, *they have to understand what the business is all about.*

They need information—a ton of it, and on a regular basis, just as a manager does.

They need a basic understanding of the financials, so they can evaluate and act on all that information.

Without information and understanding, the pioneering companies believe, empowerment is just an empty word. Ignorant employees are always dependent on someone else to tell them what to do.

Without information and understanding, profit sharing or stock ownership is at best no more than a nice extra benefit. Unless you *act* and *think* like an owner, you don't *feel* like an owner.

The pioneers put their principles into action in various ways:

• Southwest Airlines, the only air carrier in the United States that consistently makes money, encourages workers—even pilots—to pitch in cleaning planes or handling baggage or doing anything else that needs doing. An employee's job: Get the plane quickly and safely into the air. Satisfy the customers. Help the company succeed. The airline pays generous profit sharing, which employees choose to take mostly in the form of Southwest stock. Chairman Herb Kelleher writes periodic letters to employees, explaining the company's cost figures and financial prospects almost as if the recipients were Wall Street analysts.

### Thinking like an owner:

Employees in one fuel-cost crisis chipped in hundreds of thousands of dollars to help Southwest buy jet fuel. Employees in several stations have volunteered to paint their facilities themselves. "They know how expensive it is to get it painted," says Vice President Ann Rhoades. The airline's pilots recently agreed to an unprecedented ten-year contract that froze wages for five years but granted them additional shares of stock.

• Wabash National is a truck-trailer manufacturer that zipped from start-up to $100 million in sales in its first three years and is now one of the industry leaders. It entrusts its production to teams of workers and divvies up 10 percent of pretax profits among its 2,700 employees. But founder Jerry Ehrlich also wants "to make sure everyone understands how we make a profit." So Wabash puts nearly every employee through six hours of financial-education classes. Every quarter Ehrlich or another manager projects Wabash's financials onto the side of a trailer in the factory and walks employees through them.

### Thinking like an owner:

"We may have an order for, say, a hundred trailers, and we get paid when that last trailer gets delivered," says Ehrlich. "So maybe the customer owes us $1.5 million. And if a defect or something keeps that last trailer from being delivered, we run up our receivables by $1.5 million. Our people understand that sort of thing."

• Herman Miller, the big office-furniture company, operates according to the Scanlon Plan, a scheme developed in the 1950s by a onetime steelworker named Joseph Scanlon. The principles aren't so different from the ones you'll read about in this book. Herman Miller encourages widespread stock ownership, to the point where nearly a quarter of the company is owned by directors or people on the payroll. It pays quarterly bonuses pegged to key financial and operational targets. It sends information about the business out to all six thousand employees every month—on video.

### Thinking like an owner:

"Our shipping group had been loading trucks bound for other Herman Miller facilities," says Jim Schreiber, a top HM executive. "We'd been doublestacking on semitrailers, using pallets. The crew, the people in shipping, said, if we hand-stacked this it would take longer but we'd probably get twice as much on a trailer." They tried it, evaluated it, put it into practice—and, says Schreiber, eventually discovered it was saving the company nearly $3 million a year in freight costs.

Plenty of other companies could fit into the pioneer category as well. Wal-Mart makes sure employees own stock (and has watched many get rich as the stock appreciated). Employees—oops, associates—see their store's sales and earnings every week and talk about how to improve things. Chaparral Steel makes sure its employees see and understand the company's budgets and financial statements. "We try to focus people's attention on the business because they participate in profits," says Vice President Dennis Beach.

And then, of course, there's Springfield ReManufacturing Corp. (SRC), a company that may have had more impact on American managerial practices than any ten of the nation's business schools.

In 1983 a guy named Jack Stack was both desperate and creative—a productive mixture.

Stack and twelve other managers had recently bought out a struggling factory belonging to International Harvester (now Navistar). The Renew Center, as it was known, remanufactured engines.

The purchase was a buyout that was highly leveraged even by Wall Street's freewheeling standards. The thirteen managers had scraped together exactly one-ninetieth of the purchase price, which was close to $9 million. They had borrowed the rest—at 18 percent interest. The new company was called Springfield ReManufacturing Corp., but it wasn't exactly a going concern.

"We were nearly comatose as a corporate entity," says Stack. "We couldn't afford to make a $10,000 mistake."

The only way to survive, Stack decided, was to make sure everyone in the whole plant, all 119 employees, knew exactly how iffy things were.

He began distributing the income statements, along with the various operational and budget numbers that made the income figures move one way or the other.

He taught the managers and supervisors how to read the financials. They, in turn, gave an abbreviated course to hourly employees.

Stack had laid the foundation for this basics-of-business education by working one-on-one with people such as Denise Bredfeldt.

Bredfeldt, who started at the Renew Center in 1975, worked on the line building hydraulic pumps, valves, cylinders. She remembers Stack asking her if she was making the company money.

Sure, Bredfeldt replied.

Prove it, said Stack.

"Then he gave me a two-hour lecture on how to determine costs," Bredfeldt remembers. "I took two weeks and scrambled around, digging up information. I didn't know anything—I had to learn as I went along.

"Finally I proved that we were making money. But I had thought we were making more than we were. Transmissions were making more. Jack said, 'Suppose we took your area and gave it to the transmission group?'

"They say numbers don't lie—and it was obvious from the numbers what we had to do. He armed us with the information we needed to make wise decisions."

Stack developed an open-book system that relied on people hearing the financials every week and working for bonuses pegged to financial targets. He christened it the "Great Game of Business." Employees, like players in any game, needed to know the rules of business. They needed to be able to follow the action. They needed to have a stake in winning.

Knowing the rules of business meant learning, as Bredfeldt did, how to make money. Following the action meant following the weekly and monthly income statements.

The stake at SRC was partly stock ownership. Through a stock ownership plan, employees came to own 30 percent of the company. The stake was also the bonus. Each year, Stack and others would figure out the financial goals that were most important to SRC's survival and growth. A certain level of pretax profits, for example. A balance-sheet goal such as liquidity. If the company made those goals, everyone got their bonus.

SRC under Stack's system proved to be a phenomenal success.

Its sales for the first several years grew 40 percent a year. Income rose. The debt-to-equity ratio plummeted. The value of its stock—the wealth that employees were creating for themselves—rose from 10 cents a share to $18.60 in just ten years. The company today does close to $100 million in revenues, operates several different divisions, and employs nearly eight hundred people.

Stack's system also proved to be a phenomenal attraction.

Written up first in *Inc.,* it was soon being featured on the *MacNeil/Lehrer Newshour* and on *CBS News,* and later in *The Wall Street Journal.* Other companies began asking Stack if they could come visit. Stack was swamped with speaking invitations. In 1992, he published his book, *The Great Game of Business,* written with Bo Burlingham. In the book he used the phrase *open-book management,* describing it as "the key to SRC's success."

I had coined this phrase in a 1989 article on three other companies that shared financial information. None of them actually used the term, but we writers always like to come up with what we hope will be catchy phrases. Stack picked up on it and popularized it. In 1993, he gave a speech at a national conference on labor relations, presided over by Bill Clinton. He again used the words open-book management in describing SRC's system.

"And the phrase . . . that made the biggest impression on me here was 'open-book management,' " said Clinton later. "If we could do nothing other than convince people that somehow the only way to get everybody on the same team is to give them the same information, the same capacity to evaluate the information, I think that would be a terrific thing."

I'm not telling you all the details of SRC's system because Stack does that himself in his book. Read it. What you won't find there, however, is how many other companies have been discovering open-book management. Some have learned about it from Stack and SRC. Others have developed a homegrown system of their own. Still others don't have a system yet, they just have an intuitive sense that it's the right way to go. Consider:

• So many companies asked for tours of SRC that Stack set up an Executive Training Institute. Once a month or thereabouts, representatives from businesses all over the United States and Canada gather in Springfield for a two-day seminar on the Great Game, complete with attendance at one of the "huddles" described in Stack's book (see chapter 6). Influenced by Stack, Allstate's Business Insurance division has mounted its own version of the Game. So have scores of other companies—some of which you'll read about in the pages that follow. At last report, some 1,200 people had attended the SRC seminar.

• Homegrown open-book systems have been sprouting all over as well. Bob Argabright at Chesapeake Packaging Corp. created a system he has dubbed "Net Results" (chapter 9). Rhino Foods, a Vermont company that supplies specialty ingredients for Ben & Jerry's ice cream and other products, calls its system the Game of Business—and CEO Ted Castle says he was "amused to hear about a similar strategy" at SRC. Most companies don't have a name for what they do, they just do it. Stonyfield Farm, the yogurt maker, plasters its financials all over the cafeteria wall. Ashton Photo, an Oregon photo processor, puts a P&L up next to the lunchroom door—and pays its teams a percentage of the sales that they're responsible for, along with a bonus tied to profits. A Coopers & Lybrand survey of four hundred fast-growing companies found that 60 percent "furnish their employees with frequent, regularly scheduled reports that detail key operating and financial information." More than 80 percent of the three-hundred-plus companies responding to an *Inc.* poll on the subject said that opening the books was a good idea.

• Open-book management seems to make intuitive sense to a variety of people in a variety of situations. When Walter Kiechel III began a brief stint as managing editor of *Fortune* in 1994, the *New York Times* reported, the first thing he did was give employees "an unusually detailed rundown on the budget, including information about expenses and profits." When U.S. congressman Jim Bunning, the former big-league pitcher, was asked what he would do to solve the 1994 baseball strike, he replied, "I would say, 'Management, open your books completely to the players.'"

Spend a little time in Springfield, Missouri, and you get a sense of how quickly open-book ideas can catch on when people are exposed to them. Lynn Thompson, who runs the local Pontiac-Cadillac dealership, makes a point of posting information about sales, income, and the like up on the walls of his office. Units in his company meet weekly to review budgets and expenses or to set forecasts. David Zapatka, owner of Z-Tech Companies Inc., a commercial cleaning service, teaches employees a "Business 101" course and pays bonuses pegged to profitability. "It's quite similar to what Jack Stack does with his company," says Zapatka.

My most interesting conversation along these lines was with Capt. Randy Clutter of the Springfield Police Department, who was eagerly figuring out how to apply Great Game, open-book management techniques to his organization. Clutter had a few problems in making the translation to the public sector. He couldn't exactly hand out bonuses to the cops. Nor was the SPD supposed to make a profit.

But, Clutter decided, it wasn't out of the question that police employees—all of them—should understand and track the department's budget.

That, he reported, had several benefits.

"Once they understand the budget process and how it works, they help us create a better budget. It's more understandable, so we can sell it more easily to City Hall. And City Hall can more easily sell it to the customers, which is the citizenry.

"They also start seeing where the money's going. And they see, oh, my gosh, we've used 30 percent of our overtime budget in two months; we're going to have to watch how we do things or we're gonna run out of overtime money.

"And with the officers knowing what our budget is—well, the preponderance of our budget comes from a sales tax base. They can see there's just so much pie there. So when it comes time to negotiating wages and benefits, maybe we can do a little bit better if we're prepared to do our jobs better."

So this is where we are in the evolution of management. Companies all over are groping toward a system, a way of thinking, to replace the old, outmoded one. A handful of them have hit on principles to get people working cooperatively, toward the same ends, in the same direction. One pioneer has invented and codified a system so appealing that even the local cops want to implement it.

Stack's name for the system is the Great Game of Business, a phrase that's now a registered service mark of SRC. The generic name is that phrase Clinton picked up on: open-book management. It's time to see exactly what it involves and how to put it into practice.

## CHAPTER 3

# Open-Book Management

## What open-book management is—and how it can transform a company

## The Basics

Open-book management is a way of running a company that gets everyone focused on helping the business make money. Nothing more, nothing less.

It gets rid of the old approach to management, in which bosses run the show and employees do what they're told (or what they can get away with).

It takes the best new ideas—empowerment, quality, teams, and so forth—and gives them a business logic. In an open-book company, employees understand *why* they're being called upon to solve problems, cut costs, reduce defects. And they have a reason to do so.

If you could tear apart an open-book company and compare it to a conventional business, you'd see three essential differences.

**Every employee in an open-book company sees—and learns to understand—the company's financials, along with all the other numbers that are critical to tracking the business's performance.**

That's why it's called open-book. They know whether they're making money. They know how much. They know why. They have a pretty good idea of what the future holds—all because they see the numbers that most companies show only to top management.

**Employees assume that, whatever else they do, part of their job is to move those numbers in the right direction.**

They may be salespeople or software designers, machine operators or telephone operators, book editors or bookkeepers. But they are also part of the business and are accountable to each other for their unit's performance.

**Employees have a direct stake in the company's success.**

If the business is profitable, they get a cut of the action. If it's not, they don't. In effect, open-book management teaches people to quit thinking of themselves as hired hands (with all that implies) and to start realizing that they are businesspeople (with all *that* implies). Their financial security depends on their joint success in the marketplace. Period.

The first several chapters of Part Two take up the many ways by which companies are implementing these principles. They tell you how to do it—or at least how to begin doing it, since you'll probably invent a lot of it yourself.

This chapter explains the logic of the open-book system. In a nutshell it is this: Companies in which everyone helps make money will *outperform* companies in which only a few people at the top see that as their job. In the new economy, creating a company of businesspeople is the ticket to survival—and prosperity.

But since one story is worth a thousand lectures on logic, let's first check out open-book management in action.

# The Turnaround at Pace Industries

I don't know who named Monroe City, Missouri. Maybe he or she had plans or hopes or dreams that didn't materialize. If Monroe City is a city, then this book that you are holding is the *Encyclopedia Britannica.* What we're talking here is a pleasant hamlet of maybe 2,200 people out in the Missouri hinterlands, twenty miles west of Hannibal, itself no metropolis in spite of its fame as the boyhood home of Mark Twain.

Near the railroad tracks in Monroe City is a plant that makes die-cast metal parts, mostly for the automotive and electric-motor industries. It's a fair-sized factory, employing about three hundred people, and without it Monroe City would be even less of a city than it is today.

A few years ago, the plant looked as if it was about to go the way of so many small midwestern manufacturing facilities, which is to say belly-up.

First the plant's owner went bankrupt. Then another company—Pace Industries, out of Fayetteville, Arkansas—leased the building and equipment. Henceforth the plant would be known as the Cast-Tech Division of Pace Industries.

But Pace didn't seem able to turn things around. The plant had work, but it lost money every month. Morale, already low, kept sinking. People in the die-casting department didn't talk to people in machining. Managers didn't mix with workers, except to give orders. ("The only communication you got back then," says one employee, "was when they came around on Friday and said you had to work Saturday and Sunday.") Hourly employees figured that management was clueless. On the floor the word was, if you didn't like one set of instructions, wait a while. You'd get some different ones. Some people in the shop, mad at the whole situation, supported a unionization effort. Everyone, pro-union or anti, was fearful for the future.

In December 1992 Pace appointed a manufacturing engineer named Andy Crowder as plant manager. Crowder decided he got the nod mostly as a holding action until Pace could decide what to do with its investment.

But Crowder was not the kind of guy who put his name up on the manager's door and sat around waiting for something to happen. He had some ideas about how people should work together in a business. So he started going out in the plant and talking to employees.

Out there, he said things that no one had ever said before.

He told them that the future was in their own hands, not someone else's. A union didn't make much sense; what they needed was to make money. If the plant was profitable, Pace wouldn't walk away. If it kept on losing money, no corporation in its right mind would keep on writing checks forever.

More to the point, employees *could have an effect* on whether the plant made money. "We started talking about responsibility, about what we had to do to turn this company around."

Then Crowder began teaching himself about why the plant wasn't making money—which meant, for starters, understanding the numbers.

Of course, first he had to *get* the numbers. "I was in this office two months before I ever saw a profit and loss statement. I was livid! What am I doing? Where am I going?" At least Crowder was in better shape than most. None of the plant's sixteen other managers had ever even seen a P&L. Some wouldn't have understood it if they did.

Crowder finally got the attention of the accountants at Pace headquarters and began receiving monthly statements. Figuring that every manager ought to know what he knew, he distributed them to his staff. Every Wednesday night the little group would go to a nearby Holiday Inn and work their way through the most recent figures, learning as they went.

One thing they learned was that spending was out of control. Maybe that was putting it mildly. No one was watching where the money went. No one even *knew* where the money went. So week by week, the managers began scrutinizing line items, figuring out where each number came from. They looked to see whether—and how—expenses might be cut.

Then came the crucial step. Crowder opened the books to the whole plant and gave employees an incentive to make wholesale changes.

As manager, Crowder was entitled to a bonus of 2 percent of gross profits, should there be any. Suppose, he suggested, we divvy up that 2 percent among everybody in the plant. If we make a profit, everyone gets an equal bonus.

Sure, said the other managers. Sounds good to us. By now, they had heard of what Jack Stack was doing at Springfield ReManufacturing Corp. down in the southwestern part of the state. Opening the books. Teaching employees to understand the numbers. Paying bonuses pegged to key financial targets. The Great Game of Business, Stack called it. Over time, people from Pace attended SRC's seminars on the Great Game. Experienced SRC managers visited Monroe City to teach the basics to those who weren't able to attend.

So Crowder announced Pace's version of the Great Game at a series of meetings. He sat down with groups of workers, maybe thirty-five at a time, each meeting lasting for as long as ninety minutes. He told them of the profit-based incentive he was offering. He showed them how the numbers that led to it were calculated. He said those numbers would be posted in the shop, and that they could keep track of the numbers themselves.

The first reaction, he remembers, was chilling. Dead silence. In other words: Sure, pal. We'll believe it when we see it.

A month later, the skepticism wasn't quite as thick. It had been a good month, and everyone was slated to get a few dollars in bonus money. Attitudes began changing. Wait a minute, said one employee at that second meeting. I know the bonus isn't much. But as long as we're making a profit I have a job.

With Crowder's encouragement, managers and employees formed teams in the plant's various departments to figure out how to cut costs.

One group attacked what they felt was an inane time-clock requirement. Employees punched in when they arrived, punched out at break, punched in at the end of break, punched out at lunch, and so on throughout the day. Why? Same reason that most companies do most things—it's how they had always been done. There were only three time-clocks in the hundred-thousand-square-foot plant, so 250 hourly employees spent many minutes each day just walking back and forth. The team asked 65 people to record that time, then calculated the cost. It came out to $133,000 a year.

The rules were changed.

Another department decided to hire a worker to go through all the scrap iron produced in the plant, salvaging what was usable. "We're rebuilding valves we used to buy," explains Steve Ryan, a master mechanic. The savings average $4,000 a month.

Some departments didn't even need a team. Cleanup at the plant is handled by Danny Hardcastle, the janitor, working under the supervision of safety director Todd Young. Young took the cleaning-supplies line item—about $6,000 a month—to Hardcastle and asked him if it looked right. Nope, said Hardcastle, no way. Six thousand a month? A hospital wouldn't spend that much.

Young and Hardcastle investigated where the number came from. One problem, they discovered, was a computer glitch worthy of a Pentagon procurement system. Every roll of toilet paper taken from the stockroom was charged out as a *case* of toilet paper, $52 a pop. The plant's accounting system was misallocating thousands of dollars a month in toilet paper alone.

There were real savings to be had, too. Hardcastle found a cleaning agent that was cheaper than what he had been using. He and Young served on a team that came up with a plan to recycle the cardboard boxes then being thrown away. That saved the company $200 a week in haulage fees.

Meanwhile, Crowder set up two plantwide contests to reach objectives that were critical to the plant's efficient operation. Like Stack, he called the contests "games." Each would carry its own incentive, paid for from the savings that it generated. Each would also tie in to a healthy bottom line.

Game #1 was about inventory accuracy—the correspondence, month to month, between physical inventory and recorded inventory. For any goods-handling company, inventory accuracy is a critical number. No one wants to be in the position of a sales manager, say, who promises next-day delivery of three thousand valve covers and then finds out that the inventory records are wrong and he doesn't have three thousand valve covers.

At Pace, inventory accuracy had been as low as 54 percent. Improve that figure by three percentage points in a month, said Crowder, and we'll pay a bonus of $10. Today inventory accuracy is consistently close to 90 percent.

Game #2 was scrap reduction. "Scrap" is bad product that must be melted down and recast. Every die-caster makes some scrap. Every die-caster wants to make as little as possible.

Pace's scrap had been as high as 20 percent. Crowder showed employees what they'd save by reducing it, and proposed that savings from scrap reduction be shared four-fifths for the company, one-fifth for the workers. Today, scrap is consistently below 10 percent.

But the real game at Pace Industries was the game of business, which is to make money.

Big boards out in the shop tracked how the plant was faring in terms of sales and earnings. Full profit and loss statements handed out at monthly meetings told employees the bottom line. Bonuses—everyone's share of that 2 percent of the gross—were paid out quarterly.

And slowly, fed by the more accurate information, by the cost cutting, and by the increased efficiency, profits at the Monroe City plant began to grow. Month to month. Quarter to quarter. Today, Pace Industries' Cast-Tech Division is solidly profitable. Large customers such as AlliedSignal are giving the plant big new jobs, so the future looks bright. "Congratulations to Pace Industries Inc. on your turnaround capabilities and your quest for excellence," read an ad in the local paper, placed by the Monroe City Chamber of Commerce. "We are proud to have you in this community."

What has changed most dramatically, though, are the attitudes and actions of the people in the plant:

*In my opinion it's a whole new world. This open-book policy is—I don't know how we ran so long without that policy. I feel I have a stake in my future.*

—ORIE PERKINS, MACHINE OPERATOR

*I noticed the people out on the floor were putting in a lot more effort. We're learning different stuff as far as working on our machines.*

—DONNA DODD, MACHINE OPERATOR

*Instead of having people coming up to you and bitch about a situation, they come up and . . . give you not only a problem but an idea of what their solution is.*

—RONNIE MILLER, SENIOR MANUFACTURING ENGINEER

*Just about everybody [in our department] knows where we're at, where we spend our money. It makes a difference. 'Do we want to go with a brand-new motor?' Or—'No, we're a little close this month, why don't we go ahead and have this one rewound?' You make a lot of decisions with that in your mind.*

—STEVE RYAN, MASTER MECHANIC

*Before, if you came from machining into a die-cast area and saw a man sitting there doing something wrong that was costing us money, [if you mentioned it] that die-caster would kick you in the rump and tell you to get out of there. It's just not like that anymore.*

—LINDA TEAGUE, MACHINING SUPERVISOR

The three hundred employees at the Cast-Tech plant have learned—are still learning, as they're quick to point out—to be businesspeople. Not hired hands.

# The Homely Truths of Open-Book Management

I better say it right out: Pace Industries' Cast-Tech Division is not the be-all and the end-all of open-book management, the perfect exemplar.

There isn't any such thing. Too many companies are implementing the concept in too many different ways. Some, like SRC, have been at it a whole lot longer than Pace. Besides, what works for a die-caster may be irrelevant to a delicatessen or a bank. And what's important to a turn-around like Pace may not matter to a company that's already making money.

But the Pace saga illustrates a few homely truths about this process of learning to think like a businessperson rather than like a hired hand. And it shows a few of the reasons why open-book management can transform a company.

**Homely Truth #1: There isn't anything mysterious about open-book management.**

You put the numbers out there and teach people to understand them. You give people a chance to move whatever numbers they're able to affect. You offer them a share of the proceeds if the numbers move in the right direction and the company therefore makes more money.

To put it slightly differently: *If you reward people for making money, you teach them that's what business is about. If you give them the right information and control of their job, they can begin figuring out how to make more.*

The how-to chapters in the next part of the book go into lots of variations on these principles and on methods of implementation. But you don't need an MBA to begin putting this idea into practice.

A corollary of this Homely Truth, by the way, is that *just about anybody can learn to understand basic financials.*

I know—people go to school for years to learn the fine points of accounting. And as Andy Crowder discovered, even managers may need a while just to get comfortable with conventional income statements and balance sheets. Since most of us don't learn finance in school, business numbers at first are about as intelligible as earned run averages to an Englishman.

But income statements and balance sheets can be simplified to emphasize the important stuff. People can learn—and can teach each other—what they don't understand. Most Pace employees don't have college degrees. Some never finished high school. But they all understand the difference between making money and losing it. And now they can track that difference on paper.

**Homely Truth #2: The things that change in an open-book company are ways of thinking and acting. The basic structures of the corporation may or may not change.**

The die-casting plant in Monroe City is still owned by Pace Industries. Hourly employees still tend the machines. Managers still manage. The Cast-Tech Division has not become a democracy, and the distinctions among jobs and people haven't evaporated. Open-book management doesn't make everybody equal. It just assumes that everybody on the payroll has a stake in the business's success—and that companies work better when people understand that stake.

Sure, there are issues here. Some of the practitioners of open-book management, for example, believe that employee stock ownership is an essential ingredient. Others don't. We'll get into this debate later. Pace employees, at any rate, have begun thinking like businesspeople. The only structural change at the company was the addition of a few modest bonuses.

And, saving the most important for last. . .

**Homely Truth #3: Open-book management works.**

The employees at Pace Industries' Cast-Tech Division turned their business around, and in the process saved themselves from the unemployment line. Notice something important here: *Pace had no big infusion of cash, no huge new customer, no fancy new technology, no costly consultants, just a new system of management.*

That's what happened at SRC, too. And at Chesapeake Packaging's Baltimore plant, and at Cin-Made, and at a dozen other struggling companies that have stumbled upon or invented the principles of open-book management. A turnaround—done from the inside.

But open-book management isn't only for companies in trouble.

Manco Inc. may be one of the most successful consumer-products distributors in the country. It uses an open-book system to help keep its blistering growth under control. Phelps County Bank has passed its two chief competitors to become top dog in its market, even though both are owned by big bank holding companies and Phelps is independent. Open-book management at Phelps supports its strategy of offering customers top-of-the-line service.

Managing by the open book, of course, isn't the only thing these companies do right. On the other hand, when you talk to executives and employees at these companies and many others, there's no doubt in anyone's mind that open books—teaching employees to think and act like businesspeople—is a central element in their success.

# Why It Works

OK, so what's really different? *How* does open-book management do what it does?

The simplest answer is this: People get a chance to act, to take responsibility, rather than just doing their job. And they know enough to understand what actions will have a positive effect on the business.

It's a day-in, day-out difference. Open-book management is Danny Hardcastle figuring out how to spend less on cleaning supplies. It's Steve Ryan, the master mechanic, making a decision to rewind a motor rather than throw it out and buy a new one. Out there on the front lines is where any company's battles are won or lost. "The moment of truth? It's when that guy is standing in front of somebody's house making a delivery," says Leslie Fishbein of Kacey Fine Furniture in Denver.

"That's when things have to be done right." Fishbein ticks off her mental list of things that can go wrong anywhere along the line. The salesperson oversells the product, so the customers expect more than they're getting. Someone in the office does the contract wrong, so the paperwork isn't in order. The customer asks a question and no one knows the answer. And then, in front of the house, the delivery person drops the dresser.

No supervisor or department head can anticipate or handle all such situations. A company that hired enough managers to do so would go broke from the overhead. Open-book management gets people on the job doing things right. And it teaches them to make smart decisions, decisions that reflect the company's best interests, because they can see the impact of their decisions on the relevant numbers.

So that's the simple answer. And it's the truth. Unfortunately it's not the whole truth.

If it were, we'd all be practicing open-book management by now. We aren't.

The reason, of course, is that nothing involving human beings and society is ever so simple.

Companies are social organizations. They're complex structures shaped and affected by history, by law and custom, by people's motivations and ambitions, by a wealth of different economic interests. Companies are labor and management, they're bureaucracies with half a dozen or half a hundred different departments and divisions and business units. They're avenues for the advancement of careers.

Then, too, no one creates a company from whole cloth. Start a business or take a new job and you bring a whole set of expectations with you. Expectations about who gets to do what. About what each department's responsibility will be. About how people will work together, and how they'll be compensated.

Changing the accumulated weight of all this history is like redirecting the flow of water over Niagara. And yet the beauty of open-book management is that it cuts a whole new channel, all at once. It works because it steps outside of the mind-set we inherited from the last industrial revolution. It says, *we're all in this business together and we're all accountable to each other for making sure it succeeds.*

That by itself is a powerful statement. It also has some powerful implications.

- The usual sources of mistrust and resentment simply evaporate.

When people don't know how a business is doing—or how their particular unit is faring—they speculate. They suspect the worst. Or maybe they don't suspect the worst, and then are caught by surprise when the worst turns out to be true. The result? Bitterness. Animosity.

Open-book management builds trust because it builds understanding. "We came through a couple of very tough years," says Ken Anderson of Anderson & Associates, an open-book engineering firm. "In 1990, 1991, 1992, the economy was down. We had plenty of work, but profitability was low, and there were very few raises during that time.

"We didn't have people coming in to complain. They all understood where we were because they could see the numbers every day. And we had some lines of business that we just couldn't do well on. People liked to do them, but when they saw time and again that we couldn't make money there, we just dropped them."

• People can see that common goals outweigh parochial ones.

In the typical business, labor wants more money. Management doesn't want to give it. Or maybe the dispute is between manufacturing, which is lobbying for new machines, and marketing, which needs more people. The average business is a lot like Washington, D.C. Everybody knows there are common objectives somewhere. But the common objectives get lost amid the cacophony of turf wars and special-interest pleading.

Special interests don't disappear in an open-book company, they just get put in the right perspective. The terms of the debate shift. People want higher wages? Great—how do we boost margins so we have more money to spend on wages? Manufacturing wants new machinery? Fine—give us a detailed plan showing how the new machinery benefits everybody.

A side benefit for unionized companies: Open-book management consigns the adversarial relationship between unions and management to the historical dustbin.

Unions always want "more," as Samuel Gompers said, and figure they have to take it out of management's (or the stockholders') hide. "We are set up by law to fight," mused one labor leader recently. "We had to fight to get the union, then we had to fight to get a contract. Labor laws just set the rules for fighting." Management—particularly these days—is usually happy to fight back. Both sides act as if business is a zero-sum game, and the only thing to decide is who gets how much.

*But business isn't a zero-sum game. Make more money and there's more to be shared. The important decisions have to do with how to enlarge the pie, not how to divide it.* That's the basis of open-book management.

Suppose a company says to the union something like this:

Right now, we'll set our base wages and benefits equal to the average for our industry and region. That way we know we won't start off at a competitive disadvantage. If we make money and grow, your members will share generously in the profits. You'll know from month to month how we're doing—indeed, we're expecting the employees to help us do better every quarter. In return, they'll have a say in figuring out whether we should spend our surplus on wages, better benefits, improved working conditions, or something else entirely.

What would be left to fight over? Plenty, no doubt. In any company, managers fight with each other and with stockholders. But these are the disagreements of people who know they're on the same side and who want the company to succeed. They aren't the disputes of sworn enemies.

• Open-book management can focus attention like a laser beam on operational goals. At the same time, it keeps people from blowing them out of proportion.

Companies often need to get employees focused on some critical operational number. Sales goals. Quality levels. At Pace, the two biggies were inventory accuracy and scrap reduction. Until those numbers began moving in the right direction, the bottom line was iffy. Opening the books allowed employees to see that. The extra bonuses Crowder paid for improvements on those two measures focused everyone's attention. They began to move.

And yet: It's all too easy for operational numbers and targets to take on a life of their own.

You see it happen all the time in sales departments. Salespeople nearly always want to sell more, to boost that top line (and thus their commissions) even when the sales aren't that profitable for the company. You can also see it in Total Quality programs. Varian Associates Inc., a maker of scientific equipment, went wild in the late 1980s for quality-related measures such as on-time delivery. Varian's vacuum systems division boosted its on-time rating from 42 percent to 92 percent. Trouble was, reports *Business Week*'s David Greising, everyone at Varian got so obsessed with meeting production schedules that they neglected to take care of matters like returning customers' phone calls. Result: loss of market share. Red ink on the bottom line. "All of the quality-based charts went up and to the right," a Varian vice president said, "but everything else went down."

Too bad the books weren't open for inspection, along with the quality measures. Open books provide the missing link—they turn the operational numbers into dollars.

• Open-book management facilitates profitable innovation—and builds continuous learning into the organization.

Every company these days has to innovate. It has to come up with new and better (or just different) products and services. It needs ever more efficient work processes.

And what's the biggest obstacle to innovation, after coming up with the idea?

Sorry—no simple answer. It depends on what business you're in.

For old-line businesses, insurance companies and metal-bending manufacturers and department stores, the chief difficulty is that people are set in their ways. Managers protect their turf. Workers want to do what they always did. Everyone's scared of trying new things. Open-book management doesn't make those all-too-human feelings go away.

But it's amazing how persuasive numbers can be. Think of the difference between being *told* to do things a new way and seeing *why* you have to do things a new way. When job security is at stake, people learn quickly.

In new industries, in the software and telecom and medical-technology businesses, for example, the problem may be exactly the opposite.

Innovation—the latest project, the hottest new technology—is where the action is. Everyone wants to be out there on the edge, doing the glamour work. Any venture capitalist with more than three weeks of experience has watched companies pursue that glamour right down the tubes.

Open books are a reminder, day in and day out, that someone needs to be watching the store. Innovate, yes—but watch the cash flow, watch the return on investment, protect one niche while you explore others. The numbers never tell the whole story of a business, particularly one that's venturing into new turf. But the numbers don't lie, either. If you're hemorrhaging cash, you're hemorrhaging cash.

"Continuous learning," the hot buzzword of a few years back, is an idea not to be sneezed at: It means pursuing hundreds of tiny innovations of product and process, all the time, constantly learning to do things a little more effectively and a little more efficiently, constantly learning to provide customers with a little more of what they want and need. It's one of the hardest organizational chores there is. It probably wins the prize—in American corporations, anyway—for Most-Talked-About, Least-Done.

But open-book management helps build the continuous-learning mentality right into the organization, because the report cards—the financials—are out where everyone can see them.

"A company that decides to be an open-book organization," says *Training* magazine's Chris Lee, "is making a commitment to become a learning organization."

• Opening the books helps managers manage better.

Any company's bottom line is made up of—and therefore affected by—a zillion other numbers. Departmental expenses. Inventory turns. Labor efficiency. Sales efficiency. Materials costs. Warranty costs. On and on, down all the tabulations, every day and week and month and quarter.

Managers in conventional companies are supposed to track these numbers, watch for trend lines, get a handle on budget variances, identify problems before they get too big. Sometimes they actually do.

But most managers know the sordid truth: They're so busy putting out fires, answering the phone, responding to the latest memo from corporate that they're lucky if they get time even to look at the numbers. Somehow that $6,000 for cleaning supplies slipped by Pace's management, month after month.

If you think that never happens at your company—um, I hope you're right.

I said it in the introduction and I'll say it again: Open-book management is open-book *management*. It's a system for ensuring that what's supposed to get done actually does get done.

And how does it do this? Three ways:

## One: It forces managers to know their own numbers.

"If every department knows they've got to turn in these numbers at least once a week," says Mike Chiles, co-owner of Heatway Inc., "it forces a certain rigor in their thinking. It means that their own tracking procedures tend to become more automated because people get tired of adding up all these things. So they implement their own spreadsheets, their own processes. It makes them more aware."

## Two: It forces managers to understand their numbers.

When the books are open, the numbers are up where everyone can see them. They're reported at meetings in front of employees and in front of top management. They're posted on the wall. As one practitioner said, when the boss says, Harry, why is that variance so high—and you're in a meeting with all your peers—you really don't want to answer, "Gee, boss, I don't know." At least not more than once.

**Three: It builds dynamism—a driver—into the system.**

The point of a business is to *move* those numbers. To grow and to make more money. That's not the only point of business, granted. But if the numbers aren't moving in the right direction, they're probably moving in the wrong one. Growth and healthy profits are the sign of a healthy company.

Open-book management pegs a part of people's income to improvements—to higher profits, to better margins, even to improvements in the balance sheet. That gets everyone thinking about how to boost growth and earnings. It builds the basic logic of business into the very sinews of the organization. Managers and executives are no longer alone in worrying about whether the company is making money. They'll have a lot of help—which means that they can spend less time issuing orders and more time coaching employees in how to make money effectively.

Remember: Reward people for making money and you teach them that's what business is about. Then they can begin figuring out how to make more.

# The Power of Metaphor

No, I'm not going to wax poetic here. But there's something intangible that changes in a company when the books are open. People begin thinking about their jobs differently.

What's the usual metaphor for business? War. Companies are like armies. They have missions and strategies. They have officers, noncoms, privates. The people at the top map out campaigns and issue orders. The people at the bottom carry them out.

The reality of business life, of course, is less dramatic. It's more like a peacetime army.

People have jobs. (Yawn.) They have superiors and subordinates. Work consists mostly of learning the job, doing what you're told, not getting in the boss's way, trying to stay out of trouble, hoping for a raise or a promotion, schmoozing at the water cooler. Beating the competition is about as relevant to everyday life as beating the Americans was to the Red Army just before the collapse of the Soviet Union. As for how the business is doing, well, that's something that's shared (or not) at the end of a quarter or a year. It isn't exactly a pressing concern.

Open-book management, by contrast, turns business into something resembling a game. A contest. It offers a chance to win, every week and every month.

Business-as-game is the most common metaphor of open-book companies. Springfield ReManufacturing Corp. calls its system the Great Game of Business. A lot of other practitioners use the same language. Opening the books lets people "follow the action" or "know the score." Making people accountable for moving those numbers turns them into "players." A bonus is a "win."

The game metaphor isn't perfect. The outcome of most games, for example, doesn't matter once you stop playing. (That's why they're called games.) The outcome of business matters a lot. Livelihoods and economic futures are at stake.

But the metaphor is immensely powerful because it captures basic aspects of the open-book philosophy. As in a game, people do need to know how they're doing—otherwise they can't take part. They need to know the rules, which means understanding how their company makes money. They're expected to be active players, not just automatons who show up every day, perform some tasks, and then go home. And they will win or lose depending on how their company performs.

The metaphor of games has another pleasant aspect as well. Games are fun. Work in an open-book environment can be fun, too.

Most companies are pretty dreary. Big ones are like government agencies: drab, bureaucratic, impenetrable. You never know what's going on. Work consists of doing whatever lands on your desk. The high point of the day is lunch. Small companies have problems of their own. The boss is often secretive. Maybe he or she is indecisive or unpredictable. Work at some small companies consists mostly of figuring out what the boss wants today, as opposed to yesterday.

The fact is, we spend more time at work than we spend in any other single activity except sleeping. It ought to be enjoyable. And it can be, because *business* is enjoyable. Entrepreneurs, venture capitalists, even a few big-company executives know this, but they somehow manage to keep it a secret.

What makes business fun? Every day you get to match wits with the marketplace. Every day you face the challenge of doing something a little better, a little smarter, than before. Unexpected obstacles and opportunities crop up as frequently as in a video game. Every day you can find out the score. Every month or quarter you can tally up the results.

Winning, moreover, means something. If you win at business you get food on the table, money in the bank, a more secure future. And you get to play again tomorrow.

Not everybody can be a chief executive or a venture investor or the owner of a small company. But can't everybody share in the excitement of working together, trying to make money? Sure they can.

By now I hope you're excited about open-book management. Part Two will tell you how to begin implementing it in your company.

# Part Two

# IMPLEMENTING OPEN-BOOK MANAGEMENT

# Introduction
# Changing a Company

*If at first you don't succeed, fish the directions
out of the wastebasket.*

—ANN LANDERS

This book is about changing the way a company works. As anyone who has tried it can tell you, this is no small task. You need a clear idea of where you're going. You need a plan of attack. You need perseverance.

The following chapters should provide everything but the perseverance, which you'll have to come up with on your own. Not that they're a cookbook-style recipe for implementing open-book management. There isn't one, because every company is different. But they'll tell you how other companies have put this philosophy into practice. They'll show you the different pieces of the open-book system and how they fit together. They'll describe what works and what doesn't.

Before you plunge in, though, let me ask you three questions. Knowing the answers to these questions can save you from some blind alleys.

### First, look at your business situation. What do you hope to achieve?

Pace Industries needed a turnaround. Springfield ReManufacturing Corp. needed to dig itself out of debt. Allstate's Business Insurance division was doing so poorly that employees worried it would soon be shut down. Plenty of open-book companies got into it because they were in difficult, even desperate, straits and badly needed to get everyone pulling together. One small company's owners decided to open the books because they had been burned by not one, not two, but three crooked bookkeepers in succession. Posting the financials seemed the only way of preventing what felt like a chronic disease.

Other open-book companies mounted what was essentially a preemptive strike. They were profitable. They wanted to stay that way.

Sprint's Government Systems Division, for example, was doing fine when its executives made the decision to begin open-book management. But they knew that competition in their industry was—is—fierce beyond belief. They knew they needed every possible advantage, and they figured that open-book management would provide advantages that couldn't easily be copied.

Still other companies use open-book management as a critical ingredient in pursuing specific strategies or solving specific problems.

Phelps County Bank builds its competitive strategy around top-flight customer service. Opening the books has helped Phelps County's employee-owners learn how to deliver sterling service while keeping costs under control.

Manco has grown at a startling rate. Open-book management helps the company keep a lid on costs and focus on profitability as well as revenue growth.

The point here is simple: Any company, large or small, should understand the connection between open-book management and its business objectives. That's the only good yardstick for measuring your success in implementing the philosophy.

Of course, maybe your objectives are more modest—and more personal. Maybe, like Jim Sandstrom, owner of a specialty-coatings company, you just want to sleep a little better at night.

Any entrepreneur—and a lot of overstressed corporate managers—will recognize Sandstrom's situation.

"One night my phone rang at three o'clock in the morning. It was twenty-some below zero, windchill in the seventy-below range—and I'm being called. Some problem at the plant. I realized—many nights I'm awake and staring at the ceiling. I was thinking, how come I'm the only guy staying awake trying to figure out how to keep the company from going bankrupt? I said to myself, wouldn't it be great if *everybody* in the company stayed awake trying to figure that out? Then we wouldn't have a problem."

Sandstrom opened the books, taught employees to manage more of their own affairs, and set up a system through which they could earn sizable bonuses for improvements in the business. The payoff: "Now I can sleep."

## Second: Is there anything else that needs to be changed in your company?

I'm thinking, for example, of downsizing. Wholesale payroll slashing.

Granted, you can open the books to show employees how high your costs are and why you have to let all these people go. Some companies do—and then go back to old-style closed-book management once business turns around.

But if you use open books only to justify layoffs, your employees will figure, rightly, that this thing called open-book management is a scam. A snare. A ploy designed mostly to scare the bejeezus out of them. That doesn't quite jibe with the purpose of open-book management, which is to build trust and get everyone working toward the same ends.

Moral: If you're about to downsize, maybe you want to wait a while before you introduce open-book management. If you do it at the same time, be prepared for a tidal wave of skepticism and hostility.

Of course, even if downsizing isn't in the offing, you'd be wise to examine the level of trust and communication in your company.

Doubtless you've worked in companies where the hostility between labor and management was thick enough to slice. Where people regarded each other with all the trust of drug dealers toward their suppliers. Need it be said? Opening the books in such a company will not immediately usher in a utopia of warm fuzzy feelings. Open-book management will seem at first like yet another tool of exploitation or manipulation. Make sure that it isn't—and then be prepared to ride out the storm of skepticism.

### And finally: Don't forget that perseverance.

Even in the best of circumstances, implementing open-book management is the beginning of a long journey, hugely exhilarating but arduous and frustrating. Are you prepared to see it through?

In the last decade, any number of companies have mounted multiple attempts to change. Excellence. TQM. Reengineering. Self-managing teams. Some of these efforts brought huge payoffs. Others foundered. None came without costs—disarray in the organization, departures of key people, disappointment and disillusionment among the employees.

Today, people in those companies will regard yet another new idea with a jaundiced eye. Is it management's latest Flavor of the Month? Where are the hats, the T-shirts, the coffee mugs? Who are the consultants this time around? Most important, when will this horse manure go away so we can get back to work?

There are antidotes to such skepticism. Give them this book to read. Talk about it. Get people turned on to the idea. Most employees will relish a little more responsibility for the business, not to mention the chance of earning some more money. When you begin implementation, set your system up so that an immediate reward is built in. The chapters that follow should give you plenty of ideas.

Still, don't kid yourself that it's going to be either easy or quick. Some people will laugh (or sneer) at what you're trying to do. Others will quit. Most will just roll their eyes and bide their time. So be patient. An old farmer in the town I grew up in liked to say that God took a week to create the world and it might be a durn sight better if he'd taken two. Since we're only human, transforming a company through open-book management will take not one week or two but many. Jack Stack likes to say that SRC can teach employees to rebuild engines in a couple of months. Teaching them to understand the business can take a couple of years.

*But the reward for this patience is exceptional. The reward is that you will then be part of a different kind of enterprise—a company designed to thrive in the economy of the twenty-first century, not a company designed to thrive in the economy of the twentieth.*

A word on what you'll find in the following pages:

Open-book management is a system, a whole new approach to running a company. I've broken it up into four "principles," meaning four things that need to be done before an open-book system can work.

- Get information out there (chapter 4).
- Teach people business literacy, meaning teach them how to understand and use information (chapter 5).
- Develop a system of responsibility and accountability—that is, empower employees to act like businesspeople (chapter 6).
- Give everyone a stake in the company's success (chapter 7).

After that, the chapters focus on specific real-world experience—how companies get started (chapter 8) and how they implement and utilize open-book systems (chapters 9 through 13). Chapter 14 addresses some of the many questions and problems that arise when companies consider open-book management or actually begin putting it into practice.

## CHAPTER 4

# First Principle: Information, Please!

## Everybody has to know what's going on in the business

Get the information out there! Tell employees not only what they need to know to do their jobs effectively but how the division or the company as a whole is doing. That's the first step to open-book management.

Now this is not an original idea. I didn't realize quite how unoriginal it was until I reread Peter Drucker's classic book, *The Practice of Management.* The book was published in 1954, when Eisenhower was president and the New York Giants won the National League pennant.

The employee, wrote Drucker, needs information. Enough information to "control, measure, and guide his own performance." He "should know how he is doing without being told" and should understand "how his work relates to the work of the whole." He should also know "what he contributes to the work of the enterprise and, through the enterprise, to society."

Drucker advocated widespread information sharing not because employees wanted it, necessarily, but because "the best interest of the enterprise" demanded it. Only by providing full information could a company expect workers to take responsibility for their work. If a worker lacks information, "he will lack both incentive and means to improve his performance."

No kidding—1954. Talk about being beaten to the punch. This was so long ago that Drucker could get away with using "he" to refer to "the worker."

And it was so long ago that Drucker had to admit he wasn't sure *how* companies could get information out to people quickly. "The figures themselves are usually on record, but new tools are needed to get them speedily to the worker whose work they measure." Financial information would be especially tough to convey. "Most of the conventional data mean nothing to [workers], especially if presented in conventional form and with the conventional time lag."

In other words: It doesn't help people a whole lot to see the usual public-company income statement twenty-nine days after the close of the quarter.

As it happened, Drucker needn't have worried about the practical difficulties. For decades, most American companies weren't about to share more information with employees than they absolutely had to.

Top executives feared that information would be used against them, by union organizers or maybe by competitors. Keep people in the dark and you keep 'em off balance.

Middle managers realized that control over information was the source of whatever power they might enjoy. We don't pay you to think around here. I'll do the thinking.

Frontline employees, unionized or not, were well trained by years of experience in the mentality of hired hands. Just tell me what to do and I'll do it.

Besides, when Drucker was writing, the timely communication of information throughout a company's ranks would have been a herculean task. Income statements were prepared with the help of adding machines, not spreadsheet programs. Copies were made with carbon paper, not Xerox machines. You'd have needed a small army of clerks just to prepare and distribute the data.

But then times changed. In the new economy, a few companies began to realize that Drucker was right all along—that at least some kinds of information should be shared and distributed.

Times changed technologically, too. The logistical obstacles to timely distribution of information evaporated.

Sit in, for example, on a staff meeting at Springfield ReManufacturing Corp., a company that has turned information gathering and dissemination into something resembling a fine art. .

The meetings take place every other Wednesday morning at eight o'clock. Some thirty-five or forty people representing SRC's divisions and departments gather around a big U-shaped table. Controller Sydney Moore has a laptop computer loaded with the company's financials for the current year. The laptop is hooked up to an overhead projection system so that everyone can see the screen.

One by one, every unit calls out its numbers for the two-week period just ended. Sales or revenues. Cost of goods. Gross margins, selling expenses, and so on down the income statement, the relevant figures varying from unit to unit. On the screen, everyone can see how the performance numbers compare with the company's plan. Unit reps also give their forecasts as to what those numbers will be in the weeks to come. Moore pops the figures into the laptop. The computer automatically adjusts the totals.

When the reporting is done and the meeting moves on to other subjects, Moore quietly excuses herself. She feeds the laptop's new data into the company's computer system and prints out a full set of financials. *By the time the meeting is over,* every person there has a hard copy in his or her hand. The attendees then take that copy back to their departments or units for more discussion.

Today, if you want to share information, you can. But do you want to? Yes. Here's why.

# The Power of Information

It's an aphorism of good management: Managers need information. Lots of it. Up to date. What gets measured gets done. The more information you have, the better off you are. It's not hard to imagine a scene like SRC's in any well-run company. Managers get up-to-the-minute figures and compare them to forecasts. Problems are spotted, opportunities identified, marching orders handed out. Information is power—the power to run a business effectively.

But Peter Drucker and SRC know something else about information: When it's dispersed throughout a company, made available to all, it provides a power boost of a different sort entirely.

One reason: As Drucker said, *information lets people figure out what to do on their own, without being told.* It gives them feedback. It's a measuring stick, a scorecard, that tells them how they're doing.

Charles Coonradt, author of *The Game of Work,* tells a little parable of the importance of immediate feedback. The story has been repeated by numberless after-dinner speakers, so maybe you've heard it. Never mind—it's worth hearing again.

Work, says Coonradt, is a lot like bowling—"except there's a guy called a supervisor who stands in front of the pins with a curtain."

He can see the pins, but the bowler can't. The bowler throws the ball, hears something, and says, "How'd I do?"

The supervisor says, "Change your grip."

The bowler says, "But how did I do?"

The supervisor says, "Move your foot." The bowler changes his grip and moves his foot and throws another ball.

He hears the pins fall and asks, "How am I doing?"

"Don't worry about it. We've got a review coming up in six months. We'll let you know then."

Cute, right? But its lessons apply in real-life business situations.

Bill Palmer runs a company called Commercial Casework, located in Fremont, California, on the east side of San Francisco Bay. Commercial Casework builds and installs cabinetry and custom furniture for offices. Jobs average between $40,000 and $50,000.

As with any construction-related business, Palmer's big problem is to get the work done on schedule and on (or under) budget. His managers do up detailed plans for every part of every job. So many dollars for materials. So many labor hours. For most of Commercial Casework's corporate life, they didn't communicate these budgets to the employees. They told them they wanted the table or the countertop built as fast as possible. Employees were like Coonradt's bowler. They didn't know how they were doing unless somebody told them to do it differently.

In the first six months of 1993, Commercial Casework's jobs were running about 6 percent over budget. That was pretty typical.

Then Palmer made a change. He began posting the budgeted labor hours and costs for every part of every job. Employees could see the budget. They could keep track of how long it took to build a given part. People being what they are, some workers figured they'd beat the budget. Palmer also posted the actual totals. If a department beat its budget on a given job, the accomplishment was up on the lunchroom bulletin board for everyone to see.

Result: Suddenly jobs were averaging 2 percent under budget, a swing of eight percentage points.

So information is powerful as feedback, as a score sheet. *Business information—financial data—is particularly powerful because it shows people the reasons for doing something.* And when people see a reason, they're likely to act. Before anybody can get around to telling them to.

I think of this as the Rob Kellow principle.

Kellow is a friendly, burly software designer who works for a company called Acumen International in San Rafael, California. Acumen produces what are known as 360-degree personnel-assessment systems, which it sells to large companies. Typically, customers buy a system from Acumen, gather up questionnaire data from employees and their colleagues and supervisors, and send the data back. Acumen then generates a customized report on each person. The reports are used by the client for leadership development, team building, and the like.

Anyway, Acumen not long ago began holding monthly state-of-the-business meetings. The chief financial officer taught a series of classes to make sure that employees understood basic finance. Then, at the meetings, he or the CEO would take them through the income statement and forecasts.

Rob Kellow wasn't wild about the meetings. They seemed like a waste of time. He figured he'd be better off doing something he got paid for rather than sitting there listening to a bunch of numbers.

But in one meeting he heard something that surprised him.

One of Acumen's new products, an assessment system launched without much fanfare, was selling like hotcakes. Much better than expected. In fact, the sales department was projecting that it would soon account for 30 to 40 percent of Acumen's business.

The operations manager, Ornaith Keane-Fowler, spoke up at the meeting. She had a problem. The assessment reports that Acumen generated for customers of this new system were taking too long to produce. Each one took 7.5 minutes. At that rate the company wouldn't be making much money on the product. Thanks to the income projections, everyone could see a disaster in the making. More and more sales from a barely profitable product. Not exactly a recipe for success.

Kellow remembers leaving the meeting room thinking, I've got to do something about this.

That night, he got together with another developer, Rodney Kam. The pair wrote a little computer code so that they could try generating reports on a faster computer. The experiment worked—reports came out in only two minutes. They calculated the time difference for the number of reports the company expected to produce, and translated the time into money. Then they investigated the cost of a faster computer.

Bingo. The computer would pay for itself almost immediately. It was bought and on the job in a few days.

So there's the Kellow principle: *Given the relevant information,* people often act like businesspeople, not hired hands. They do what makes sense. Without being told.

Just think, dreary though the exercise may be, about how a problem such as this might have been addressed if Acumen were managed in traditional fashion.

Some overworked executive notices the problem, probably when Keane-Fowler makes enough noise.

At some point (when?) the exec contacts Kellow's boss and asks for help fixing it.

Kellow's boss gives Kellow the assignment when she gets around to it. Kellow solves the problem—when he gets around to it. (*Nobody* tells programmers to drop what they're doing this minute and do something else.)

Kellow provides the solution to his boss. She takes it, looks at it when she has time, asks someone to investigate the costs involved and get back to her. Eventually she makes a recommendation to the executive. *Maybe* at that point the executive orders Purchasing to buy a new computer.

In fact, Acumen wasn't so far from just that pickle. "The operations manager was asking for a new machine but wasn't being heard," says Tom Martin, the chief financial officer. "It was, 'Yeah, well, I have other things to deal with.'"

But instead Acumen became the model for the Kellow principle. Get the information out there and things begin to happen—just because people can, for once, see what needs to be done (or at least the logic of what they're being asked to do), and can decide for themselves to do it quickly.

## What's the Right Information?

Every company has some pivotal operational numbers.

Where I work, at a magazine, one key number is the ad pages sold for every issue. That number has a huge effect on profitability. Once you've sold enough pages to cover your costs, every extra page is almost pure profit.

Where my wife works, at a health maintenance organization, one of the key numbers is patients' hospital days. Hospital usage is one of the organization's biggest variable costs. Too many hospital days can turn a projected profit into a loss in the blink of an eye.

What are your essential numbers? A manufacturer of optical instruments says he watches order entry and on-time shipments most closely. The owner of a chain of lumber yards keeps a careful eye on scrap. The CEO of a home-health-care company focuses on hours worked per week by each of her caregivers—the higher the average, the lower the costs of turnover and recruitment among the staff. Operational numbers by definition vary from one industry to another.

These days, plenty of companies make a point of posting some of these numbers.

If you've seen a state-of-the-art 800-line customer-service operation, for example, there's likely to be a big electronic board tallying the number of callers on hold and the number that have had to wait longer than sixty seconds.

And any company that's mounting a quality drive will have a chart showing the trend in defect rates.

All this is great—as far as it goes. Whatever the vital numbers are in your business, those are the right numbers to tell people. But operational numbers alone don't go far.

Sure, employees will keep an eye on them, particularly if they think they (or their department) will get in hot water if the goals aren't met or the trend lines begin heading the wrong way. But the tabulations are as likely to be a source of resentment—Big Brother is watching us—as a source of inspiration. The classic example for clerical workers is the software that counts each employee's keystrokes per minute. But even in less Orwellian circumstances, operational numbers by themselves get old fast. If people don't understand *why* they're supposed to lower the defect rate or take those calls faster, pretty soon they'll stop caring. Like traditional employees, they'll do just what they have to do to get by.

Open-book management, by contrast, is all about the why—and in a business, the why is told by the financials. The Kellow principle.

Financial measures, moreover, define and constrain what any business can do. Rapid growth doesn't do a small company any good if the company runs out of cash in the process. Hitting defect-rate-improvement targets in one production area doesn't help the business if warranty costs stay high because of problems elsewhere. (IBM's blunt finance chief, Jerome York, acidly pointed this lesson out to some of Big Blue's operations managers who were bragging about quality improvements.)

So along with the operational figures, publicize the financial measures that are critical to your business. The income statement, of course. The cash-flow statement and its "second bottom line," operating cash flow. The balance sheet when it's appropriate. But what else?

• At Commercial Casework, the key financial number is budget variances. So along with the labor-hours targets, Bill Palmer posts "Job Cost, Over and Under" up on the lunchroom wall. At weekly meetings, he explains how variances affect the income statement.

• At Acumen—still small and growing—employees keep a hawk's eye on the company's cash. "What hits everybody's gut? How much money we have in the bank," says operations chief Keane-Fowler.

• At Sprint's Government Systems Division, revenue per employee is one of several critical financial gauges that employees are learning to watch. "It's one way of looking at how well the organization is doing," explains Rick Smith, a senior federal account manager.

Needless to say, the numbers must be "good." Accountants (and a lot of managers) know that numbers can mislead. But if you know your business, you'll know what the right numbers are—and what they do or do not tell you. Get them out there.

# How to Do It

Some companies have *scoreboards*—big boards up on the wall of the office or shop—that show all the essential numbers.

Dwinell's Visual Systems, in Yakima, Washington, may have one of the snappiest. "We're in the sign industry," says owner Dave Dwinell, so it was fairly easy for us to make a relatively sophisticated board." On the board: Dwinell's daily cash position, monthly sales and profit levels versus budget, gross margin percentage ("That's key for the production department"), on-time deliveries, rework costs, and so on.

Or maybe you'd like just to generate tables and charts on ordinary paper and tack 'em up.

Go look at the wall behind the receptionist's desk at Macromedia, a software company in San Francisco, and here is some of what you see:

Service revenue vs. plan

Revenues for every product line

Total revenue vs. plan

International revenue vs. plan

Products shipped to original schedule

Accuracy of product delivery dates

Marketing-driven calls per month

Departmental expenses

Annualized revenue per employee

And this is what's on the lunchroom wall at Manco, a consumer-products manufacturer and distributor located outside Cleveland:

Year-to-date sales vs. budget and vs. prior year

Year-to-date departmental expenses, current and prior year

Return on operating assets

Manufacturing direct support, dollars and percent of net sales

Daily sales picture, including sales budget, month-to-date sales, open orders, monthly sales

Stock value [Manco is an ESOP company]

Profit before ESOP and bonus vs. budget and prior year

Scoreboards don't have to be stationary! Manco also has those little electronic signs with the dancing letters positioned strategically throughout its facility. The signs report daily sales totals. Eaton Corp.'s engine-valve plant in Kearney, Nebraska, reports daily sales on a TV monitor in the cafeteria. But an electronic message isn't enough by itself—employees need to be able to come up to the board, study it, compare this month with last (or this year with last), talk about the numbers with one another.

Scoreboards (or score sheets) don't have to be big, ponderous things that get updated only once a month. Someone at Manco hand-letters the sales totals every day. Nor do they have to be unduly complex. Ted Castle, CEO of Rhino Foods in Burlington, Vermont, puts out what *Inc.* magazine dubbed the "profit-promoting daily scorecard." A mini-income statement, it's just a piece of paper posted at noon every day near the entrance to Rhino's production area. "We post a new scorecard every day," says Castle. "If we have any production problems, they show up on the scorecard the very next day."

Another way to get the information out there: *meetings*.

Manco and Pace Industries have monthly meetings. Rhino's people get together weekly. SRC asks its divisions (which are essentially stand-alone companies) to meet weekly; division representatives then get together every two weeks for a companywide meeting. At small companies, everybody attends every meeting. Larger ones such as Pace and SRC ask those who attend to take back the data and post it or discuss it in their departments.

Meetings are important! SRC or any other company could just have managers e-mail in the numbers and have a staff member distribute the resulting reports and projections. The point of looking at the numbers in a meeting, as most companies realize, is to talk over what the numbers say—to bring many different intelligences to bear on the problems and opportunities they suggest. People who attend the central meeting can then go back to their departments and report not only the numbers but what was said about them.

Of course, not every company can get people together in meetings.

That's when you use faxes or computers to get the data out. Crop Quest, an agricultural consulting firm, has professional consultants spread over five states. The company gathers them all together only once a year but sends them detailed financials every month. Commercial Casework always has some of its employees out on job sites, installing the company's custom-built cabinetry. Bill Palmer's brother Tom goes out to the sites once a week for a quick financial meeting—or simply calls people on their cellular phones and walks them through the weekly income statement. Herman Miller, the furniture maker, produces videos that detail and explain the company's financials. Anderson & Associates, the engineering firm, puts the information out on its computer network.

This is the age of the Information Revolution. If you can't figure out how to get data out to people quickly, you probably don't want to.

## Confronting the Great Fear

The Great Fear, of course, is that if you begin sharing information, the numbers will somehow be used against you.

Who are you afraid of?

Your employees, maybe. In companies where labor hates management's guts, yes, indeed, a union might try to take advantage of the figures. The whole point of open-book management is to get beyond that enmity. The open-book system gives everyone a stake in the company's success. The information sharing is a way of building the trust and cooperation that's essential to success.

Conclusion: If management and employees are locked in conflict in your company and you don't want to change the situation, don't share the numbers. They will be used against you. If you want to change the situation, get the data out there. It's a first step.

Then again, if you run a closely held company, you may be worried about something else, which is that employees will figure out how much you take home. If the number is large, you feel awkward and defensive—and that it's none of their business.

I hope this won't come as news, but the fact is it's already their business.

They talk about you and speculate about how much you're making. Their speculations are probably a whole lot higher than the reality. "Most people thought that our incomes were far and away more substantial than they really are," says Leslie Fishbein of Kacey Fine Furniture, which recently opened its books. Co-owner Mike Chiles of Heatway makes the same point. "If they don't know what's going on, and they see a $50,000 shipment go out, they think, golly, Mike and Dan Chiles are making a lot of money out of this—not realizing that when we get to the end of the year there might be 3 percent left over after taxes."

But if you don't think you can explain the logic of earning a fair— even large—return on the investment and risk that you or your family took in setting up the company, you're doing your employees an injustice. Americans believe that risk takers are entitled to a reward. They believe that company presidents should earn more—a lot more—than receptionists and machine tenders.

*It really isn't so hard.* Listen to Jim Sandstrom, owner of that specialty-coatings company, who opened up his books to his employees and says he has no trouble explaining a healthy profit:

> There's money invested here! The investor has a right to a return. If the net return gets so low he can take the money and go buy T-bills, 7 percent with no risk, what is he entitled to get here, with risk?
>
> To me that's a very answerable question and I'm willing to debate it with anybody, including the employees. They're not a bunch of fools. They understand that. So we share the financials. Yes, it's an ongoing learning process. Many of these people don't have a financial background. But they learn, and they learn fast.

But maybe your biggest fear isn't of employees, it's of competitors.

It's silly to be naive. There are often a few numbers that companies simply don't want to let out. If employees know these numbers, you have to explain why they need to be kept confidential—and you need to figure out how badly (really!) you'll be hurt if one renegade employee leaks the data.

But don't be naive on the other side, either. How many secrets do you really have? Your competitors are in the same business. They know your technology and your costs. They watch what you're doing with prices. They can see if you're growing or not. So probably they know your key numbers anyway. Kacey's Leslie Fishbein:

> In furniture retailing, all you do is take your number of salespeople, multiply that number by the published (and generally accepted) averages of what a retail furniture salesperson sells every month, and you can tell almost any store's volume in the country.

A furniture store in Iowa called me. They were worried about opening the books because of information their competitors might glean about the business. They were worried they would lose a competitive advantage.

I said to the guy, "You do between this and this. I don't even know who you are, I've never met you, we don't even share the same lines, and you're in Iowa." I said, "You think your competitors don't know?"

Mostly, though, the open-book managers just don't worry about competitors because they figure competitors will be too busy worrying about them.

Says Steve Wilson, the no-nonsense West Point graduate who is president of Mid-States Technical Staffing Services (chapter 10): "We think our numbers would scare the crap out of our competitors."

Putting out the numbers, of course, does no good if people don't understand what they mean. Which brings us to the second principle of open-book management: People in an open-book company need to know the basics of business. If they don't understand what profit is, or how you figure it out, or what difference it makes to turn inventory more quickly, or a hundred other issues and questions, they won't know how to make money. "Business literacy" means just that: knowing how a company—their company—makes money, and how to gauge whether it's making as much as it can.

## CHAPTER 5

# Second Principle: Business Literacy

## Everybody has to understand the information they get

To most people, which is to say 99 percent of those who don't sport the letters "CPA" or "MBA" after their name, financial statements—the fundamental data that show how a company is doing—might as well be written in Sanskrit.

We can't explain the difference between making a profit and generating cash. We stumble over gross margins, stutter over whether a borrowed $100,000 counts as an asset or a liability, and gaze in blank pitiable helplessness if asked to explain the variance on the income statement's SG&A line. What's an SG&A line, anyhow?

Notice that embarrassing pronoun "we" in the above sentences. I'm not being unduly modest here. It wasn't so long ago that I was a serious business illiterate—*even though I had already been president of a research company for several years.*

The memory makes me shudder. This was like standing up to conduct the symphony orchestra and saying, nah, I don't need the score, I'll just do it by ear. Unless your name is Mozart you're probably making a big mistake. My name wasn't Mozart, and I was indeed making a big mistake. I discovered just how big when my company came within a smidgen of going stone cold broke.

OK, I was young. And stupid. Plenty of older and smarter business-people do have a pretty good intuitive sense of their business's financials even if they rely on the accountant to walk them through the income statement. They're like old-style jazz musicians—they can play by ear.

But too many managers operate the way I did. When it comes to the financials, they're tone deaf. Which means they just aren't as good at their job as they might be.

It gets worse. The business-literacy story, I mean.

At least if you have owned or helped run a company, you know a little about where the money comes from and where it goes, even if accounting isn't your strong suit.

But suppose you have worked as a hired hand all your life. Or suppose you're just coming out of school—and your education, like most people's education, didn't teach you a whole lot about how companies work.

In that case you're likely to be burdened with misconceptions about business even more fundamental than mixing up assets and liabilities.

Maybe you think that revenues are the same as profits, for example. You wouldn't be the first. Or that profits are whatever a company has in the bank. You wouldn't be the first to think that, either.

Or maybe you understand that companies obviously can't keep a hundred cents of every sales dollar that comes in the door. But you figure profits must come to 40 or 50 percent of sales. Companies are rich, aren't they?

Chances are you have little idea what your employer spends its money on. "Employees don't realize that telephones cost thousands of dollars a month, and advertising costs this, and utilities are that, taxes, insurance, on and on and on," laments one chief executive.

Business illiteracy of this sort isn't confined to those without much formal education. It lurks in the hearts of people from all walks of life.

Not long ago there was a guest column that appeared in my local newspaper, the *Boston Globe*. It was written by a guy who worked in a bookstore.

The guy was also a graduate student—a candidate for a doctoral degree at a well-respected university—so he figured he was grossly overqualified for the job. And he was *ticked*. "I'm miserable," he wrote. "Not to mention maligned, mistreated, and mad at my boss." One of his gripes: low pay, even though the store seemed to be coining money. Why, he would "ring up a week's earnings" in five minutes on a busy day.

Well, maybe the guy *was* overworked and underpaid. But despite his fancy education he didn't know the difference between gross and net. Nor did he seem to realize that bookstores aren't exactly famous for their high margins.

An isolated case? Hardly. Sprint's Government Systems Division surveyed its (mostly) well-educated white-collar employees to find out how many understood the organization's financial objectives. Answer: few. Did they know how their own job or unit contributed to the bottom line? Nope.

And Kacey Fine Furniture in Denver discovered that even its managers weren't too familiar with financial measures and concepts.

None of this, of course, should come as a surprise.

Companies in America have never expected their employees to understand the fundamental financial data of business. They've never provided them with financial information or taught them to understand the snippets they might pick up on their own. Schools and colleges don't do much better. (On the very day I am writing this, *The Wall Street Journal* leads a story with the sentence: "Accounting courses: many college students avoid them like the plague.")

Then, too, many of us came of age in the days when giant corporations ruled the economic roost and sort of made money without thinking about it. Costs didn't matter much. Budgets were guidelines, not constraints. No one really cared about the delicate relationships between revenues and expenses and cash because all those numbers just seemed to take care of themselves. And so no one other than those CPAs or MBAs figured they had to learn.

# The Power of Business Literacy

Now, there may be a skeptic or two reading these words. If so, I venture they're muttering something like this:

*So what if we're a nation of business illiterates?*

*Sure, managers ought to understand the financials—though financial smarts probably aren't as important as operational expertise or good people skills. But employees? Come on. It's hard enough to teach workers their jobs, let alone train them to be accountants.*

Bear with me. We'll discuss how to do it in a moment. First, imagine how different a company could be if people really did understand the financials.

You might see, for example, a sudden drop in the animosity and mistrust that pervades most businesses.

The bookstore clerk and a zillion other workers assume that their employers' bank accounts are sizable, and wonder why they're not getting more of the stash. Must be because those jerks in the executive offices are getting rich. "When you're doing well, the question everyone asks is, gee, that money must be stacked up in the basement—we want more of it," says Clark Kawakami, chief financial officer of Black Diamond Equipment, a maker of mountaineering hardware.

If they understand the financials, by contrast, employees can see whether there's money in the bank or not. If profits have been growing, if labor costs have been dropping, if revenue per employee is rising, well, maybe they can reasonably expect a raise, or better benefits, or some other reward. If all those pleasant things are not happening, they won't be caught by surprise when budgets are tightened or raises postponed. They may even have some ideas about how to change the situation.

One of Bob Frey's major objectives at Cin-Made, the container manufacturer, was to teach this connection between how the company is doing and how employees can expect to do.

Conditioned by years of unionization, Frey's employees were accustomed to making demands. They demanded a raise. They demanded more vacation. A few kept on making these demands even after Frey opened his books and earmarked a generous share of profits for the employees.

But Frey budged nary an inch. You can have a raise only if you give up profit sharing, he told them. You can have more vacation only if you give up something else. "There's nothing here to negotiate, I said. There are no concessions you can squeeze from me. Or, to put it the other way around, there are no concessions I won't make. It's your money. You can distribute it any way you please."

A second improvement: less waste. If you assume your employer is rich, then you figure that the issues the boss gets all bent out of shape over can't really matter all that much. What if we did lose a customer? What if we do turn out 5 percent defects? What if our expenses are up a little? Lighten up, for Pete's sake.

It's human nature: If we don't know the impact of spending a little extra money, we don't give it a second thought. Hey, the company's paying for it. Don't worry about it.

This attitude affects conscientious employees as well as the not so conscientious. I have a friend named Bob, whose buddies call him Bobby even though he introduces himself as Bob or Robert. (What can I say? He *looks* like a Bobby.) Anyway, Bobby is a sales rep. He's good at his job. Well respected. And honest. Though he travels all over the country on expense account, I believe him when he says he doesn't pad his reports.

But neither, he says, does he worry for more than a nanosecond about staying in a Hyatt Regency rather than a Holiday Inn. Or spending $60 on dinner rather than $20.

Nor does he worry about getting the hotel to do his laundry for him at $3 a shirt. Or bringing his rental car back with an empty tank, thereby incurring the fill-up charge. Or taking a cab rather than the bus home from the airport.

Bobby isn't stupid—he knows all that spending costs his employer money. He knows he wouldn't disburse the cash quite so recklessly if it were his own.

But he has no idea what his company spends on travel, no clue how the travel budget affects his department's expenses (let alone the company's bottom line), no idea whether his profligacy is more or less than the company expects.

Result: Conscientious employee he may be, but Bobby spends his employer's money lavishly. It's a safe bet that the other two dozen sales reps do, too. And the company is the worse for it.

Waste gets built into the system whenever people feel there's plenty of money to spend. When IBM finance chief Jerome York was making his rounds looking for spending cuts, he discovered he could save $5 million a year simply by consolidating the purchase of office supplies—and $50 million by sending out computer instruction manuals electronically rather than on paper. No one had ever thought to look at those numbers before.

Third improvement: People make better decisions when they understand the stakes. And in a business, the ultimate stakes are financial.

*Decisions* (I hear you say). *Ahem. It's management's job to make decisions, not employees'.*

Well, yeah. Certainly many managers think so.

But the fact is that line employees and frontline supervisors make dozens of business decisions every day. Whether to throw out or remachine a problem part. How hard to pursue that new prospect. Whether to get maintenance to investigate the funny noise the truck motor is making, or just wait till it breaks. Whether the irate customer on the phone is entitled to a refund. Not to mention those little nigglies like what hotel to stay in.

You, the decision-making employee, can have the best intentions in the world. But if you don't understand the financial impact of your decision, you won't be able to make the decision like a businessperson. You'll do what you think your boss wants, or what will make you look best, or even what you think is right.

But "right" almost always involves financial considerations. You can't give every customer a refund if the company is going broke because of it. And you can't go all out for quality if doing so means your costs are no longer competitive. You can't make a Mercedes and sell it for the price of a Hyundai.

One last point: It isn't only a matter of watching costs. That's fine; that's helpful. But business literacy also enables everyone to understand, and get excited about, the magic of business.

You heard me right: magic. Business creates wealth. A successful company creates lots of it.

Think about what happens as a company grows. Revenues go up. Profits rise. Most important, the value of the company increases.

Add a million dollars to the bottom line, for example, and you haven't just put another million in the corporate coffers. You've added $5 million or $10 million or maybe even $20 million, depending on the industry, to the value of the company. It's the magic of the multiple: What the company is worth depends in large measure on its earnings stream. Ultimately, one way or another, the stockholders will share in that increased value.

If employees are shareholders, they're creating a secure economic future for themselves. They might even be making themselves rich. Thousands of ordinary employees who worked for Wal-Mart or Southwest Airlines or Microsoft wound up with tidy sums simply because they got some stock when the company was smaller and held on as it grew.

Even if employees aren't shareholders, they're creating wealth for those who are. They're building opportunities—and a chance for ever more generous compensation—for themselves.

Watching a business grow in value is exciting. People get caught up in the enterprise, become committed, work hard, work smart.

But I don't know a soul who gets excited about a process that he or she doesn't understand.

# How to Do It

Here's the truth: It really isn't so hard for people to learn the basics about where the money comes from and where it goes and what difference it all makes.

No one needs to become a certified public accountant. No one even needs to spend a year in night school.

All people need is a little education (with a bit of cleverness in the presentation) and then some reinforcement on the job.

**The first step—I'm afraid it's unavoidable—is classroom instruction.**

Wabash National, the trailer manufacturer, puts nearly all its employees through six hours of financial training. "You're studying financial statements, balance sheets, how a company makes money, gross profit, net profit, depreciation, all that," explains CEO Jerry Ehrlich.

The Body Shop USA, the natural-cosmetics company, does the same thing in a daylong orientation program for headquarters employees and new franchisees. A team at Sprint's Government Systems Division developed a three-day training program for managers and a daylong session for employees, both focusing on business basics. These three companies use staff people as instructors. Others hire consultants, trainers, even local professors to do the teaching.

*You don't have to be a big, rich company to do this.* If your business is small, or new, or still struggling, do it yourself. Learn from Chuck Mayhew.

Mayhew is both president and chief operating officer of Foldcraft Inc., a $20 million manufacturer of institutional seating in Kenyon, Minnesota. The company is employee owned, and Mayhew wanted people to understand that they could have an impact on the stock value and hence on their future. But first they had to understand business. So he developed a six-hour course of his own. He teaches it to employees in groups of thirty or thirty-five at a time, one hour a week for six weeks.

I loved hearing about this course. It makes the financial side of business seem downright simple. Mayhew's curriculum:

First, build up a personal balance sheet using home, car, boat, and so forth. Explain assets—the "what you have" side—and liabilities, the "who owns them" side. (You get a car loan from a bank. The car you buy is an asset. The debt you owe is a liability.) Explain stockholders' equity (in this example, the value of the car minus what you owe on it). Then walk through a personal "income statement"—the paycheck and what it gets spent on. Show how people build equity.

Second, create a cookie company. Just on paper. With simplified financials. Explain the manufacturing terminology Foldcraft uses by drawing an analogy with chocolate chip cookies. The cookies' ingredients are the same as Foldcraft's bill of materials. The steps in the recipe are routings. Look at the cost of ingredients. Analyze the effect of variances in the price of flour. See what happens if the baking takes more time than expected.

Third, move from production to marketing. Explain about markups and selling prices and profit. Show the effect of branching out into oatmeal-raisin cookies, which might have a different cost of production and a different selling price. Compile income statements and balance sheets.

Bonus in this lesson: Bake some chocolate chip cookies at home, bring them in, eat them.

Fourth, look at Foldcraft's financials. Compare Foldcraft's balance sheet and income statement to their individual counterparts, and to the cookie company's simplified ones.

Fifth, get into the more complex stuff. Talk about inventory and inventory costs. Discuss accounts receivable. Explain the difference between "cash" (money in the bank) and "profit" (what you've earned after allocations for depreciation, taxes, etc.). Look at the effect of purchasing variances, usage variances, labor variances. Discuss marketing expenses.

And sixth, bring it all home. "Then I go around the room," says Mayhew, "and try to get an understanding of who's in there and the jobs they have. I actually try to talk to them individually in the classroom about—What is your job? How do you see it impacting profitability? We talk about some real-life things that go on in your job."

Incidentally, if you find the prospect of starting from scratch too daunting, there are plenty of outside curriculum materials available. Bill Palmer of Commercial Casework uses a little volume called *The Yo Yo Company,* written by Denise Bredfeldt of SRC. Steve Wilson of Mid-States Technical uses business-education materials developed for Junior Achievement.

One other tip on classroom work: Have fun.

To most of us, financial education is boring, scary, or both. The numbers have to be demystified, the process made interesting.

That's why Mayhew bakes those cookies. "A silly thing," he says. "I do it to add a little flair and interest."

And it's why professional financial trainers such as Educational Discoveries, Inc., marketers of The Accounting Game, have their students blowing whistles, singing songs, jumping around the classroom, and generally acting nutty as they watch the instructor create a lemonade business.

And neither Mayhew nor The Accounting Game folks have anything on The Body Shop, where training manager Karen Delahunty runs the one-day course.

The class starts a fictitious company to make facial creams—and Delahunty is up on the podium breaking eggs and smearing stuff on her face.

The class learns about balance sheets using the medium of a wooden seesaw. When an asset is piled on one end, a corresponding liability has to go on the other—otherwise it will be out of balance.

When they study the income statement, they sing "When the Income Goes Marching In" and parade around the room.

The hoopla goes on and on. Silly? Sure. But Delahunty is a firm believer in having a good time. "People," she says, "don't learn unless they're having fun."

## Reinforce the lessons.

The best reinforcer of business education, of course, is the open-book system itself.

Get the information out there and people will start paying attention to it. Tie a bonus to the attainment of a gross margin target, and suddenly the gross margin line on the income statement looms large in people's consciousness.

But you can move the process along—by asking people to help each other, by giving people exercises, by finding other ways to reinforce the lessons taught in the classroom. For instance:

• Web Industries, a converter of roll materials such as foil and film, distributes its income statement every month—and often asks a frontline employee to take people through it at the monthly plant meeting. The employee, usually a machine operator, sits down with someone in accounting a day or two ahead of time, and like any teacher has to learn the material better than the students.

Over time, says Web's Charles Edmunson, more and more people learn—really learn—the meaning of terms like SG&A (selling, general, and administrative expenses, or what's often called "overhead"). A side benefit: Hearing the information from a colleague persuades employees that it's trustworthy.

• Jim Jenkins of Jenkins Diesel Power, a truck dealership with eighteen service technicians, gave the technicians an exercise to do at home. They had learned how much the company billed their time out for. They had learned what costs had to be paid out of the revenues they brought in.

Now, said Jenkins, figure out how much more the company could earn if each technician could improve his productivity by one-sixtieth—that is, if he could do in fifty-nine minutes what now took him sixty. The answer: $21,000. "Right to the bottom line," says Jenkins.

• Terry Fulwiler, president of Wisconsin Label, had his shop print up $2 million worth of play money, then called a meeting of all his employees. Before the meeting he went around and gave out big hand-lettered signs to selected people. "Labor," read one. "Paper." "Supplies." "Unemployment insurance."

You've guessed it: At the meeting, Fulwiler held up the $2 million and explained that that was about the amount Wisconsin Label received from its customers in one month. Then he began working his way down the income statement, asking each "line item" to come up and take its share.

At the end—surprise!—there were a few bucks left in profits. Not many. "The meeting ran for an hour and a half," he says. "People didn't realize how many dollars were spent on certain items."

• Intel Corp.'s Embedded Microcontroller Division (EMD) in Phoenix bought a board game called Profit and Cash, developed by a Kansas City consulting firm called Capital Connections. Profit and Cash was developed to teach the basics of business, and Intel customized it so that the game cards reflected actual Intel situations. Then an EMD program manager put together a contest: Teams of four players would play Profit and Cash against each other. The winning team would get a dinner for two (up to $100) for each team member.

"We ran it for eleven weeks," says the program manager, Jeannette Hendrych. "Two sessions a week." The game took about forty minutes, and players would spend another hour or so talking over what they had learned and comparing the score sheets in the game to actual financials." Ultimately nearly 350 people played the game—and had a good time doing it. "People were very competitive! When one team really got ahead, other teams wanted to audit their sheets! They wanted to know the secret! And some teams even started to benchmark—to compare their methods and strategies—with the other teams, which is what we need to do in business."

There's a lot else you can do—show business-education videos, give people books or newsletters to read, start discussion groups, get some of the clever new software designed to teach business literacy. Allstate's Business Insurance division even developed its own computer-based training course, a five-hour self-directed program that employees can go through at their convenience. (It prints out a diploma when you have passed the course.)

When it's done right, what you'll find is that business education develops a life of its own. It takes time. But once people learn what business is all about, you better be prepared for the consequences.

It makes me think of two stories. One is told by Bill Fotsch.

Fotsch is now a consultant, but at the time was vice president for business development at J.I. Case, the big farm-machinery company. He was flying down to visit Springfield ReManufacturing Corp., which his boss had described to him as a "small but innovative supplier." Fotsch had heard that SRC employees were supposed to understand their business, but he was skeptical. When he came across a guy polishing crankshaft journals he figured he'd ask him a question.

"Good morning," said Fotsch. "My name is Bill Fotsch. If you don't mind, I have a question for you. I understand that most SRC employees really understand their business. I'm curious: What is the price of that crankshaft you are working on?"

At Case, thought Fotsch, such a question would probably provoke a grievance for trying to embarrass a union worker. He figured he'd get no answer and that he'd probably wind up explaining the difference between *price* and *cost*.

The guy looked up. "List price or dealer net?" he asked. Then he went on to explain both prices, how they compared with SRC's cost, and what his own component of the cost was.

"At that moment I became a convert," says Fotsch.

The other story is told by Jerry Hatcher.

Hatcher is a consultant out of Nashville. One year he was working in a plant belonging to a *Fortune* 500 company.

He did a lot of the process-overhaul things that a good manufacturing consultant does these days. He and his team taught employees statistical process control and the other techniques of quality management. They reengineered the changeover process so that what had once taken 2.5 hours now took less than twenty minutes.

He also brought in a friend named Don Barkman, who has developed a training program called Biz Wiz. The program helps people learn the fundamentals of business, with a heavy emphasis on the financials.

It was a successful project, and the savings mounted. Soon the president of the plant's parent company decided to pay a visit. He sat down with the workers in the plant and asked them how they had made so many improvements.

A guy named Marty, a second-shift extruder operator, explained things. Let Hatcher pick up the story from there.

"Marty said, 'We figured out all the variables, and then we figured out where the real pinch points were.' He went on using all these statistical process control terms. And the president is sort of looking—his eyes aren't rolling back in his head, he's trying to stay interested, but it's clear he hasn't got the faintest idea what this guy is talking about.

"So then the president says, 'Boy, I really appreciate you guys. Now do you have any questions for me?' Well, it turned out Marty had been through Biz Wiz. So he looks at the president. 'I do,' he says. 'I've been looking through the annual report.'

"And then he says, 'You know, your cost of sales is rising a little bit. We're not getting the same return on investment that we did a year ago. Could you explain what it is that's causing that and what you're doing about it?'

"Well, the president's mouth dropped open. He was stunned—and delighted. He knew the answer, just as you would hope. But what he couldn't believe was, a line employee would know enough to ask that kind of question."

Too bad more hourly employees aren't asking questions like that of more company presidents. If you do the training right, they will be.

In the meantime: Go on to Principle Three and Principle Four. They're the drivers, the movers, the dynamic forces behind open-book management. Distributing the numbers and teaching people to understand them does no good unless they can then act on what they know—and unless they have a reason to do so.

## CHAPTER 6

# Third Principle: Empowerment (with Brains)

## Does empowerment make sense? Sure—but only when people understand the financials

Sometimes you hear about some big trend, some Major New Development in Society, for years and years, and you quit believing it because you've heard about it for so long and it never happens. And then, one day, you realize it might happen after all.

My favorite example: cashlessness.

Way back in the 1960s we began reading about the Coming of the Cashless Society. Soon, said the articles, financial transactions would all be electronic. Money would be obsolete.

Didn't happen. Still, we heard about the cashless society again in the 1970s as credit cards came into vogue. And again in the 1980s, when automatic teller machines were sprouting all over. (Granted, the cashless-society visionaries had trouble explaining why so many people used ATMs only to pick up some greenbacks.)

The weird thing, at any rate, is that one of these days we might actually find ourselves in a cashless society.

Not totally cashless, of course, but nearly so. Supermarkets are now taking ATM cards and credit cards. Liquor stores take them too. Heck, even high-class prostitutes carry one of those little card imprinters in their bags. (So I hear, anyway. I can't help wondering what shows up on your bill.)

Over time, people have grown accustomed to carrying no more than a few bucks in cash. Over time, computers have evolved to a point where a no-cash society is technologically feasible. Innovations are on the horizon: "Banks, credit card companies, and even the governments of some countries are racing to introduce 'electronic purses,' wallet-size cards embedded with rechargeable microchips that store sums of money for people to use instead of cash," reports the *New York Times*. So maybe this particular Big Trend will really happen soon—even after all these years of false prophecies.

# The Trend That Never Happened

I embark on this digression because something similar has happened with a notion about business management that goes by any number of names. Sometimes it's called *workplace participation*. Or maybe *participatory management*. *Employee involvement* and *empowerment* are right up there, too. Depends on which book you read and which consultant you hire.

Whatever the name, the idea itself is pretty simple. Rather than being watched over and ordered around by a supervisor all the time, employees in a company should have some autonomy. They should involve themselves in running their corner of the business. They should have a say in the decisions that affect their work area. They should be empowered, when possible, to solve problems and make changes on their own.

The logic: On-the-job decisions will be made faster and better when the employees directly involved are making them. People who have a say in their company's affairs will be happier and more productive than people who are always carrying out somebody else's orders.

This is an idea that has been around for a long time.

The dominant business paradigm in the twentieth century was always the one described in chapter 2—the bureaucratic chain of command, with do-as-you're-told jobs and tight supervision of the ranks. But participatory management was like a backwater, always there, never quite disappearing, even as the mainstream of history seemed to pass it by. It would turn up in one company here and another company there. It would catch on, fade, then reappear somewhere else.

In the 1920s, for example, the Baltimore & Ohio Railroad set up labor-management committees to improve efficiency. The committees started in the maintenance department but soon spread throughout the company. Over several years, the B&O got more than twenty thousand suggestions from the committees and implemented more than eighteen thousand.

In the 1950s, a former steelworker named Joseph Scanlon invented what he called the Scanlon Plan. Employees in companies that adopted his principles contributed ideas for reducing costs or boosting efficiency, then took home bonuses representing a share of the resulting profits. Several dozen companies signed on. (Many, such as Herman Miller, continue to practice Scanlon principles today.)

In the 1960s and 1970s you could read (if you knew where to look) about "work redesign" and "quality of working life" experiments. These were yet another version of workplace participation. Consultants and journalists swapped stories of the Procter & Gamble plant in Lima, Ohio, and of the Gaines dog-food plant in Topeka, Kansas, and of dozens of other places where some form of participatory management was being tried out. Every year, so it seemed, someone pronounced participation the wave of the future. "It pays to wake up the blue-collar worker," argued a *Fortune* article in 1970. "The growing popularity of employee participation programs isn't really in doubt," stated another *Fortune* article in 1981.

And then, in the late 1980s and 1990s, came empowerment. Or involvement. And everybody's favorite vehicle, the team.

Go back and check out the discussion in chapter 2 if you missed it: Empowerment is hot. Teams are widespread. More than two-thirds of *Fortune* 1000 companies were using teams in 1994, according to a University of Southern California study. The Clinton administration is pushing workplace participation. The administration's Commission on the Future of Worker/Management Relations defines part of its mission as investigating "new methods or institutions" to "enhance workplace productivity through labor-management cooperation and employee participation."

So maybe—just maybe—the participatory-management revolution is upon us. The cashless society, so to speak, has arrived.

Then again, maybe not.

# Empowerment with Brains

The trouble with empowerment as it's usually conceived is this: It's like empowering a guy to drive a truck without telling him where he's going.

Think of all the empowerment/team projects that you've heard of or read about or maybe even had something to do with.

One kind, for example, is the cross-functional team. A collection of employees from a variety of departments is assembled and given a mission. Fix the quality problems on the No. 3 line. Come up with recommendations for a new line of services aimed at senior citizens. The group meets, works, makes its report, disbands.

Another kind: the self-managing work team. Here the team structure is supposed to be permanent. Employees, working as a group, take on scheduling, job allocation, and other tasks traditionally done by supervisors. They may even have a hand in hiring and disciplining team members.

Both kinds of teams get access to whatever operational information they need—or at least we hope they do. (If they don't, they won't be around long.) Cross-functional or project teams are told the parameters for their mission. Self-managing teams track their own production and quality levels. Walk into a team-based factory and you'll see big charts in each team's area recording the week's output.

What these teams *don't* get, typically, is access to financial information. Or instruction in what the financials mean. Or an understanding of how their work contributes to (or detracts from) the bottom line.

They get the authority, in other words, to drive the truck. They start the engine, shift the gears, work the pedals, steer. But they don't know where they're going. They don't know how to get there, or what difference it makes if they take one route rather than another. Someone else has to spell all that out for them—to give them instructions.

As a result, it's easy for teams and team-based companies to get lost.

Maybe, for example, a manager makes a decision without consulting team members. The team gets annoyed and decides to skip its weekly meeting. Before long everyone is disillusioned. *Empowerment, right. They'll never listen to us, anyway.*

Or maybe a team goes off in a wrong direction. One team I heard of was charged with ensuring 100 percent on-time delivery—and suddenly its members were flying everywhere, damn the expense, to make sure every part was where it was supposed to be and every finished product went out the door on schedule. Meanwhile the company was going broke. ("If you empower dummies, you get bad decisions faster," opines Rich Teerlink, chief executive of Harley-Davidson.)

Or maybe the company just gets busy and puts the whole thing on hold for a while. We'll get the teams together in a couple of weeks. For now, you folks just do your job. Wait till things ease up a little.

Pretty soon: *pffft.* Empowerment is just something we used to do around here. One more fading fad.

The tragedy is, it doesn't need to be that way.

What empowered employees need, not surprisingly, is a map—and instruction about what the destination is and how to gauge their progress toward it. They need open-book management.

More specifically, empowerment doesn't work unless two conditions hold—conditions you can't get without the open-book approach.

**First: The operations of the business must be transparent.**

It should be plain to everyone how their own work affects their department's or their unit's numbers. It should be clear how those numbers affect the company's bottom line. (People need a clear "line of sight," as John Schuster of Capital Connections puts it.) That way, employees will get the information they need to make smart decisions. And they'll be able to learn from the dumb ones.

To put the matter differently: *Employees have to be empowered to make money, not just to hit operational targets.* "When employees are kept in the dark about the real objectives and workings of the business— how the company generates cash and makes a profit—empowerment is a hollow concept," says *Training*'s Chris Lee.

**Second: Empowered employees must be willing—indeed, should be required—to assume responsibility for their decisions and hence for their numbers.**

Accountability of this sort cuts through the confusion of empowerment like a knife through angel cake.

If you *know* you and your teammates or colleagues are responsible for your unit's numbers—if, for example, someone from your unit will be reporting them to management and if a hefty part of your bonus depends on making those numbers—your mind-set changes in a whole helluva hurry. The empowerment game stops being a charade or an exercise and becomes real life.

If someone makes a decision that's rightfully yours to make, you won't stand for it. Too much is at stake. If someone proposes skipping a meeting, your reaction is likely to be, *Are you kidding? How can we know that our week's numbers are on track unless we go over them?*

Some open-book practitioners call the system *no-excuses management.* That's a phrase that has been used in plenty of other contexts as well, but it captures the essence of open-book management. If your unit doesn't have the tools you need, it's your responsibility to ask for them—and in the meantime to figure out how to get by without them. If you need a new machine, or if you need more people to get your job done, well, get busy preparing the financial justification. If some of your colleagues don't understand the financials, see that they get some instruction.

Too often, conventional-style empowerment just means getting a bigger job to do—and maybe a new T-shirt with a brightly colored team logo on the front. You still do as you're told, you're just told to do more. Open-book empowerment, by contrast, is empowerment with brains, and with accountability. It means taking ownership of the numbers—forecasting them, tracking them, making them behave. It's like owning your own business. Like an entrepreneur, you can't pass the buck.

Or, to go back to the original metaphor, under open-book management you're responsible for getting the truck where it's going and on time. You're responsible for making your numbers. If you need help, you can ask for it. But you can't wait for someone to tell you what to do.

# How to Do It

OK, so how do you get people to make decisions, to take responsibility for them, to begin acting like businesspeople?

Simple—give them the power to do so. But you can't just announce it, any more than the Founding Fathers could have just announced that the country they were creating would have a democratic government. You need structures. You need procedures.

The good news: You don't have to invent these structures and procedures all by yourself. At least not all of them. Because the pioneers of open-book management have hit on at least three different approaches that seem to work pretty well.

The first, developed by Springfield ReManufacturing Corp.: Set up a huddle system.

The second: Turn your big company (even if it isn't too big) into several small ones that are just like the original. You'll see what I mean in a minute.

The third: Turn departments into business centers.

These three are *not* mutually exclusive. Let's plunge in, and you'll see how they fit together.

### SET UP A HUDDLE SYSTEM.

Stack calls his get-togethers "huddles" because his system is dubbed the Great Game of Business and—well, you get the idea. You can call them assemblies or turnips or anything else you want to. What they are is meetings structured around a very specific agenda of accountability.

Here's how it works at SRC and at most of the companies that have patterned their open-book systems after Stack's:

1. The company creates an annual plan ("game plan," in Stack's lingo): a sales forecast, a capital-expenditure budget, projected month-by-month income statements, and so on. (In SRC's manufacturing environment, as in most, a standard-cost system allows an income statement to be projected for a given sales volume.)

This is a six-month process and is itself highly participatory. "The planning process is a time to think about the future, to dream a little," says Stack. "This is everybody's big chance to say exactly how he or she thinks [the game] ought to be set up. The whole idea is to come up with a game that people will play with a lot of enthusiasm—that they will care about winning." When people set their own goals, of course, they buy into them a lot faster than if the goals are handed down by management.

The annual plan is partly about operational goals—about parts to be manufactured, products or services to be launched, branches to be opened. People in each department talk about what they'd like to accomplish in the coming year. The plan is also financial, because business reality always has to be reflected in numbers.

2. Numbers, in turn, let you assess your performance as you go along—which is just what SRC does.

Every week (in the company's business units) and every two weeks (in the corporate offices), representatives from every department or division get together to see how they're doing compared to the plan. Remember that scene described in chapter 4? People sit around the table watching the spreadsheet projected onto the big screen. They read off performance numbers and measure them against the plan. They offer opinions as to the upcoming weeks and months, and compare those to the plan, too.

The result: Stack and his managers, along with the supervisors or hourly employees delegated to sit in on the meeting that day, know instantly where the deviations are. They can spot sales that are higher or lower than plan, analyze costs that are out of line, watch for pressures on the company's cash. The numbers are incorporated in the spreadsheet and printed out before the meeting is through.

3. And then, of course, people can go to work.

Department reps take the financials back for discussion at the shop-floor level ("posthuddles"). Managers work with employees to address problems. Every unit is accountable for its own numbers—and every man and woman in that unit shares in the accountability. In a week or two, shop-floor meetings will look (in "prehuddles") at the new numbers they'll be bringing to the next main meeting. If the numbers are on target, fine. If they're off, they better have an idea as to why, and how to fix it.

You'll see the huddle system doing real-world work in the case studies later in this book, notably in the chapters on Sprint and Mid-States Technical. For now, let's go on to the second approach.

## TURN THE COMPANY INTO A COLLECTION OF SMALLER-BUT-IDENTICAL ONES.

Not every company can do this. But I bet more can than think they can. In a fast-growth situation, it can utterly transform the way employees view their jobs and how they view the business.

Certainly that's what happened at Published Image Inc.

Published Image is in my mind a sort of quintessential new-economy company, a world apart from a gritty engine remanufacturer such as SRC.

It's in a service business—producing customized newsletters for mutual-fund houses and other financial-service companies. It trades heavily on the professional skills of its employees.

It's entrepreneurial. Founder Eric Gershman started it in a loft. He financed the enterprise with $5,000 he had saved up.

It has grown fast, fed by the trend toward outsourcing. Why publish our own shareholder newsletter, figure a lot of mutual-fund houses, when there are hotshots like PI to do it for us?

As it turned out, PI almost gagged on its growth. "It happened to us about a year ago," says Gershman. "The feeling got to be, growth was bad."

Gershman himself, the owner, welcomed growth. But the employees who had to do the work groaned and complained every time a new customer turned up. Not that you could blame them. Organized into conventional departments—editorial, art, production, and so on—employees were working hard but inefficiently. Bottlenecks developed as each newsletter crept through the pipeline. "People were working hard, but they were often sitting around waiting for other departments to do their job."

Gershman's solution: Abolish the old Published Image. Create a new one in its place.

The new one—you can see it in action if you visit PI's tony Boston offices—has half a dozen teams. Or at least that was the number as this book went to press.

Each team has its own editor, art director, salesperson, and a couple of junior staffers. "Little Published Images," Gershman calls the teams.

In many ways the teams do act like self-contained businesses. They line up their own clients and negotiate prices. They take responsibility for producing their clients' newsletters, start to finish. They collect their own receivables and are learning to keep their own books. They are still part of Published Image, to be sure—Gershman and other veteran managers oversee the teams, coach and train their members, and set companywide policies on matters such as compensation. But the teams' relative autonomy encourages members to think like businesspeople rather than like hired hands. Team members pitch in to help get the product out the door. They see—and take responsibility for—their team's business results. The companywide compensation system provides for rewards commensurate with team-level business success.

A unique situation? Not really. Any "project" company can operate much the same way. "Each of our project teams is like a little company under the umbrella," says Ken Anderson of Anderson & Associates, a civil-engineering firm in Blacksburg, Virginia. "They get help from the parent company, so to speak, with their accounting and with their marketing support. Otherwise they're running their own company."

Even team-based manufacturing companies can extend their workers' authority in this way. "There's no management on the floor of our Framingham plant," says Rob Zicaro, a machine operator with Web Industries. "Instead, we use self-directed work teams. Every team gets its own P&L. It focuses the people who do the work on how they can impact the numbers. It also gets people thinking about business issues—about what's profitable and what's not."

Web, adds Zicaro, knows exactly how many dollars per hour each team needs to bring in if the company is to meet its goals. "We do up a report at the end of each shift. If the shift isn't up to its profit goal, they know they have to change something—the method, the price, whatever."

## TURN DEPARTMENTS INTO BUSINESS CENTERS.

Tom Peters calls it "businessing" a company. Make everyone into "real, whole businesspersons," he advises in *Liberation Management,* "responsible for customers from order to delivery of a service or product."

The idea: Every department becomes like a company within a company.

Unlike the Published Image model, the departments still have specialized tasks. But they're responsible for satisfying their customers, whether internal or external. *And* they're responsible for their finances.

The granddaddy of the company-within-a-company practitioners is Chesapeake Packaging's Baltimore box plant, described in chapter 9. But this particular idea is spreading rapidly:

• At Macromedia, a San Francisco developer of multimedia programming tools, the technical services department is structured as an internal business. Its revenues are a share of Macromedia's service contracts. Its expenses include personnel and overhead. Department head Sherry Flanders and her staff of thirteen track their own performance and watch the revenue and expense lines like hawks.

• At YSI, a scientific-instrument maker in Yellow Springs, Ohio, the work groups that used to be called self-managing teams are now called business centers. Each center is responsible, as a group, for handling customer orders from the time they are placed to the time they are shipped— and for keeping its costs on budget.

• At Zingerman's, the famous delicatessen and catering company in Ann Arbor, Michigan, founders Ari Weinzweig and Paul Saginaw are creating separate companies that will be part of a "community of businesses." Even the firm's administrative arm will be a separate company, its services sold to (and paid for by) operating companies.

• Foldcraft, the seating manufacturer, has divided itself into fifteen "process units," each with its own budget and levels of expected performance, to be reported every week. "If you're the marketing department you report on your expenses," explains Chuck Mayhew. "If you're a shop, you're going to report on your variances" (that is, how actual costs differ from the "standard" cost figures used in the company's plan). "Those are the things that take away or add to profit."

The business-center idea isn't so different from what big companies have always done. Any company beyond a certain size divides itself into business units. Executives at the top of each one have P&L responsibility. Managers heading up departments are held accountable for their budgets (though they may or may not have much of a say in determining them).

Everybody else, however, might as well be drones. Employees get no reward for improving the performance of their department. No one but the manager is held responsible—which means that he or she is always running around trying to tell everyone else what to do.

When you create internal companies or business centers, you're carrying the idea of P&L responsibility to a logical conclusion: You're telling small groups of people that *they as a group* are accountable for their performance. The books of their department or division are open. They're co-owners, so to speak, of their own little company.

"'Business' is a magical word, it turns out," writes Tom Peters. "It implies autonomy, practicality, action-taking, self-sufficiency, and self-responsibility." That's exactly the opposite of the do-as-you're-told mentality that pervades most corporate units.

## Some Final Advice

Some of the earliest practitioners of participatory management got a little carried away. They set up "industrial assemblies" modeled after the U.S. government. Goodyear Tire & Rubber literally had a House of Representatives and a Senate, elected by employees. The system lasted from 1919 until the mid-1930s.

You don't need to get carried away. Open-book management is experimental, fluid, not set in stone. It doesn't lend itself to big constitutional-type structures. Nor does any set of structures exist that could be copied exactly. The most successful companies mix and match their approaches, invent some of their own, use what works and throw out what doesn't.

Then, too, don't get hung up on the idea of democracy.

I like Jack Stack's comment in his book, *The Great Game of Business*. "A political democracy derives its authority from the consent of the governed. A company derives its authority from the consent of the marketplace."

*Participation,* from a manager's point of view, means giving people a say. It means explaining the options and then listening (carefully!) to their opinions. But managers in a business still must assume responsibility for their decisions. The CEO is ultimately responsible for the health of the whole company.

This isn't so different from the best of conventional business practice. Smart executives have always delegated decision making. They have provided their middle managers with the information they needed to make good decisions, and they have coached them until they were confident in the subordinates' judgment. They have encouraged the decision makers to listen to a variety of opinions, particularly from people who knew more.

It's no different with open-book management. Only now the playing field doesn't include only the managers, it includes everyone in the company. They're all empowered—because they're all businesspeople.

The one big issue remaining? Compensation. If people don't have a stake in the outcome—a chance to win, so to speak—they may not see much reason for playing.

## CHAPTER 7

# Fourth Principle: A Stake in Success

## Make sure people share directly in the company's success—and in the risk of failure

Businesspeople have a lot riding on the prosperity of their company. It does well, they do well. It gets into trouble, they take a bath.

Open-book management teaches employees to think of themselves as businesspeople rather than hired hands. To make that real, they need a stake. Part of what they earn must be tied to the company's performance.

Besides, look at open-book management from the employees' point of view. They're being asked to learn new stuff, take on new responsibilities, conceive of their jobs in different—and much broader—terms than before. Anyone who did this with no prospect of reward would feel like a sucker. And would probably be right.

"If there's no reward, why does anybody give a damn?" asks Roger McDivitt, production manager at Patagonia, the outdoor-apparel company. The question answers itself.

## The Pitfalls of Profit Sharing (and Bonuses)

This principle, alas, takes us into one of the murkier morasses of American business practice. It's called variable compensation, and companies find more ways to screw it up than the S&Ls found to lose money.

First we better be clear what we're talking about here.

Variable compensation, as I'm using the term, refers to *group* incentives such as across-the-board bonus plans, profit sharing, stock distribution, and so forth. I'm not discussing *individual* performance-related pay, which is another can of night crawlers entirely. This limitation is a good thing, believe me. Otherwise this chapter would go on for another two hundred pages and you would be holding a book about compensation rather than one about open-book management.

American businesses' bonus and profit-sharing plans come in all shapes and sizes, much like the businesses themselves. They're bounteous or chintzy. They're paid in cash or they're paid into tax-qualified retirement accounts. They're paid monthly or quarterly or yearly or just every so often. The bonus pool is calculated by a hundred different methods and divvied up by a hundred more.

In theory, variable-compensation plans are supposed to accomplish exactly what we would want an open-book-management pay system to do. Tie people's fortunes to the prosperity of the company. Let everyone share in success. Give people an incentive to work hard, go the extra mile, use their brains as well as their hands. In consultantspeak, the plans are supposed to "align" employees' objectives with the company's.

But for the most part, they fail. They don't get people working harder and smarter, figuring out how to help the company make more money. They don't have an effect on people's *behavior.*

The reasons aren't hard to fathom. Most bonus or profit-sharing systems get bogged down in one or another pothole. Some get stuck in many all at once.

### Pothole #1: The plan is discretionary.

Management determines the payout each year.

This is the most common failing, for the simple reason that company owners and managers despise bonus and profit-sharing arrangements that they don't have direct control over.

You can sympathize with their feelings. What if we need the money? they figure. What if we decide to build a new plant next year? What if we make an acquisition? What if we anticipate a business downturn?

In an open-book company, of course, employees would be privy to such thinking—and might agree to set aside funds for the purpose rather than paying them out in bonuses or profit sharing.

In a conventional company, though, all they'll see is that the bonus or profit-sharing check depends on the whim of management. The money may or may not materialize.

This is not what you'd call a world-class incentive. All it takes is one year in which management decides it really can't afford a bonus, for reasons that it explains to employees after the fact. Boom—the motivating effect is gone. Would you bust *your* butt for money that you might or might not receive, for reasons beyond your control?

## Pothole #2: The plan is incomprehensible.

Formal profit-sharing plans are regulated by the government, meaning that you need a law degree to interpret the fine print. And companies rarely go out of their way to make the plans simple and understandable.

When Bob Frey wanted to set up a profit-sharing plan at Cin-Made, he bought books and sent away for materials and studied a variety of plans. The complexity was staggering. "There were threshold limits; there were profits behind, above, and beyond the normal expected rate of return; and there were minimums and maximums and categories and schedules and language that struck me as pure bafflegab."

Good word. How are people supposed to be motivated by a plan they can't fathom?

The effect of potholes 1 and 2, at any rate, is that employees don't trust the plan.

It's an axiom of business, and maybe of life: People don't trust what they don't understand. If a bonus or profit-sharing system is discretionary, so much the worse. "They pay us what they feel like paying us" is the most common response when you ask line employees how their company's system works.

## Pothole #3: The payment is always the same.

It staggers the mind, but some companies actually treat profit sharing or bonuses the way AT&T once treated its dividend. Always the same. Year in and year out. You can bank on it.

If you can bank on it, of course, it probably bears no real relation to profitability. In the real world, profits go up, go down, sometimes vanish entirely. Employees know that.

And if you can bank on it, well, people will. They'll count it as part of their regular pay. It becomes an entitlement, not a reward for performance.

## Pothole #4: The plan is invisible.

This too may seem far-fetched. But some profit-sharing plans are virtually invisible to employees. Maybe the payout is tiny. Maybe it's determined by a management board, at a meeting that no one knows about, and then communicated in a letter that no one understands. Maybe there's no cash payout; all the money is deposited in a retirement account. So every now and then employees get a statement telling them that they have a little money in an account they can cash in twenty or thirty years from now.

**All these potholes, however, are mere dips in the road compared to the biggest pitfall of all, which is that employees typically have no clue as to whether, or how, what they do day in and day out affects the payout.**

A bonus, when it comes, is pennies from heaven.

The memo that accompanies it always makes a point of thanking employees for their outstanding efforts, which made it possible for the company to enjoy such a profitable year, etc. etc. etc. Employees wonder what they did this year that they didn't do last year.

And if the bonus doesn't arrive, no one knows why.

The memo in this case will blame the market, or the tough competitive situation, or the slow economy. (Anything but management!) Employees will figure they worked just as hard as ever—and now, for reasons they don't understand (and probably don't believe) they aren't getting their bonus.

Remember my friend Carole, the mental-health clinician who works for the big health maintenance organization? This HMO offers a textbook case of the Meaningless Bonus.

The company's bonus is paid in cash, twice a year, to all staff. OK so far.

The bonus is apparently nondiscretionary. It's calculated according to how well the HMO does in hitting certain performance targets. Some years it has been zero. Other years it has ranged as high as 10 percent of salary. That's OK, too.

The rub: Nobody has a clue as to how it's figured out.

You could scrutinize one of the recent memos purporting to explain the system. You would still, like Carole and 99 percent of the HMO's other employees, be in the dark.

According to the memo, the company has four divisions, including "management offices." Each of the divisions has four goals. Carole had never heard of any of the goals.

The divisions' performance on each goal was rated anywhere from zero to two—"two," in this case, meaning twice as much as management had hoped for. Who did the ratings? Management, of course—by criteria that no one else understood. "Management offices" scored better than any other division. (Surprise.)

The bonus was then calculated from those ratings. "Eligible employees," read the memo, "will receive the above designated divisional percentage of their 1994 compensation as of 6/30/94 (1/1/94–6/30/94 wages excluding the Planwide bonus and any noncash compensation received in 1994)."

Oh.

# The Open-Book Approach

The stake that employees have in an open-book company can take the form of profit sharing, or bonuses tied to some target other than profit, or stock ownership. (More on stock ownership below.) On the surface it might look like any company's system. But the concept is different.

The payout isn't a reward that management decides to hand out to employees when the company has a good year (or when the CEO is feeling benevolent). It isn't charity. It isn't a benefit. If they get it, employees know they have earned it. If they earn it, they get it. It isn't discretionary.

Nor is it some reward that descends from the sky (or not), for inscrutable (and unpredictable) reasons. People *know* what they have to do to get it. They know from week to week and month to month whether they're on track for a bonus or not—*because they can see exactly how the business is doing.*

Open-book management gets everyone in a company thinking like businesspeople. Like businesspeople, they're rewarded when their company makes money.

On the other hand, a company is an ongoing organization, not a sidewalk lemonade stand. People can't decide to pay themselves everything the business earns in a year—not, at least, if they hope to be in business in the future.

And an organization always has multiple goals. Earning a profit is always one of them. But others may be equally important. Sales growth or market share. Liquidity. Long-term increase in the value of the company. Businesspeople learn to balance those goals, one against another, from year to year.

A good bonus or profit-sharing system rewards employees generously when their company does well. It also focuses their attention on balancing all the goals—so that the company can continue to do well.

Here's how to set it up.

# 1. Establishing goals

What's important to your company? The bottom line, of course. What else?

Financial goals are as varied as business itself. Small companies must watch their cash. Manufacturers must worry about return on assets. Maybe your key financial number is gross margin, or free cash flow, or return on sales.

Operational goals may be as important as financial ones, if only because they're a kind of leading indicator. Lose control of them, in some cases, and you're sure to lose control of the bottom line. Thus, an airline watches cost per available seat mile, a hotel its occupancy rate, a retailer the number of returns. A steel minimill's key number is conversion cost— what it costs to turn a ton of scrap into finished steel. (Nucor's is thought to be between 70 and 75 percent of the competition's.)

So here's the idea: *Pick one or two or three of your company's key measures—whatever will be most important to the company's health and prosperity in the coming year and over the longer haul. Set goals. Pay a bonus if and only if those goals are met.*

The simplest goal: to make money.

For some companies, that's enough. Pace Industries' Cast-Tech Division divides up 2 percent of the plant's gross profit among its employees. Heatway, the heating-systems manufacturer, divvies up 20 percent of the net.

A profit goal can be combined with other objectives. Engines Plus, which buys diesel engines and converts them to stationary power plants, pays bonuses pegged both to profit before taxes and to inventory accuracy. For Engines Plus, inventory accuracy is one of those pivotal operational numbers. Kacey Fine Furniture paid a bonus in 1993 based on net profits and return on assets. In 1994, the company included a factor designed to minimize customer returns.

Some companies change their goals regularly, depending on their business needs. Vectra, a Columbus, Ohio, printing and marketing-materials company, creates a new combination of objectives every six months. In 1993 the goals included sales growth, inventory accuracy, operating expenses, and what accountants call the current ratio. (The current ratio shows the strength of a company's cash position.) In the first half of 1994, return on assets and customer satisfaction replaced operating expenses and the current ratio in the lineup.

Think about this goal-setting process for ten seconds and a few lessons will leap right out at you:

## PEOPLE HAVE TO UNDERSTAND WHY THE GOAL IS IMPORTANT.

Everybody understands "profit," though people may need a little instruction on the various ways it can be measured (operating profits, net profits, earnings before interest and taxes, etc.). Get into inventory accuracy or return on assets, though, and you better make sure your business-literacy programs cover the subject. (*And* that managers and supervisors can explain it clearly.) Vectra's objectives—including such accounting terms as return on assets and the current ratio—put even more of a burden on the business-education end of open-book management.

## IT'S WISE TO INVOLVE AS MANY PEOPLE AS POSSIBLE IN SETTING THE GOALS.

People buy into goals faster when they've had a say in choosing them. That's why smart managers make a point of talking about goals and eliciting opinions about what's most important for the company. People get a voice in the process. The discussion itself produces a better understanding of the business.

## THE GOALS MUST BE TRACKED IN PUBLIC, ACCORDING TO CRITERIA EVERYBODY UNDERSTANDS.

You say part of the bonus is pegged to customer satisfaction? Let's see big customer-satisfaction charts out in the office or the shop, along with a written explanation of exactly how that all-too-elusive concept is being measured. If it's inventory accuracy, you'll want a graph showing the figure from month to month.

Public scorekeeping like this is a matter of building trust—of proving to people that the numbers aren't rigged, that there are no secrets. An open-book company has to operate by the sunshine principle. Get the numbers out where everybody can see them and can watch what happens to them over time.

Besides, watching the score is part of the excitement of open-book management—not to mention a big part of the incentive.

## PEOPLE SHOULD BE ABLE TO AFFECT THE OUTCOME . . .

You can't make a goal out of "interest income" if—as at most companies—the financial officers are the only ones whose actions affect the figure. At least part of any bonus must be tied to numbers that employees have some control over.

## . . . BUT THE PAYOUT MUST BE FISCALLY RESPONSIBLE.

Companies can get themselves into hot water when they focus *only* on numbers that employees can affect directly.

Suppose, for instance, employees do a bang-up job of controlling inventory accuracy, or watching gross margins, or whatever. They've apparently earned their bonus.

But suppose the company isn't making much money, or is running short of cash, for reasons that have nothing to do with what the employees did.

Result: Management decides not to pay the bonus even though people believe (rightly) that they've earned it. Whatever credibility management might have had goes right down the toilet.

If there's a chance this could happen to you, do what SRC (and a lot of other companies) do: Build protection right into the system from the start, and make sure employees understand it. Don't pay profit sharing unless profits exceed a certain level, agreed upon in advance. If cash is a potential problem, set a goal for liquidity or some other measure that will ensure an adequate supply of money to pay the bonus.

Chuck Mayhew, president of Foldcraft:

> The single most impressive result of our financial education program and open-book management was the elimination of a gain-share program that was paying out of profits we didn't have. This program was reducing our cash and lowering our stock values. It was the hourly employees who recommended discontinuing the program, and they assisted in developing a program to take its place. The new program is based on profits and is measured every week.

## FINALLY, THE GOALS SHOULD BE AMBITIOUS BUT ATTAINABLE.

How will you know if they're right? Through experience.

ECCO, a backup alarm and strobe-light manufacturer in Boise, Idaho, was paying part of its profits in bonuses even when the company was barely making money. "We were rewarding mediocrity!" says president Ed Zimmer, incredulously. Today, ECCO creates no bonus pool until profits climb above 4 percent of sales, and the pool percentage rises as profits increase, up to a maximum of 10 percent. Says Zimmer, "Now we max out about every month."

Vectra set its goals for operating expenses and current ratio too high in 1993. That caused discontent in the ranks as people began to see that the bonus targets were out of reach. "You had people being negative," remembers CEO Craig Taylor. "It was—'See, they're going to screw us.'" In 1994 Vectra's objectives were more realistic. You learn by doing.

# 2. Making the payout

Setting goals, alas, is only the first part of establishing your compensation system. You also have to figure out the mechanics for making it work, which in turn means answering three questions.

## HOW MUCH SHOULD EMPLOYEES RECEIVE IN BONUSES OR PROFIT SHARING?

The short answer is, all your company can afford.

The reason: The more that people have riding on the company's success, the more they'll be inclined to think like businesspeople.

I'm not advocating cutting anybody's wages. That's a surefire recipe for starting off on the wrong foot. But why not, as Bob Frey did, freeze wages where they are now—and make sure that employees see a hefty increase in their pay as long as the company grows and makes money? Today, Frey's workers get close to one-quarter of their total pay in profit sharing.

If you want, give people a choice.

Vectra CEO Craig Taylor offered employees a deal when he installed his open-book system. They could get a raise and play for a bonus pool of $200,000. Or they could forgo a raise and play for a bonus pool that was twice as big. They chose the latter option—by an overwhelming majority. And even though they didn't earn their whole bonus that year, most people wound up better off than if they had taken the raise.

In ordinary circumstances, anything less than a payout of 5 percent of salary won't seem like much. But not all circumstances are ordinary. Remember Pace: Employees at last report were getting only a few hundred dollars in bonus money every quarter. But the bonus meant they were making a profit, unlike before, which meant that the plant wasn't about to be closed down, unlike before, which was *considerably* better than the prospect of being thrown out of work. Everything's relative.

## HOW SHOULD THE BONUS POOL BE DIVIDED UP?

I wish I could stay out of this one. Few issues get open-book practitioners so excited.

Andy Crowder at Pace took the pool and split it equally among every man and woman in the factory regardless of job, salary, or any other distinction.

This egalitarianism was not lost on the company's rank and file. "The guy in that office gets the same amount as the guy out in the pit," mused Steve Ryan, master mechanic, gesturing toward Crowder's quarters. "That's a nice way to do it. It's hard to knock yourself out for profit sharing when you get $10 and the guy in the office, in the air-conditioning, is getting $500. This way, it makes us all equal. That's kind of the feeling of the place."

Emma Lou Brent of Phelps County Bank thinks egalitarianism of that sort is dead wrong.

At Phelps County, your share of the bonus pool is figured as a straight percentage of your total compensation, period. Your compensation, figures Brent, is a pretty good proxy for your level of responsibility and thus your importance to the company. It's only right that people with more responsibility get a higher reward—and have more at risk.

Manco takes a still less egalitarian approach: The percentage of your salary that you get from the bonus pool goes up as you climb the corporate ladder.

If the company "makes bonus"—if it hits 8 percent profits and 22 percent return on operating assets—hourly employees get a payment equaling 10 percent of their base pay. Supervisors and middle managers get more—20 percent, 30 percent, on up to the 50 percent of salary earned by President Tom Corbo. The thinking? Not so different from Brent's. The more responsibility you have for the company's operation, the more of your total compensation should be at risk.

The fact is, the variations here are endless. Mid-States Technical divides its bonus pool 75 percent by total earnings, 25 percent equally. Vectra pays different amounts to individual employees depending on how well they did on a list of personal goals. The important thing? Whatever you do must seem fair. That's partly a matter of how fair it really is—and partly of how good a job you do explaining it.

## WHEN SHOULD THE BONUS BE PAID OUT?

Here, too, you can find all manner of answers.

Companies have historically paid an *annual* bonus, usually determined after the books are closed. That's what Manco does, even now. "We want everyone to be in the boat till the end of the year," says controller Charlie MacMillan. Besides, he adds, the company's business is highly seasonal, which would make more frequent payouts difficult. "Our last quarter is astronomical compared to our first three quarters. So we'd basically pay the majority of it at the end of the year anyway—and often we wouldn't be paying anything in the two middle quarters."

Annual bonuses have one big plus: They're large. People don't factor them into their monthly budgets. They really seem like something extra. They have one big drawback, which is that they're hard to get excited about. How far away does next February seem when you're in the doldrums of this February? And what can happen between now and then to impact your bonus?

For my money, the two best compromises are SRC's 10-20-30-40 system and Mid-States Technical's bucket plan.

At SRC, the bonus pool is determined by the annual plan. Employees know from the beginning what they're shooting for and what they stand to get if they make it.

Hit the target for the end of the first quarter at SRC and you get 10 percent of the total bonus pool for the year. Hit it for the end of the second quarter and you get 20 percent. For the third quarter it's 30 percent; for the fourth, 40 percent. That system, explains Jack Stack, keeps people focused all year long. The stakes keep going up.

Most interesting, though, is what happens if people miss those interim targets: That quarter's pool is rolled over into the next quarter and will be paid out if the company hits its cumulative (year-to-date) target for the end of *that* quarter. So even if one quarter is a disaster, the game still hangs in the balance. "We can win one quarter at a time, or we can pull it out on a Hail Mary pass in the final seconds," says Stack.

At Mid-States Technical, CEO Steve Wilson forgets the calendar entirely. He pays a bonus to his employees every time the little company records $75,000 in earnings. "Filling up a bucket," he calls it.

You'll read more about Wilson and his bucket plan in chapter 10. For now, the important point is that there's no fixed formula for payouts—and that you should invent one that's appropriate to your business.

## What About Stock Ownership?

Let's get one thing straight right off the bat: Open-book management works even when people don't own a single share of stock in the company that employs them.

Maybe this defies logic. (Why would people learn to *think* like owners unless they *are* owners?) But it's true. I've seen it at Pace Industries, at Chesapeake Packaging, at Mid-States Technical, at Vectra, at a dozen other companies. Even in an ordinary company, after all, people have both an economic and a psychological stake in their employer's business success. And a successful open-book company provides not only the usual rewards—steady work, chances for advancement—but some unusual ones, such as the chance to make the company's goals and thereby earn a bonus.

Employee ownership just isn't in the cards for a lot of companies anyway. If you work for a division of a large corporation, the decision is out of your hands. If you work for a smaller business, maybe an employee stock ownership plan (ESOP) is too cumbersome. Or maybe the family that owns the company simply isn't ready to share (or transfer) equity.

Having said all that, however, I have to add the inescapable truth, which is that *employee stock ownership and open-book management go together like love and marriage, a horse and carriage, pork and beans, and all the other pairings that poets and pundits have dreamed up over the years.*

Employee ownership in one form or another is much more widespread these days than you might think.

A handful of giants—Avis, Publix Supermarkets—are owned outright by their employees. So are hundreds of smaller companies, from Republic Engineered Steel (five thousand employees) all the way down to businesses such as Phelps County Bank (fifty-five employees).

Many, many more companies have partial employee ownership.

Workers as a group own sizable chunks of Wal-Mart, Procter & Gamble, Polaroid, and scores of other big-name companies. They hold big stakes in thousands of smaller companies. A few years ago, Congress bestowed generous tax benefits on employee stock ownership plans that met certain specified conditions. Today, more than ten thousand companies have a formal ESOP, while another four thousand or so have another kind of stock plan for employees. An estimated fifteen million people work in employee-ownership companies.

Managers at these companies like to think that their underlings will magically transform their behavior when they become stockholders. Not so. Study after study has shown that employee ownership by itself has no discernible effect on corporate performance.

But study after study has also shown that employee ownership coupled with some form of participatory management—empowerment—does make a difference.

And where open-book management is concerned, ownership helps provide the long-term perspective that's required if employees are really going to think like businesspeople.

The kind of ownership provided by an ESOP or similar plan, after all, is quite different from owning stock in IBM. You can't get your money out just by calling your broker. Like an entrepreneur, you have to make sure that it's being used wisely. "The feeling is, 'I'm tied to this company, and it's up to me and the people I'm working with to make it succeed or not,'" says Charles Edmunson of Web Industries. "That's a different relationship than the typical big-corporation stockholder."

Business is always a game of trade-offs between the short term and the long. You can see the tension between the two in the ongoing debate over Wall Street's myopia, and in the pressure on public companies to boost earnings every quarter. You can see it in the quiet success of Japanese companies over the long haul, boosting market share even at the expense of quarterly earnings.

It doesn't matter how big a company is, or whether it's public or private—it always must decide how much to pay out in earnings or dividends, how much to reinvest, whether and when to expand, whether and when to launch new products or services. The decisions are numberless, and they always involve a calculation about long-term payoffs.

*Those long-term payoffs redound primarily to the company's owners.* If the decisions are good ones, the company will grow and will create wealth. Its stock value will rise. That's how company builders get rich.

If employees don't own a share, their immediate interests will lie in the direction of more payouts, now, and less investment in the future. It's a tension that just doesn't need to exist. Which may be why so many open-book companies are also employee-ownership companies.

"Equity is the basis for all long-term thinking," writes Jack Stack. "It is the best reason for staying the course, for sacrificing instant gratification and going after the big payoff down the road. If you have equity and understand it, you know why it's important to build for the future. You can make long-term decisions. You still pay attention to the day-to-day details, but you're doing it for the right reason: because it's the best way to achieve *lasting* success.

"Companies that don't share equity are making a mistake. They are leaving up a barrier that should be taken down. They are setting limits on how far people can go."

So that's the end of the four principles of open-book management— information, business literacy, empowerment, and a stake in success. Now for the fun part: how to get started. It isn't as hard as you might think.

## CHAPTER 8

# Ten Ways to Get Started

## If you're not ready to dive in, here's how to dip a toe or two in the water

You *can* plunge into open-book management all at once. It isn't easy, and you can't expect it to catch on right away. But it *has* been done.

You put out the information and teach people to understand it. You structure the company so that employees can act on their newfound knowledge. And you revamp the compensation system to give everybody a stake in the business's success.

Maybe you kick the whole thing off with a big meeting and hoopla. Leslie Fishbein of Kacey Fine Furniture orchestrated a whole show, complete with songs and skits. (Both the show and subsequent meetings were professionally videotaped for the benefit of new employees.) Neil Schmid of Viking Glass invited a healthy fraction of Sioux Falls, South Dakota, to his company's kickoff. ("We had all the employees, all their spouses, and about a hundred invited business guests!") Eric Gershman of Published Image dubbed the event United Day and gave all the employees bright red T-shirts.

If you're the boss and you're ready to take the plunge, more power to you. As you'll see from the case studies in the following chapters, it can work.

But if you're the pragmatic, experimental type, the beauty of open-book management is that you're not obliged to do everything at once.

Open-book management is not an operational overhaul like reengineering that must be done in toto or not at all. It's a philosophy, a way of thinking, a new paradigm of management. People can learn it—and can begin to implement it—a step at a time.

So what follows are some first steps, some ideas about how to get going. All are tested by experience. They work. They'll begin teaching employees to think of themselves as businesspeople, even as co-owners, rather than as hired hands.

They are just a way to start. They won't revolutionize a company all by themselves. Nor will they automatically lead to a next step. Taken alone, they'll engage people—for a while. If nothing else changes, they'll soon come to seem meaningless (at best) or manipulative (at worst).

If you want to go swimming, you have to get wet. And if you want the benefits of open-book management, you have to transform your company.

But here's how to test the temperature before you dive in.

# 1. Play "guess the gross" or "guess the costs" or any other game that gets people thinking about key numbers.

Do what Southwest Airlines did not long ago: Send your employees a card with a quiz on it.

Southwest's had a little cartoon—"climbing the ladder to success"— and every step on the ladder had a question about the airline's costs. (Do you know how much office supplies cost Southwest last year?) The answers then appeared in the company's newsletter, one each week. Employees who checked out the cost data could fill out the card. A filled-in card was a ticket to enter a drawing for free travel.

Silly? Sure. But it gets cost data out where it can be talked about— which is more than most companies do.

Myself, I like the "guess the gross" game invented by the two brothers who run Heatway, the heating-systems manufacturer.

Every month Mike and Dan Chiles circulate a form among their forty-two employees. "It's like a horse-racing form," says Dan—"with a tip sheet at the bottom."

The objective: Guess Heatway's gross revenues for the following month.

The tip sheet is exactly the information a CEO would have at his or her disposal in making a forecast. Last month's gross. The gross for this month a year ago. What's on the projections that the chief financial officer gives to the bank. The latest forecast from the sales department.

The winner gets $25. If there's a tie, the tiebreaker is who comes closest in guessing net earnings. Suddenly people get a sense of how much the company brings in each month—and how much (or how little) shows up on the bottom line.

# 2. Start open-book management—but only among the managers.

Any company or business unit has five, ten, maybe as many as twenty key managers. The executives. The department heads. The people who gather for the weekly staff meeting.

These are *managers,* right? They're supposed to know—and to take responsibility for—what's going on. They may even get a bonus tied to some measure of performance.

But if your company is like most, they know what's going on—in their own department. The others? They could care.

And as for responsibility, well, yeah, they're accountable—*except if I don't make my numbers it's not really my fault because you remember that slowdown I warned you about and there's no way I can hit the forecast without three more people and I didn't really sign on to that forecast anyway and—*

In a bureaucracy, even a little one, there are always excuses.

There are also turf battles, me-firstism, politics, feuds, butt-kissing, and deals to make one person look good at the expense of another.

Managers in smaller companies—and even in a few bigger ones—face another enemy, one they're loath to admit to: ignorance.

You know people like this. The sales manager is a great saleswoman but doesn't really think about the relative profitability of various accounts. The plant manager is a dynamite production guy but can never figure out why his costs are so high.

So go ahead—start open-book management among this group.

• Teach people about business

David Zapatka, Z-Tech Companies Inc.: "Every month we—the management team, twenty-three people—meet. We spend a couple of hours together. The controller has an entire selection of business material to cover. We teach them what an asset is, and a liability, and how they relate to each other. We're getting into cash flow. We're beginning to understand how the balance sheet and profit-and-loss statement and cash-flow statement tie into each other, how they affect each other.

"As a result, we spend much less money frivolously. Maybe we could have made a piece of equipment or a tool last longer instead of replacing it. People don't understand, unless they get this training, where all that money's going. They don't realize that telephone bills are thousands of dollars a month, and advertising costs this, and utilities are that, taxes, insurance, on and on and on. Line item by line item, we're teaching them about every single cost and revenue producer in the company."

• Distribute complete financial statements, not just departmental ones.

Jim Jenkins, Jenkins Diesel Power: "Prior to last year we provided managers with financial statements about their own departments. But they didn't see the overhead for the whole company, and they didn't know anything about other departments. So you're in your own little world. You may be doing fine—but some other department might be losing their ass."

• Have people initial the numbers they're responsible for.

Ed Zimmer, ECCO: "We've put initials on the income statement. When it prints, it shows who's responsible for that line item. That has helped increase awareness, and also filled in some holes. There's no more 'I thought you were doing that!'"

• Create an SRC-style system of week-to-week accountability for managers.

Chuck Mayhew, Foldcraft: "Every Wednesday afternoon we hold a managers' meeting. In the first fifteen minutes we build an income statement. Every line item is assigned to the person who actually makes those numbers happen. There are four sales lines, for example, because we have four sales managers. The standard cost of those sales is the responsibility of our cost accountant. The variances that are shop-related—labor efficiency, labor price variances, overhead—well, there's a line item there for every one of our process units in the shop.

"So each manager is expected to come in and say, this is what my variance is, or this is what my number is, for the month. They come in with opinions—a new opinion every week—of what the current month is going to look like.

"Then we take that same income statement—we have one of those electronic overheads that shows on a screen—and they just drop in the numbers, and at the bottom it says, our profit is going to be $X$ dollars. Then we go on with other agenda items. But our cost accountant takes that disk out and has copies run. In half an hour everybody has a copy of all that information. They take it back to their units and review it in their staff meetings.

"Our philosophy is, if you know the process well enough to predict the number accurately, that's the first step. The second step is, if you know it well enough you can change the number. You can manage the outcome."

# 3. Announce the end of annual raises.

"OK, ladies and gentlemen, this company will pay no more across-the-board raises, even for cost of living. Starting now." This kind of statement has a way of getting people's attention.

Unless you want a wholesale rebellion or defection on your hands, of course, you'll have to offer something in return. Like a generous bonus tied to profit sharing.

That's what Bob Frey did at Cin-Made.

And it's what Eric Gershman did at Published Image. "What we say is, we're not going to give you a raise. We're never going to give you another raise." Instead, PI employees can earn a bonus of up to 50 percent of salary, depending on how their team performs.

It's also what Jim Sandstrom did at Sandstrom Products. "We slammed the door on automatic pay increases two years ago. But we opened the door that says, let's start looking at the bottom line. We'll give you a share of that number."

The mechanics of this are very, very important, because the annual raise is an institution in American business. Until recently, people expected it as a matter of course. Even today, people expect it as long as the company is doing well.

So the bonus better be generous—and expandable over the years if the company is successful. And the targets that it is pegged to better be reachable.

In principle, a share in the earnings of a growing, healthy business is worth more—a lot more—to employees than a few percent more in wages or salaries every year. That's a fundamental principle of capitalism. The aim of open-book management is to help everyone in a business understand that, and thus to think a little more like capitalists.

# 4. Start distributing information—with a bonus attached.

Another way of getting people's attention.

Eric Paulsen of Engines Plus taught the basics of business to his shop employees. He began distributing the income statement. "Their attitude was, well, this is nice, but so what? It really didn't develop any serious meaning until the time we set up a bonus program that was tied to our PBT [profit before taxes] number. And I'll be damned! At the end of a couple of months I could go out in the shop with an income statement and every employee could show me exactly where on that income statement the PBT number was."

Steve Ashton of Ashton Photo, a photographic processor, did the same thing. "We distributed a copy of the P&L and let them know they'd get a percentage of the profits. That was a pretty good kick in the head to get people's attention."

Extra added attraction: Pay the bonus retroactively.

When Kacey Fine Furniture's kicked off its open-book system, Leslie Fishbein passed out an actual check for the bonus employees *would have earned if the system had been in place the previous quarter*. "It was a very pragmatic move. I figured, I know how to get everybody's attention!"

# 5. Play a business game (part one).

Mike Ansara and Evan Grossman had a problem that's only too common among entrepreneurial businesses.

Ansara is CEO and Grossman chief financial officer of Share Systems Inc., a $5 million telephone fund-raising company in the Boston area. One year, Share had overexpanded, and the company was losing money. By the third quarter of that year, Share was $140,000 in the red.

Ironically, Share had plenty of clients. Its problem was to keep the phone stations staffed. Share's callers are highly trained and well paid. They do high-stress work. Many work only part-time. If management leans too hard on them to work more, they leave. And they're expensive to replace.

So Grossman set up what he called The Challenge. The goal was to boost the total number of hours that callers were actually working the phones and generating revenue.

The incentive came in two parts. Extra paid vacation for part-timers. A cash bonus for full-timers. The cash pool was to be 20 percent of all net income over $40,000.

The effect was electric.

As the game began, scoreboards went up in the calling area. Number of hours called last night. Total hours called so far this month. Callers began staying an extra fifteen minutes one day, a half hour the next. They urged their colleagues to work more, too. Managers watched calling-station utilization more closely—making sure, for example, they had back-ups for callers who missed a shift.

By the end of November, Grossman thought Share would be marginally profitable for the year. By December he could see the outcome was far better than he had expected. "We ended up making $70,000 for the year," says Grossman, shaking his head in disbelief. It was a $210,000 turnaround in just three months.

# 6. Play a business game (part two).

Business games come in all shapes and sizes. Pace's inventory-accuracy game. The Holiday Inn game, with a bonus paid out as long as the occupancy rate stayed above a given level.

Samuel Smith of Smith & Co. Engineers set up a remarkably simple one. Like most professional-service firms, Smith & Co. makes its money on the billable hour. Billable hours weren't where Smith thought they should be, and the firm was barely breaking even.

So Smith talked with each professional: How many hours did he or she think was reasonable to shoot for? He then toted up the hours, multiplied the sums by the individual's rate, and came up with a goal: so many dollars of revenue for each engineer, so many dollars for the company as a whole. Hit the goal, he said, and we'll pay a bonus.

In the first month—it was December—the firm played for $100 a head. Everyone saw the weekly chart of hours billed, so everyone knew where they stood. Presto. Billable hours suddenly increased, up to and even beyond what people had said they would do. The company made money. People got their C-notes.

Starting in January, Smith upped the ante: Now the bonus would be 5 percent of salary. That worked so well—the firm made so much money—in the first six months of the year that he increased the bonus to 10 percent for the next two quarters. At this writing, it looks as if they'll make it.

Note a couple of things about this game playing.

One is that it works, and works quickly. People change what they do so as to make more money. As both companies found, it can turn things around almost overnight.

The other: Unless it becomes part of a whole open-book system, it can backfire.

Remember that news story a few years ago about Sears Auto Centers in California? The division was charged with defrauding customers by making unnecessary repairs. The apparent reason was that service managers were paid partly on the basis of how many parts they sold. So they allegedly pressured mechanics into installing unneeded parts.

Employees will do what they get paid to do. But a business needs people thinking about the long term as well as the short term. Employees *can* do that only if they know how, and if they have the necessary information at their disposal. They *will* do it only if they have some reason to care about the company's long-term health. (Smith & Co. started an employee stock ownership plan in early 1994. Share was considering one as this book went to press.)

So set up a game, by all means. But use it as a way into open-book management, not as a stand-alone incentive.

# 7. Set up an ESOP (and use it as a vehicle for open-book management).

An ESOP—employee stock ownership plan—is a government-regulated trust that holds stock on behalf of employees. Some ten thousand U.S. companies have such a plan, thanks in part to the tax breaks Congress has bestowed on them.

Plenty of ESOP companies have been practicing a kind of homegrown open-book management for years without necessarily calling it that. Reflexite Inc., a Connecticut manufacturer of reflective materials, puts out an annual report with every line item annotated in plain English, so that employees with no financial training can understand it. The company's monthly profit-sharing check is dubbed an Owner's Bonus. Reflexite and many other ESOP companies hold regular meetings to go over the financial results in detail.

But a truly startling number of ESOP companies seem to believe that employees will act like owners just because they now hold title to a few shares of stock. It doesn't happen. You need open-book management.

Consider the mistake that Dick Bohnet made, for example.

Bohnet is president of Acumen International, the software company. He ran a pretty conventional start-up business for a while, though he had installed a gain-sharing plan that paid out quarterly bonuses.

When the company got big enough, he began looking into an ESOP. He believed it was the right thing to do "to make a real team effort."

After a lot of research and hard work, the ESOP was in place. Since setting up a plan can cost several thousand dollars, Bohnet assumed employees would forgo the gain-sharing bonus that quarter. "We'll save those dollars to make the ESOP happen," decided Bohnet. He "just assumed" that everybody would go along.

"Everybody," of course, had no clue. Some had already spent their bonuses—in advance. They expected to be paid, ESOP or no ESOP.

Bohnet got mad. "I wondered, 'What the hell are you guys thinking about? How could you not understand and think this through? What's the matter with you?'

"Literally, I said that! I was really angry. And I felt depreciated. Damn it, I'm working hard to make this thing happen."

Then Bohnet realized that Acumen's employees didn't really have much of a sense of the business. They didn't understand the financials. They missed the immediate money in their pocket and didn't know how the ESOP would ultimately benefit them.

He set up what he called "ESOP 101" to teach them about profits, and equity, and wealth building over the long haul.

ESOP 101 led to Finance 101. "In this company, two-thirds of the people had never read a financial statement. They didn't know how what they were doing ended up on the balance sheet or the income statement." If they were going to be owners, they'd need to know that.

Finance 101 led Bohnet to learn about open-book management. He read *The Great Game of Business* and attended some conferences. He set up Acumen's huddle system. He commissioned a group of employees to explore short-term bonus arrangements. People such as Rob Kellow, the software engineer who solved a problem on his own just because he could see how much money it was costing the company, began learning to think like owners (chapter 4).

Now, Acumen is on track for the future. Bohnet: "It makes a radical difference to people to know they control their own destiny."

# 8. Ask people to show how they make money for the company.

I once heard a CEO reflect on the hiring process. When you're hired on, he mused, you're given a particular task to do. Nobody ever tells you that your real job is to make a profit for the company.

Turn the tables! Ask people for a short report, maybe during their quarterly performance review, *not* on what they've accomplished but on how they helped the company make money.

This is a different way of thinking from the normal here's-what-I-did report that managers and supervisors often expect.

If you're the employee, for example, you have to look at whether what you did was cost-effective. Could the job have been done better through some other method? Could you have done it more efficiently with different tools? A different work environment?

You also have to consider whether your time and skills and resources are being used to the greatest advantage.

When Jack Stack asked Denise Bredfeldt of SRC to show him whether she was making money for the company, neither one was going to be satisfied with proving the hydraulics unit was profitable. It had to be at least as profitable as other activities that might have occupied the floor space.

Mike Chiles of Heatway explains how a similar way of thinking improved the performance of his company's sales department.

Heatway's salespeople work with regional representatives scattered around the country. Like salespeople everywhere, they used to focus exclusively on the top line. The reps' production was added up to show how much revenue each salesperson brought in.

Chiles said, in effect, wait. Let's figure out how much *profit* each rep is producing for us.

That meant toting up the cost of the literature Heatway sent out to the reps. It meant considering how much it cost to fly salespeople out to the reps' territory to put on seminars, or to fly reps in to Heatway. It meant factoring in the time spent at Heatway headquarters preparing heating-system designs for the reps' customers.

"Add together those numbers," says Chiles, "and it tells us how much each rep costs. It tells us whether they're making money"—and by extension whether the salespeople who work with them are making money.

Soon the salespeople began listing reps by profitability rather than by gross revenues. Soon they were leaning harder on reps that used a lot of literature or design time without much to show for it. Suddenly they were more receptive to new strategies—like sending out nearly free copies of Heatway's system-design software so that reps could do more of their own design work.

How do *you* make money for the company? The question itself can change the way people think.

# 9. Make a game out of learning.

Intel Corp.'s Embedded Microcontroller Division played the Profit and Cash business-simulation board game in a tournament: Teams of four players competed against each other to win dinners for two for each team member. It was voluntary. It was played during the day, two hours a pop, meaning that people often had to stay late to get their work done. (The division's four hundred employees are mainly technical or business professionals who don't get overtime.) Yet in the entire eleven-week tournament, all the teams showed up—and *only one team failed to show up with the necessary four players*.

# 10. Don't make decisions.

This was the strategy of Jim Sandstrom, the man who introduced open-book management because he didn't want to be the only one worrying about how his specialty-coatings company was doing.

A guy comes to Sandstrom one day, for example, and tells him that the pay system at the company stinks.

Sandstrom says, gee, he thinks his own pay is pretty good. So it's really not his problem. Whose problem does the guy think it should be?

The guy is silent. "He says, 'I don't know. I don't know what you're getting at. It's certainly not *my* problem,'" remembers Sandstrom.

Sandstrom points out to the guy that he's the one doing the complaining and asks if anybody else feels the way he does. Yeah, says the guy, a lot of people out in the plant feel that way.

Good, says Sandstrom. "You get those people, you form a committee, and I will approve any pay plan you come up with that meets certain criteria."

Sandstrom set two conditions. The plan had to be fiscally responsible. And—since the original complaint was that some people were working harder than others for the same pay—it couldn't be the same for everybody. After a while the group came back to Sandstrom with a plan they admitted was essentially the same for all. Sandstrom sent them back to the drawing board.

Finally, nearly seven months later, an idea occurred to one committee member at 4:00 A.M. The group considered it, modified it—and eventually implemented it. It's essentially a pay-for-knowledge system that allows people to work up from $10 an hour to $15 by learning new skills. Sandstrom's profit-sharing pool each month—25 percent of pretax profits—is divided up by another method, one that relies largely on workers' evaluations of one another. That, too, was designed by employees.

Anyway, that was the beginning of self-management-by-default at Sandstrom Products Inc. Today, people in the plant schedule their own time. Working in teams, they take responsibility for production and quality. If they need a new machine, they're expected to prepare a cost justification for it. ("We've got to be able to go through all the facts and figures and prove to them that we can pay for this new piece of equipment," says Leo Henkelman, an hourly employee.) The third Thursday of each month, says Sandstrom, the financials "are put on the board and charted and discussed." Decisions get implemented quickly because employees have already bought in.

Sandstrom is a small company, between $5 million and $6 million in annual sales.

When Jim Sandstrom was running things alone—"I thought it was my responsibility to do everything, fix everything, tell everybody what to do"—his company was going downhill. "It was a litany of mediocre performance all through the 1980s."

When he changed how the company was run, things turned around dramatically. In two years the company's head count dropped by about one-third, even though sales stayed roughly the same. Corporate overhead dropped by one-third as well. Profits rose by $1 million. The employees did well. Sandstrom did well.

"I almost regret that I'm pushing sixty now," says the bluff, white-haired midwesterner. "It's finally getting fun. I finally understand what business is all about."

As you may have divined from this chapter, there's no standard approach to open-book management. Companies implement it in a variety of situations, for a variety of purposes, using a variety of techniques. In the next five chapters, you'll see how and why five companies, all different, put open-book management into practice—and what it has meant to their business.

## CHAPTER 9

# One Company's Experience: A Fortune 500 Manufacturing Plant

## Case Study 1: Chesapeake Packaging and its "internal companies"

## The Background

The parent company here is Chesapeake Corp., close to $1 billion in sales, headquartered in Richmond, Virginia, number 388 on the 1994 *Fortune* 500, a major manufacturer in the paper and packaging industry. The subsidiary is Chesapeake Packaging Co., operator of ten plants that produce brown corrugated boxes, two others that manufacture point-of-sale-display packaging, and two consumer-graphics packaging plants. The setting for this story is one of those brown-box plants. It's a big, single-story factory located just off Interstate 695 on the outskirts of Baltimore.

In 1988, when Bob Argabright arrived, the Baltimore plant was losing money. A reasonable observer—not to mention a reasonable executive in the parent company—would have been thinking about closing it.

Argabright had spent most of his career with Chesapeake and had managed a number of plants. He was a corporate officer and had been on Chesapeake's executive management committee. As time went on, he was sent back to operate the Baltimore plant. That was in 1988.

He brought with him a down-home style of management. First names. No tie, except when customers visit. No reserved parking space. An *atti-*

*tude.* ("You're the president of the company? So what? That's a title. Does it mean you're better than this person? I don't think so. Does it mean you're important? I don't think so.")

He also brought candor and ambition and drive that the demoralized folks in the Baltimore plant weren't exactly accustomed to.

Look, he told the plant's 145 employees, neither you nor I have a future here unless we start making money.

But why should we limit ourselves just to making money? As Jimmy Carter once put it, why not the best?

"If there are 650 box plants in this country," said Argabright, "and if somebody were to list them from number 1 to number 650, can't I work hard and can't you work hard and maybe aim at becoming the top plant?"

Argabright mapped out a business strategy. His plant's prices might be a tiny bit higher than the competition's. But it would more than make up for the difference with exceptional levels of quality and service. They wouldn't just sell boxes, they'd sell packaging solutions—meaning that they'd work with customers to come up with innovative, cost-effective answers to their problems.

To make the strategy work, he would need smart, engaged, hardworking people.

He sent people from all levels of the plant out for training in subjects such as problem solving and quality management. He hired a financial officer who taught employees to understand the books so they could get involved in controlling costs. He set up teams. He got everybody working toward ISO 9001, the international quality certification.

He didn't call what he was doing open-book management, maybe because the term didn't yet exist. He dubbed his approach "Net Results" and defined it as "the total employee involvement process at Chesapeake Packaging Co., Baltimore Division."

But it doesn't matter what he or anyone else may call it. What Bob Argabright did, ultimately, was rebuild and restructure the whole enterprise from the ground up. He created an open-book company—or, as the mission statement up on the cafeteria wall puts it, "a company of owners, of partners, of businesspeople."

## How It Works

Here's the way the Baltimore division works today:

Out in the plant, the big corrugating machines and rotary die-cutters and Flexo printers hum, churning out corrugated boxes for customers such as Perdue Inc., the chicken producer. The Flexo department—to take only one example—is run by a "company" called Bob's Big Boys. The elected president of Bob's Big Boys is Winston Smith.

Back in the office, the plant's customer-service reps and purchasers and design engineers and accountants do all the paperwork and people-work involved in a $25 million business. Customer service—again, only one example—is the province of another "company," called Boxbusters. Ruth Graham is the president.

In all, Chesapeake has eight so-called *internal companies.* Quality Trucking handles shipping. Chesapeake Maintenance Services maintains the machinery. Corrugator Specialties Unlimited is responsible for the corrugating process. Other "companies" handle finishing, administration, and engineering.

What was once a conventional plant, with conventional departments and job descriptions, is now a collection of little businesses staffed by people who think like owners. Pick the system apart according to the open-book principles and you can see exactly how it works.

### Information.

The internal companies compile their own operating information—production, quality levels, whatever the relevant measures are. Accounting provides them with detailed breakdowns of their costs as compared to budget. So they know from week to week and month to month exactly how they're doing.

Then, once a month, from 2:30 to 4:00 in the afternoon, everyone in the whole plant crowds into the little cafeteria to see how the whole company did the previous month.

Every internal company has its own results already. Under the direction of accounting manager Dave Shanahan, they build an income statement, there in the meeting. They see—and cheer about or grieve over—the month's bottom line. They discuss it. Why were shipping costs high this month? What can we do about declining gross margins due to raw-materials increases?

### Business literacy.

Company controller Yong Kim began teaching business basics to employees a couple of years ago. It wasn't anything too fancy. She just drew pictures of buckets.

The top bucket on Kim's chart was for sales. Another, smaller, was for direct costs. A third, still smaller, was for contribution (overhead), and on down the income statement. She showed her students how the sales bucket filled up over the course of a month, and how money "spilled" from one to the next, each one filling up, all the way down to the bottom line.

At first, the classes were low-key, sixty minutes apiece, one shift at a time. Then Argabright shut the plant down for a whole day of business training. "That conveyed a sense of how important it was," says Kim.

Since those first classes, a committee of nonfinancial employees has prepared a basic-business-training workbook—and everyone in the plant must go through a six-hour class using it. "It really helped me because it was designed around this plant," says Winston Smith of Bob's Big Boys. "It helps me see how they get to the bottom line."

### Empowerment.

Like any business, each of the eight internal companies is responsible for managing its own affairs.

The companies track and measure their output and figure out how to improve. They track their costs. If they need new equipment, they order it—or prepare their own capital-authorization requests for the corporate office. They get involved in the annual plantwide planning and budgeting process. The members of a company review each other's performance and take part in hiring and disciplinary decisions.

Most of the companies meet as a group weekly or biweekly, with committee meetings in between. An elected president—the position rotates every six months, and carries no extra money or supervisory authority—sets the agenda and makes sure that decisions are carried out.

### A stake in the outcome.

Though the internal companies are called companies, none makes money by itself. They make money as part of a whole plant. So the employees get a profit-sharing bonus that depends not on their company's performance but on the plant's.

The profit-sharing plan works like this:

The plant must hit a certain target level of earnings before profit sharing kicks in. If it does kick in, employees get at least 5 percent of their gross monthly wages or salaries. The percentage rises as total profit rises: In one record month, Chesapeake paid profit-sharing checks amounting to 24 percent of earnings. The money is paid in cash, monthly, rather than being accumulated or put into a retirement account.

# The Payoffs

Remember what Tom Peters said? The word *business* "implies autonomy, practicality, action-taking, self-sufficiency, and self-responsibility." That's the importance of calling Chesapeake's departments *companies.*

*When they're helping to run a company, people's attitudes change.*

"The us-versus-them mentality, the management-versus-labor type thing? We don't really have that here" (Tim Green, machine operator).

"If you know what you're spending, and if you know every time you throw a box out what the effect is on the bottom line, it makes you think" (Winston Smith, machine operator).

"In our department, it has made us all work as one. It used to be, there was customer service inside and customer service outside. And the outside guy had his job and got the order and then didn't care what happened to it. Maybe I had to figure out how to unitize it [for shipping] or something else. It wasn't his problem anymore because he got the order.

"But now it's not like that. We're all in Boxbusters, so all the customer-service reps operate as one group" (Marlene Raglin, customer-service representative).

*Their actions change, too.*

"It could be something as simple as a broom handle. Yesterday, I had a guy come to me. He said, hey, these broom handles, they're just not lasting long enough. Is there some way we could get a collapsible handle, something that we could store? Or can we get a heavy-duty handle?" (Estel Martin, purchasing).

"Today, Freddy came up to me. He works on the Flexo, and he wanted information on repair-and-maintenance parts and factory supplies for last month. Gene Wolski wrote a quick-and-dirty program, and in about ten minutes had this nice report. It showed the amount, the item description, exactly what it was, the vendor we purchased it from—everything they needed to know for every part that went in that machine for all of April" (Dave Shanahan, accounting manager).

"I have a customer in Williamsport, and [to get there] the truck goes right by one of Greg's customers. I might go to Greg and ask if he has anything we can put on the same truck. If we can't get [a truckload] from one customer, we'll mix and match the customers that are close to each other" (Angel Craig, customer-service representative).

*As people take on responsibility, productivity inevitably grows.*

"A year ago we had forty-four salaried employees. Now we're down to thirty-eight. In accounting we had four people plus Dave Shanahan, the manager; now he runs the department with two people and a trainee. It's another way of empowering our people—do we really need to replace someone, or is there a way we can find ways to become more efficient?

"Just by not replacing people when they leave, last year we added approximately half a million dollars to our bottom line" (Yong Kim, controller).

*Soon the numbers that measure the business begin heading in the right direction.*

Bob Argabright has a set of slides that he uses to show the Baltimore plant's performance in the last few years.

Days lost to accidents: from a high of over fifty in 1989 to near zero.

Latenesses and absenteeism: declined to an average of one lateness and one day absent per employee per year.

Returns and allowances: cut nearly in half in two years.

Repair and maintenance costs: declined 46 percent in two years.

And, of course, the bottom line.

The plant was losing money in 1988, the first year Argabright arrived in Baltimore. The next year, 1989, it turned the corner and made a small profit.

That profit doubled in 1990, doubled again in 1991, and rose 40 percent in 1992. In 1993, with the economy recovering, sales rose 11 percent—and profits rose another 27 percent.

Bob Argabright, who speaks in the soft accent of his native Virginia, has no doubt what has made the difference.

"In a parade, everyone has sheet music, not just the drum major. And the sheet music is in the right order. If you're the drum major, you can get up there and make sure that your people play the right music. I've never seen a parade yet that was very impressive with only the drum major in step, and only the drum major with sheet music.

"That's what we're doing here. And if you do that, you unleash the power of 145 people thinking about a common goal. It's got to begin with the selection system. People have to be selected to operate in this environment. And after they're selected, you have to train them. You have to go into not only technical skills but problem solving.

"Our philosophy is, there's no sin at all in having a problem. The sin is not looking at it, not working on it, not looking at problems as an opportunity to improve. Management is not going to make that problem go away! So get yourself a problem-solving group and go to work on it.

"So you do that, you start giving them the numbers and educating them on the numbers. And then I think you sit back here, and—God, the sense of pride! You sit there and say, What can't we do? There's nothing that we can't do, that we can't take on as a challenge.

"There's a whole lot more to business than just coming in here and dreading coming to work every day. It's exciting to me to see the progress they're making. And every night I go to bed, I just pray—and I'm not a religious person—just pray hard to let me see this project through. Just let me live long enough to see it through, and see how good we can become in a very competitive—very competitive!—business."

## CHAPTER 10

# One Company's Experience: A Small Service Business

## Case Study 2: Mid-States Technical's "Bucket Plan"

## The Background

Steve Wilson, a West Point graduate with an interest in computers, founded Mid-States Technical in 1986. Five years later he had something akin to a rebellion on his hands.

The company's full name is Mid-States Technical Staffing Services Inc. It's partly a specialized temporary-help firm, recruiting engineers and other technical personnel and then contracting for their services with companies needing extra help. It also operates a computer-aided-design (CAD) facility, providing design and drafting services to customers such as Deere & Co. and J.I. Case.

Wilson, sales manager Dave McCracken, and a handful of sales and administrative employees handle the temporary-help end out of Davenport, Iowa. The CAD operation—design manager Jim Kieffer and a couple of dozen others—is in Dubuque. Mid-States Technical's total revenues are in the $5 million range, and rising. Once again.

In its first five years, the company had grown like a weed. In 1991 *Inc.* magazine ranked it 212 on its list of the 500 fastest-growing privately held companies in America.

But like a lot of fast-growth businesses, Mid-States Technical started to come apart at the seams. "Two groups formed," says Wilson matter-of-factly. "A power struggle ensued." One group was happy with his leadership. The other believed he was somehow ripping the company off. Rumors flew. Employees grew paranoid. Meanwhile, the business struggled. "Our sales dropped 40 percent and our margins went to hell. We nearly self-destructed."

Finally Wilson bit the bullet and let the disgruntled employees go.

But rather than just hire replacements, he decided he needed a new business model—one that would encourage trust rather than mistrust, cooperation rather than factionalism.

He had heard of the Great Game of Business, so he called up Jack Stack, talked with him, and paid a visit to Springfield ReManufacturing Corp.

Excited, he sent Kieffer and McCracken to SRC as well. "My key managers had to buy into the program, so I didn't do anything until I knew they totally supported it." Eventually he hired Gary Brown, a senior manager at SRC, to come up to Iowa and lead a daylong training session for all of Mid-States Technical's regular employees. Dave McCracken's mother was hired to answer the phones in Davenport. Everyone else traveled to Dubuque for Brown's session.

That day—it was in the spring of 1993—Mid-States Technical was closed for business. But an unusual version of the Great Game of Business was set in motion.

# How It Works

"It's called the Bucket Plan," says Wilson. "I'm never much good at explaining it." He gets out a piece of paper with seven colored cylinders on it.

Each cylinder, he says, is a bucket—a bucket of profits. Whenever Mid-States Technical earns $75,000, it's said to fill a bucket.

And whenever a bucket is filled, everyone gets a bonus—a specified share of those profits. The more buckets that are filled during a year, the higher the share that goes into the bonus pool.

Which means, of course, that Mid-States Technical's employees aren't waiting for the end of a month or the end of a quarter or the end of the year. They can earn a bonus whenever they fill a bucket. How many buckets they fill is essentially up to them. Their only constraints are the constraints facing any business: the marketplace, the trade-offs between growth and profitability, and so forth. They're businesspeople, not hired hands.

The mechanics:

### Information, part one.

In the beginning, says Wilson, is the budget. "We are totally budget-driven. The only document that counts is the budget. If you budgeted it, do it. If you didn't, you've got a lot of explaining to do."

The budget is assembled from the ground up, so to speak, once a year. "Employees budget line items within a profit center. The division manager budgets the division. I balance it all." Everything is zero-based. "There's no 'Add one percent to what you did last year.' You have to break it down, dollar by dollar, when you do your budget. You have to predict what's going to happen to you."

Wilson's administrative staff is a cost center, not a profit center, but the budgeting process isn't so different. "We take the budgeted gross profit from each of the revenue-generating divisions and allocate a charge to administrative services." That's the administrative staff's budgeted income, and so it too will then operate "profitably" or "unprofitably" during the year. Administration gets no more money than the budget allows—unless the revenue-generating divisions need extra services *and* can prove that they are generating enough extra gross profit to pay for them.

The point of a budget is to let people anticipate the future and thereby plan for it. Wilson's employees didn't think they could. "They said, 'We can't predict sales. Anything can happen!' I said, well, just give it a try. So for two years they predicted, to where they were predicting sales plus or minus only 5 percent. These guys realized, gee, not only can I, but I really *ought* to be able to."

Like SRC's, Mid-States Technical's budget provides a plan, a reference point, with numbers attached. What the business proposes to do during the coming year is transparent to everyone. Employees have already bought into it because they have had a hand in developing it.

"The philosophy of the whole thing is that people will pretty much do what they say they're going to do. I don't want them saying they don't think they can do something—and then giving me reasons why they didn't do it!"

### Information, part two.

Week to week, during the year, the numbers are compiled. What Mid-States Technical did last week. What people think they will do during the coming weeks.

It's a three-part system—also borrowed from SRC—and it's worth understanding in detail.

The budget itself—the plan—is the first set of numbers. It's fixed for a year. Hell can freeze over and the budget numbers for January or July won't change. A company needs to know from year to year how good it is at planning.

The actuals—what happens from week to week—are the second set of numbers. That's what you look at to see how you're doing compared to your plan.

The third set of numbers—both SRC and Mid-States Technical call it "opinion"—is what you think *today* is likely to happen next week or next month.

Opinion may be different from the budget because you know more now than you did when you were budgeting. Maybe the economy is slowing up. Maybe you've landed some unexpected new customers. The opinion line identifies problems and opportunities. If it's significantly different from the budget, you know you'll have to make adjustments.

The key numbers here, the ones that sound wake-up calls to managers and employees alike, are the variances—how much the actual or the opinion differs from the budget.

I visited Mid-States Technical in mid-1994, and Wilson pulled out some current reports to show me exactly how the system worked.

"Look here," he said, pointing to the figures for Jim Kieffer's CAD division in Dubuque. "Jim's behind plan every week. He had two contracts canceled a month ago. So he has taken a short-term hit.

"But let's go to the end of the year, over here. He's now predicting that he's only going to be $1,900 behind plan for the end of the year. So already he's working to fix the situation. He's got his whole crew working on that. This is part of their weekly discussion."

It isn't just the business's overall plan that's transparent, in other words, it's the company's entire operation from week to week and month to month. It's all there in the numbers, for everyone to see and discuss.

### *Empowerment.*

Empowerment comes with *ownership* of the numbers.

Ownership means first that authority is delegated. Salespeople are in charge of their own expenses, subject to the budget. Connie Whitcomb, sales administrator, is in charge of advertising, up to the budgeted amount.

Ownership also means that people are accountable to one another. Every line item has a name on it. That person is responsible for watching spending on that item.

The reliance on the budget means that people are accountable in both directions. At Mid-States Technical, doing better than the budget on any given number can be as big a sin as not making your budget numbers. Maybe you're not spending as much as you should be for the sake of the company's long-term health. Maybe you're cutting margins too much for the sake of additional revenue. There is no reward for, say, spending less on marketing expenses.

And because everybody has an interest in making the numbers, ownership is shared. "I have a division number to hit," says sales manager McCracken. "I sat down with my three salespeople the other day and said, we're a little short on this division for the month.

One agreed to do a little more. The others chipped in, too. "They all ponied up and figured out as a group how they could still hit their number."

### A stake in the outcome.

This brings us back to the buckets.

Wilson wanted people to focus on profitability first and growth second.

Every time Mid-States Technical makes $75,000 in pretax earnings, employees get a bonus. That's the profitability part.

If revenues are at least 25 percent ahead of last year's *during the week that the bucket is filled,* the bonus is doubled. That's the growth part.

And to keep people focused on those two goals all year long, later buckets pay a bigger bonus than earlier ones.

It isn't as complicated as it sounds. Employees typically add between 10 and 15 percent to their base wages over the course of a year through the bonus system. But the specific amounts are less important than a couple of the principles Wilson has laid down for the system's operation.

One: The bonuses take the place of all sales commissions and other performance-based individual rewards. Wilson wants people working together for the good of the company, not focusing on whether they as individuals are making their numbers. Outstanding individuals get bigger raises through a merit-pay system, not bigger bonuses.

Two: The system is automatic—mostly. When it's earned, it's paid. But it does have a couple of built-in protections. Balance-sheet numbers such as the current ratio must be above a certain threshold before any bonus is paid. That ensures that the company has sufficient cash. And Wilson reserves the right to end the program in December to allow for year-end adjustments, extra contributions to the 401(k) plan, and the like.

Theoretically, all the bonuses could be paid out by the calendar, quarterly or annually or whenever, as long as they were earned by a prescribed date.

They could be—but where's the excitement in that?

As it is, everyone watches the charts that show the buckets being filled. They finagle a little here and there to fill a bucket this month rather than next. And though there's no incentive to overperform on any single budget number, there's a big incentive, as the year goes on, to sell a little more here, cut a little more there, make a little more money—and fill up seven buckets, for example, rather than the expected six. If sales are up over last year's, that last bucket puts hundreds of dollars more into everybody's pocket.

### Business literacy.

I've saved this subject for last because it's built right into Mid-States Technical's system.

At first, Wilson did a lot of formal training in business basics.

He printed up play money, used Junior Achievement materials, and had people create an imaginary company. He walked them through Mid-States Technical's financials. He homed in on matters that particularly affect a temporary-personnel company, such as accrued vacation time and unemployment-insurance costs. Nothing too fancy, just regular lunchtime discussions, mostly led by Wilson himself. The basic training lasted maybe six months. Specific training continues.

But the budget-and-bucket system focuses people's attention on the business week in and week out. Employees watch the numbers to see when the next bonus is likely to be paid. One group even developed a custom spreadsheet built around bucket filling. "Using their financial models," says Wilson, "they were beginning to predict when the next bucket would be filled—and how much they had to get in sales to get that 125 percent number [over last year] *before* the bucket filled. They were racing sales against income."

Which, of course, is exactly what you might want businesspeople to be doing.

# The Payoffs

The logic of Mid-States Technical's system is the logic of open-book management itself: It puts responsibility in the hands of the people doing the work. "Those are the people who ultimately have control over sales and earnings," says Wilson. "I can't make them sell. I can't stop them from spending. But the system does. Operate within your budget and the company guidelines and you can do anything you want to."

The system also fundamentally alters the job of the CEO.

Wilson oversees. He coaches. He plans the company's future. He meets with customers. What he doesn't do is what owners of entrepreneurial companies habitually do: jump in and grab control of any day-to-day situation that seems to need a decision. "I don't have to decide whether we buy the high-end shredder or the low-end shredder. I don't have to decide who uses the van this week. I don't have to worry about who's talking on the telephone too much anymore. I don't even have to worry about sales.

"They do all the work. I *truly* don't have to be responsible for everything anymore."

Within the company, the system gets everyone working toward the same ends.

Mid-States Technical's divisions help each other out, because no single division can fill a bucket alone. Salespeople don't fight over who gets credit for a shared account because they aren't competing for commissions. Unlike most salespeople, they have a big incentive to cooperate. "Let's say in the group of three [salespeople] they've got ten [requests for temporary help] they're trying to fill," explains McCracken. "If one guy is working on eight and the other guys have one each, chances are not many are going to get filled. But if they can split their workload, they will."

Steve Wilson began his program in 1992. That year, sales stayed flat but profits nearly doubled. In 1993 his company grew 40 percent while profits more than doubled. In 1994, he had planned for five buckets' worth of earnings, and by the end of the year had filled *nine*. Return on sales was in the neighborhood of 10 percent—as compared with 3.5 percent in 1991.

"Open-book management has resulted in more money for everybody," says Wilson. "There's nobody in the company that would disagree with that."

## CHAPTER 11

# One Company's Experience: A Fast-Growth "Star"

## Case Study 3: Manco follows the Wal-Mart model— and opens the books more and more

## The Background

Jack Kahl used to visit the headquarters of Wal-Mart Stores in Bentonville, Arkansas, regularly. Every time he came back home to Cleveland, he had some new idea for transforming his company, Manco. His employees mostly rolled their eyes—until the day he proposed to hold regular company meetings on Saturdays, just as Wal-Mart did. Uh-uh, they said. Don't try that here. Nobody wants to work Saturday. People will quit. You'll destroy the business.

Destroy the business? Manco was Kahl's baby. He had gone to work for its predecessor company, Melvin A. Andersen, way back in 1963, at the age of twenty-two. Andersen was a tiny distributor of industrial tapes, doing maybe $80,000 worth of business a year. Kahl (rhymes with "mail") became general manager and built the company up to $800,000 in annual revenues. In 1971 he bought out the original owner and changed the name to Manco.

As it happened, that tenfold growth was only a taste of what was to come. Over the next twenty-three years, Kahl created a $100 million business—in tapes, weather stripping, and other consumer products.

His strategies were smart. In the late 1970s, for example, he sold Wal-Mart a line of hardware tapes. Five or six other big retail accounts soon followed. Pretty soon Kahl had persuaded the retailers to set up a separate section for Manco's tape products—duct tape, masking tape, and so forth, a "tape center" all in one place.

He packaged his products in bright green cardboard and plastic, creating what he saw as a distinctive "sea of green" in the store. He commissioned an artist to draw a cute cartoon duck, and he used the big-eyed bird as Manco's ubiquitous symbol and mascot. Like a Japanese company, Manco kept costs, prices, and profit margins at rock bottom, thereby expanding market share.

Kahl pushed the edges of innovation. He brought out new product lines. He pioneered cutting-edge retailer-supplier techniques, such as electronic data interchange (EDI) and vendor-managed inventory. He was an early convert to modern ideas of quality management. Somehow he hung on under the pressures of Wal-Mart's (and other customers') blistering growth—and under intense competition from the likes of 3M Corp., itself no slouch in the marketplace. In 1993 *Industry Week* named Kahl one of "America's most admired CEOs," along with such big names as GE's Jack Welch and Microsoft's Bill Gates. By 1994 he found himself heading up a $100 million company.

But the real key to Manco's success, says Kahl, were those visits to Wal-Mart.

He had always wanted to treat employees like family, to be completely open with them about the company. He had wanted to feel that everyone was on the same team. But he had doubts. His friends and business associates told him he was crazy. Employees themselves seemed dubious. "The company wasn't knit together," Kahl told a reporter.

But then he saw that Wal-Mart managers were totally open about their company. They shared information right down to the level of the store clerk. The information itself seemed to empower people. The system "gave them the facts so they could run the business for you," thought Kahl. It seemed to turn Wal-Mart into "one great exciting team."

Wal-Mart, he saw, gathered and disseminated a prodigious quantity of information in an incredibly short time. Sales data were transmitted to headquarters daily. Regional managers could fly in to Bentonville for the company's legendary Saturday meetings and have up-to-the-minute records from hundreds of different stores at their fingertips. Their discussions and decisions, in turn, would be back in the hands of store managers by Monday morning. They would be communicated to every employee in every store not long thereafter.

The information fed a constantly evolving business strategy, one that was always in close touch with marketplace trends. "They change the entire store that day," muses Kahl, reflecting on what happens when Wal-Mart's information goes out on Mondays. "Fifty-two times a year they do that. And they beat the living daylights out of the rest of the world.

"They know that information is power. And they get that information all the way out to the part-time help an hour after they're in the store."

Step by step, Kahl has created a company that, like Wal-Mart, trades on the power of information—and on how people act when they have that information at their fingertips.

# How It Works

In a way, it started a dozen years ago, with those Saturday meetings.

People said they'd quit if they had to show up on Saturday. But they didn't. The managers and several lower-level employees started to come regularly. Kahl—not a bashful or inarticulate man—used the meetings to talk to them about the company. He explained where it was going and why. He walked them through the financials to show them how it was doing. He led discussions of Manco's future. Attendance swelled, particularly once the meeting time was changed to Thursday evening. "People began understanding the business, not just their jobs," says Charlie MacMillan, now Manco's controller.

But that was just the beginning. Today, information flows like a river throughout Manco. Like businesspeople—and like Wal-Mart's staff—the company's managers and employees see, learn to understand, and act on a flood of data every day, week, and month. Through an annual bonus and an employee stock ownership plan they have a substantial stake in Manco's success.

They run the business, in other words, through a full-fledged system of open-book management, a system created on the fly by an entrepreneur who knew only that he wanted his company to look and act like Wal-Mart. The elements:

### Information.

Without a doubt, the flow of data and ideas is the single most striking aspect of Manco's operation. Information goes out through meetings, scoreboards, and the most detailed financial statements you'll ever want to see.

• At Manco, a person could get sick of meetings. Managers and executives meet every Thursday morning. They review numbers, discuss problems, look at competitive threats and opportunities, make decisions. That day or the next, each department gets together. Hot topics from the executive meeting will be passed along, questions asked and answered.

The Thursday-night meetings are broader in scope and are open to anyone who wants to come. Kahl or Chief Operating Officer Tom Corbo might talk about sales strategies. Hourly employees might give presentations on what's going on in their department. An invited guest might talk. Every department sends at least one representative, who can fill in coworkers the next day.

Once a month, Manco has an all-company meeting, focusing on the financials. "We put a graph up on an overhead," explains controller MacMillan. "It shows pictorially our monthly performance compared to prior year and to budget. We also look at a year-to-date graph that shows where we stand." People ask questions. They hear a report from the sales and marketing departments about prospects for the rest of the year. They see whether they're on track for the year's bonus—and if not, what's being done about it.

• In between meetings, you can always check the scoreboards. Manco has scoreboards for departments and scoreboards for the whole company.

Walk into the cafeteria, for example, and you're confronted with a wall of data. Daily sales totals, including open orders and month-to-date sales. Month-to-date and year-to-date performance data, for every department and for the whole company, compared to prior year and to budget. Profit before ESOP and taxes. Return on operating assets. The value, year to year, of a share of Manco stock. *(What better place to put the scoreboard than in the cafeteria—where people can check out and talk about the numbers over lunch?)*

Walk into any department and you'll see more numbers plastered up all over.

In the tiny public-relations department, PR director Kevin Krueger can show you his charts of media appearances, press releases, media publicity value, and the like.

In sales, charts on the wall track the company's profit as a percent of sales, its costs as a percent of sales, how many samples have been sent out, how many trade shows attended, how travel and entertainment expenses are doing—all by month and year-to-date, all compared to budget.

And out on the shop floor, Manco has about seventy employees packaging, wrapping, and shipping its wares. (They're called "partners," like everyone who works for the company.) All seventy work in teams, and every team tracks measures such as labor efficiency, downtime, and rework. "They measure their own performance each week," says MacMillan. "Then in their weekly meetings [!] they can discuss what's affecting their performance and how they can improve it."

• And then there are the books: Blue, Yellow, Gray, and Green. So many books, sighs MacMillan, that the accounting department at the end of the month feels like a printshop. Copies are handed out to every department and are available for inspection by any partner.

The Blue Book is the company's financial statements, the P&L that most businesses prepare at the end of every month. The Yellow Book breaks the numbers down by department, the Gray Book by product line (ultimately by item), and the Green Book by customer.

In the various books are the numbers that show, say, how the new line of children's activity supplies sold last month at K mart.

Or the numbers showing that salesman X's freight costs were a little high last month, which is why the profit credited to him was lower than expected.

Each book is a hundred or more pages—which means that you can find just about any number you might want to find. And that you can discuss—in one of those meetings—just about any number you might want to discuss.

When people see the numbers and get a chance to discuss them, not surprisingly, it affects their behavior.

Take the salespeople. According to MacMillan and his boss, Diego Perez-Stable, Manco's chief financial officer, the salespeople have undergone a kind of metamorphosis:

PEREZ-STABLE: "An interesting thing about [the books] is how they have changed the whole sales force. When we first started doing these several years ago, the sales force really didn't take ownership of their accounts from the perspective of profitability. They knew how much they were selling, but they didn't really know whether they were making money or not."

MACMILLAN: "The important idea back then was sales growth and not profit growth."

PEREZ-STABLE: "But this has been instrumental as a tool to help the salespeople take ownership of their accounts, to learn how to make money with the account."

MACMILLAN: "[Now] the sales guys ask me [for example] why their freight expense is up. And it's like, 'Well, let's take a look at your freight bill. You're shipping minimum-poundage loads to the West Coast! It's going to cost more money than if you're shipping a whole truck or if you're just shipping it to the Midwest.' So they're like, 'Oh—you gotta get more on your order.'"

PEREZ-STABLE: "Or people would ask, Why is my profit down this month? And you go and start looking, dissecting, and you say, gee, you gave a big promotion to [customer X]."

MACMILLAN: [laughs] "They tend to say, my profit can't be right! You must have done something! We say, no, we don't play with your profit."

PEREZ-STABLE: "The interesting thing is, originally, they would never ask questions associated with profit. Everything was always focused on sales."

### Empowerment.

Empowerment is built right into the system. People are responsible for their numbers, whether they're part of a team on the manufacturing floor or part of a product-marketing group. Everyone takes part in preparing the annual plan. Everyone takes part in the meetings comparing performance to plan.

### Business literacy.

This is also built in, at least for some of Manco's employees. The salespeople, for example, had to be walked through the various books. But once they understood they were held accountable for profitability, not just sales, they made a point of learning how profitability was calculated and how it could be affected. "People make better decisions once they know what they're being charged for," says Tom Corbo.

For people who don't need to understand the finances in their day-to-day work, MacMillan has begun to set up formal classes in finance and accounting—introductory classes for line employees, advanced classes for middle managers.

At Manco, employees have a two-part *stake in the company's success.*

### Stake #1: Manco pays an annual bonus pegged to the attainment of two targets.

One target is profit before ESOP and bonus, the company's basic net earnings figure. The other is return on operating assets, which in a business like Manco's ensures that (for example) it is continuing to turn inventory as fast as it needs to. The bonus is paid annually because the business is highly seasonal. The pool is divvied up unequally, on the grounds that people with more responsibility should have a larger share of their compensation at risk.

***Stake #2: About 30 percent of the company's stock is owned by its ESOP.***

Employees are allocated a certain number of shares every year and can cash them in—sell them back to the company—when they retire.

As at SRC and a lot of the other companies in this book, stock ownership gives employees a long-term incentive to stay with the company and to keep its best interests in mind. In the eight years since the ESOP was set up, the share value has risen from $217 to $385, a 77 percent increase. If Manco continues to grow at its current rate (about 15 percent a year), the shares will be worth much more.

In 1993, with the ESOP only seven years old, a couple of hourly employees retired—and cashed in nearly $50,000 of stock apiece.

# The Payoffs

Think for a moment about Manco's business.

Its "manufacturing" operations are mainly packaging and shipping of items produced by others. So it has no big capital investments and little in the way of proprietary technology or manufacturing know-how. It's essentially a sales-and-marketing organization.

*What* it markets are value-priced consumer products. Duct tape. Weather stripping. Mailing materials. Common, everyday items, available from a lot of suppliers.

And it markets these products through some of the most aggressive retailing organizations in the world. Wal-Mart and the other chains with whom Manco does most of its business are known for expecting a lot from their suppliers.

So Manco's competitive advantage lies exclusively in its selling and marketing expertise, its services (such as on-time delivery) to the customer, its capacity to come out with new products, and its ability to keep its costs and prices at rock-bottom levels. This is business at its purest. Manco can win the game it's playing only by outperforming—*and by continuing to outperform*—everybody else.

Open-book management makes that possible.

It gets every salesperson worrying about freight expenses. And every business-unit manager watching inventory turns like a hawk.

It gets shop-floor employees figuring out how to cut costs. Bill Hall, who runs the hot-melt machine utilized in some of Manco's packaging operations, heard the company needed a new melting tank—and went out and found a bargain on one. "He actually had the people pay us to take the old one away," says Corbo.

And it keeps people focused on the company's profitability and growth rather than just on their own well-being.

People can see, week after week, if a product line isn't doing well. In a transparent environment like Manco's, managers can't protect their turf if they aren't performing.

And people can see, week after week, that they'll need new products to replace the old ones as markets mature and margins erode. So there's an openness to new ideas that you don't find in many companies.

In the last ten years, Manco's sales have risen 525 percent, its sales per employee 63 percent. Its inventory turns have more than tripled. Its SG&A, or overhead, has dropped from 18.4 percent of sales to 12.4 percent.

Tom Corbo, who has been Jack Kahl's right-hand man and has recently become the president of Manco, summarizes the company's philosophy:

"Power is in the information," says Corbo, "and the guy doing the job has the information. He has more power than you do because he knows more.

"So you better trust that guy, and you better let him know you depend on each other to get that job done and done right, or the whole ship sinks.

"Without this culture it would have been difficult, if not impossible, for us to keep up with the dynamics of the retail marketplace."

## CHAPTER 12

# One Company's Experience: "The Biggest Bank in Town"

## Case Study 4: The employees of Phelps County Bank buy it out, take it over—and learn to run the business

## The Background

Rolla, Missouri, is a pretty mid-American town, a regional business center, and site of a University of Missouri campus. If you lived there and were looking for a commercial bank, you'd have three choices. Two of the banks—Boatmen's and Mercantile—are affiliated with the largest bank holding companies in the state. Everyone in Missouri knows their names. The third is independent and is known only to local residents. It has a couple of offices in Rolla and a branch in the nearby village of St. James. It's called Phelps County Bank (PCB).

Five years ago PCB was in the middle of the Rolla pack. Measured by both assets and deposits, it was a trifle larger than Mercantile but noticeably smaller than Boatmen's. Then PCB grew while the others held steady. In 1992 it passed Boatmen's on both measures. PCB was now Number One in town.

The peculiar thing about this? PCB's services are typically *more* expensive than those of its competitors. Its mortgages, for example, might be higher by one or one-and-a-half percentage points—a lot of money in a town such as Rolla.

Nor does it have as broad a range of "products," as bankers like to say. It's hard to buy mutual funds through PCB. The bank doesn't sell annuities. It was late in installing automatic teller machines.

What PCB does have is a relentless, determined, and utterly single-minded focus on customer service.

If you're thinking of applying for a loan, Leona Williamson or another loan officer is likely to spend forty-five minutes with you before even filling out the application, just getting to know you and figuring out what kind of loan makes the most sense for you.

If you show up at the bank a few minutes after it has closed for the day, knock on the door. Patti Douglas or another customer-service representative will escort you into a secure room and see if she can't help you.

Maybe you'd like to close a loan at home in the evening. No problem. Adolph Mueller, from the St. James branch, recently did just that for a couple taking out a mortgage. "They both work, and they have three children," said Mueller, "so it's a convenience for them."

One spring, the bank mounted a promotional campaign called the "You Bet We Can Can-Can," complete with caricatures of staffers doing the can-can, and advertised it all over town. Tell us a story of employees who went out of their way to help you, the bank asked customers. Each month we'll pick one. The winners—customers and employees—will each get dinner for two.

Literally hundreds of responses poured in.

A flower-shop operator told of finding herself short of cash to pay for the repair of a critical piece of cooling equipment. She called the bank while the angry repairman waited. Jody Sanders, a PCB loan officer, hand-delivered a small loan to cover the expense.

An apparel retailer reported that she had bumped into Alice Malone, a customer-service rep, at church one Sunday, and had mentioned that she was having trouble with her credit-card imprinter. "When I got to the bank Monday, there was a new imprinter waiting for me," the retailer wrote.

A professor at the university recounted how he had had his mortgage approved by PCB before he even moved to Rolla. Later, he added, the bank went to bat for him against an insurance company that had canceled its policy but tried to get its automatic monthly payment anyway.

The bank's chief executive, Emma Lou Brent, preaches the virtues of exceptional service every day. Her managers and employees are encouraged—and empowered—to do whatever it takes to satisfy customers. They can spend extra time. They can refund disputed service charges. The bank pays wages and salaries some 20 percent above market so that it can attract high-quality, service-oriented people. It devotes inordinate attention to the hiring process.

All this is expensive. Yet PCB also has a stellar record of earnings and share-value growth.

What makes it possible is that PCB's fifty-five employees think of themselves as embarked on a kind of great adventure—owning and running their own business.

# How It Works

Not so long ago, most of PCB's shares were owned by a man named Don Castleman.

Brent, who took over as CEO in 1982 at Castleman's request, had set up an employee stock ownership plan (ESOP) a couple of years before. She saw it, at first, as just a nice benefit for the bank's employees. When they retired, they could cash in the shares they had accumulated. The ESOP bought a few shares from Castleman, then a few more.

Soon Brent began envisioning a bank that was wholly owned by its employees—and that could therefore control its own destiny in a buyout-happy industry. She wondered about aiming for 100 percent ownership.

That was fine with Castleman. He was ready to cash out. Selling to an ESOP rather than to a third party kept the bank local, and provided some tax breaks besides. Over time, the ESOP borrowed money and bought more and more of his shares. By 1993 it owned them all.

Even before the buyout was complete, Brent began calling the bank's staff members "employee owners." She set up an ESOP committee to help teach people the meaning of ownership. She saw to it that the most active people, whatever their job, got a chance to attend conventions of ESOP companies.

In 1993, when the ESOP became the majority shareholder, she put on what she dubbed the "Old Settlers' Dinner" for every bank employee. There were skits and songs. There was a "Declaration of Independence" signed by everyone in the bank. Brent, dressed like Thomas Jefferson, gave an inspiring speech about fighting for independence against the big banks.

Brent sees herself as creating a proud employee-ownership culture—just as companies such as Avis and Republic Engineered Steel have tried to do.

But whatever it might be called, the culture and the ways of doing things that she has created at PCB look much—*very* much—like open-book management.

## Information.

Information, for example, permeates the bank.

Like all banks, PCB is a numbers maven's heaven. Net interest margins. Loan delinquency rates. The daily statement of condition, which is a banker's daily scorecard. There's little about a bank's operation and performance that can't be quantified. And since banks must report their numbers to public authorities, any one bank can easily compare its performance on any given measure with banks of similar size elsewhere.

At most banks, only the people at the top see this information. "I came from a bank where you didn't ask questions," recalls David Connell, now manager of PCB's St. James branch. "The financial status of the bank was kept as closely guarded as possible."

At PCB, those walls have vanished.

Employees pass around that daily scorecard, for example. "It's tough to get the daily statement of condition in St. James!" laments Connell. "The tellers want to go through it. And they don't just flip over and look at the bottom line. They look at loans and other items. I'll be looking for it and I'll hear, 'Well, I had it, but I gave it to Cheryl.'"

Employees also discuss the critical numbers for their departments. Loan-department staff scrutinize total loans for the week, the loan-to-deposit ratio, and loan delinquency, among other measures. Staff on the operations side watch noninterest income, core deposit growth, and a dozen other variables.

"All banks monitor those numbers," says Bill Marshall, vice president in charge of lending. "You have to. The difference lies in what you do with the information once you get it. Normally there's one, two, three people that get these reports, and the rest of the staff is waiting to be told how to react. We just don't feel you can do it that way."

## Business literacy.

Brent wanted her employee owners to think of themselves as owners, as businesspeople. She also wanted them to see themselves as bankers, people who truly understood what a bank does and how it makes money. Had you been an employee of PCB in the last few years, here's the array of courses and training programs you'd have had access to:

• Night classes in banking basics, taught by instructors from the American Institute of Banking. Brent arranged with other area banks to cosponsor these classes, but not many other people attended. "Out of fourteen people that took one class, thirteen were from PCB," says training coordinator Barbara Freeman.

• Several months' worth of in-house classes in the products and services offered by PCB. Each department prepared a presentation for others on what it did. To test employees' knowledge, the bank sponsored a mock "Jeopardy" game hosted by Brent, dressed for the occasion this time in fishnet stockings. Winners got two days off, with pay.

• A nine-week series of classes in problem-solving techniques, also held in the evening—but on company time. Classes in sales techniques, taught by a consultant and specially tailored to the needs of people in different jobs. Dale Carnegie courses, designed to boost people's self-confidence and communications skills. Ongoing training in "compliance," which means keeping up to date on banking regulations.

• Extensive cross-training among the bank's departments—arranged on an individual basis. "We're all pretty much cross-trained," says Patti Douglas, the customer-service rep. "We're encouraged to learn as many jobs as possible."

Besides the explicit training programs, Brent builds business-literacy education into regular meetings with employees. New employees are walked through the income statement. ("We start out with, How do we make money? And how do we spend it?") As a training exercise, customer-service reps spend one meeting a month hand-calculating items on the so-called monitoring report, a compilation of two dozen critical financial variables. "Even though we could pull them off the computer, we have to do it the old-math way," sighs Douglas, "so that we will know not only what they mean but how they were arrived at. You're going to remember how that figure was calculated if you calculate it out yourself."

### Empowerment.

The fact that employees see, discuss, and assume they have joint responsibility for the relevant numbers is one kind of empowerment. PCB employees help shape the bank's operations in two other ways as well.

One: Brent invites employees from every level of the bank to the annual planning and goal-setting meeting.

Again, banks just don't do this. "At the other bank I worked at," says one PCB veteran, "all the executives would gather up their portable computers and leave. Then they'd come back and say, 'This is our plan. This what you've got to do.'"

But what happens is that people, given the ability to understand and to participate, *do* participate.

At one meeting, remembers PCB vice president Bonita Prock, "we sat down and said, OK, if we want to pay this much into the ESOP and still increase the bottom line, what can we do? It was amazing, with everybody sitting there, how many of the loan people would say, 'We can do this. What can you do on the deposit side? Can we increase noninterest income by this?'

"People were throwing out ideas. It helps them to see—if we don't bring in deposits, the loan department can't lend it out, and if they don't lend it out we're not going to make the income we need to make. They begin to see how it all meshes together."

Two: The bank has about the most elaborate suggestion system you'll ever want to see.

Most companies' suggestion systems don't amount to much. Some are pure Mickey Mouse. Suggestions vanish into a vast managerial maw, and employees soon stop offering them. Others are downright counterproductive, because they pay rewards only to individuals. Employees thus develop ideas in secret rather than sharing them with their teams or departments.

In an open-book context, a suggestion system can be a little different. The suggestions are likely to be better, because people understand the business ramifications of an idea. And they don't need to be developed in secret. If they work, everyone will benefit.

Anyway, PCB's system is called the ESOP Challenge—and people take it *very* seriously.

Two employees researched and designed the customer survey that the bank uses to evaluate its service levels.

Another investigated whether the bank should offer its customers electronic tax filing with the IRS. (The recommendation: not yet.)

Patti Douglas compiled a twelve-page proposal for a marketing program aimed at senior citizens. Behind the proposal lay nearly two years' worth of research. Douglas had dug up demographic statistics. She had compiled information about what every other financial institution in the area offered seniors. She tracked PCB's experience with its existing elderly customers. She costed out her proposals and projected their impact on the bank's bottom line.

Now *that* is a suggestion. Only people who think of themselves as owners—and who know their ideas will get real consideration—put in that kind of effort.

Like the owners that they are, PCB's employees have a substantial *stake in the company's success.*

The bank pays an annual bonus pegged to the attainment of key targets such as return on assets. Employees can track the numbers that determine the bonus month to month. "I didn't want there to be any subjectivity in it," says Brent. "I wanted it to be measurable—so that you yourself, as an employee owner, can go into the computer at the end of any day and figure out what your bonus was going to be."

But the real stake in PCB's success is the fact that the employees hold equity—and that an equity stake in a successful bank translates into a sizable nest egg.

Once a year, the company holds a shareholders' dinner, complete with talks, skits, and songs. The high point of the evening? Distribution of the envelopes that tell each employee how much their shareholdings are worth and how much they'll be worth down the road if the bank continues to grow.

"I barely got to look at mine!" says Patti Douglas. "My husband ripped it out of my hand!"

The reason for all the excitement is that the numbers are large.

A share of PCB stock swelled more than fourfold from 1982 to 1992 and has kept growing since. The longer employees stay with the company, the more shares are allocated to their account. By the year 2003, Brent estimates, the *average* account in the ESOP should amount to some $200,000 in today's dollars. By comparison, a typical three-bedroom house in Rolla sells for perhaps $60,000.

# The Payoffs

Brent has a few key numbers that she watches besides PCB's market share and stock value.

One is asset productivity—net income per million dollars of assets. Between 1989 and 1993 that figure rose 32 percent.

A second is the bank's return on assets compared to its peer group in the national statistics. In one recent time frame, the ROA was 23 percent above peer—even though PCB, because of the ESOP, was spending 27 percent *more* on personnel costs.

What's behind this financial efficiency? The fact that so many eyes are watching the relevant numbers.

Tellers try to keep overtime to a minimum. "You don't want the company to suffer because everybody has five hours of overtime this week," explains Melanie Boyda, a teller. "So we watch the overtime real closely."

Tellers also watch overdue loans. "If a customer comes in to make a deposit," says Brent, "they can simply ask them, 'Are you aware your loan is showing past due on the computer?' Many times they just pay it."

Customer-service reps track closed accounts. "If I see a good customer who has closed his account, I'll get on the phone," says Patti Douglas. "'Mr. Brown, what is this? All your accounts are closed!' We don't want to lose a customer due to dissatisfaction and not know about it."

And people all over the bank don't hesitate to ask questions if they think something's amiss.

One employee asks Brent if anyone is watching unpaid overdraft charges on university students' checking accounts.

Another makes sure that travelers' checks and other reimbursables go out for payment today rather than tomorrow.

Everyone seems to take pride in keeping office-supply purchases to a minimum. "Our office-supplies number this year is $35,000," beams Brent. "Last year it was $45,000 and the year before that it was even higher. And our bank has grown about $10 million in the last two years."

But no business, not even a bank, is just a matter of numbers, and what keeps PCB dynamic is the investment its people make and keep on making in continuous improvement. The ESOP Challenge suggestions, the goal-setting meetings, the constant training and retraining all create an atmosphere in which people assume *it's part of their job* to make things a little bit better.

To my mind, the most dramatic example of this atmosphere wasn't the extraordinary effort put in by long-termers such as Douglas. It was the effort put in by Melanie Boyda, the teller.

Boyda's last job had been as a waitress. When she arrived at PCB she made a point of taking one of the AIB classes. "Just the basics of banking."

After a while, she and the other tellers on her line proposed an ESOP Challenge and won one of the monthly awards. They changed the way the teller drawers were organized to make their work more efficient.

Then she figured out that you really didn't need to go through the whole ESOP Challenge routine, you could just make improvements yourself. One day she and a few others cleaned up and reorganized the vault. Then they set up a system of initialing every item that was sent to another branch. That made it easier to track lost items.

She keeps an eye on the numbers. "Reading the reports that we get monthly—which is wonderful, that we get to see the financial statements—we can see what the numbers are. If deposits are down, say, maybe we need to cross-sell a little bit more.

"There are always ways to cross-sell on the teller line. Maybe you cross-sell an ATM card. Or if they want information, just explain to them all the different types of services that we have. There are all kinds of things you can do to pull people in."

What makes Boyda's performance interesting? Just this: Boyda was a music major in college. She hopes some day to land a job with a school district.

When she took the PCB job, she says, she "didn't know a debit from a credit." She figured being a bank teller was just a way of earning a few bucks—"a blow-off job."

American businesses are filled with employees like Boyda—people with other interests, people who are waiting for their "real" career, people who start work figuring that a job means no more than putting in the hours. Most companies let these employees go on thinking that.

PCB has taught Boyda to be a businessperson and a banker, to take responsibility for her economic life.

"Everything here has helped me understand—well, it has just been a whole new experience, a whole new career I can put on my résumé," says Boyda. "So many years with an employee-owned bank. If I ever leave, I think this would help me get a job anywhere.

"Everything I've learned here has been very valuable. I wouldn't give it up for a minute. I think that now, what I have, in a two-year period of time, is an accomplishment. A personal accomplishment that I take to heart and feel good about."

## CHAPTER 13

# One Company's Experience: A Telecommunications Giant

## Case Study 5: Sprint's Government Systems Division gets started in open-book management

## The Background

Chris Rooney, former head of the Government Systems Division of Sprint, was (and is) of the Tom Peters school of management. If it ain't broke, fix it anyway—because in today's economy it for sure will be broke tomorrow.

Government Systems, a three-hundred-employee unit of the big corporation, is like every division of every telecommunications company in the world these days: It must compete in a brutal and mercurial marketplace. The division was running well. But Rooney figured it could run better, and besides, he had no way of knowing what the future might hold. So he was open to new ideas—anything that would help the division respond more nimbly and more effectively to its competitive environment.

One new idea that crossed his path was the Great Game of Business, the open-book management system pioneered by Springfield ReManufacturing Corp.

Intrigued, Rooney talked with Jack Stack of SRC and met with John Schuster of Capital Connections, a Kansas City–based consulting firm that specializes in teaching the SRC principles.

Maybe, he figured, this understand-the-numbers stuff was exactly what Government Systems needed.

He knew that some of his division's employees didn't even know how to find Sprint's stock price, let alone how to use the detailed financial information he presented to them at the quarterly meetings. He suspected that too many people were just doing their jobs and didn't know how or even whether they contributed to the bottom line.

"I think he just saw a need out there," says Carl Hopkins, a product manager with the division's Kansas City office. "If people in the division knew more about how to run the business, knew more about the financials, we would all benefit from it. So he pretty much tasked Craig: 'Go out and implement this.'"

"Craig" is Craig Carter, the division's director of quality and compliance, who was then head of GSD's Leadership Forum, an office charged with helping the division's managers improve their skills and performance.

Working with Schuster and Jill Carpenter of Capital Connections, Carter established what the company calls a Challenge Team to carry out Rooney's instructions. "You task a team," explains Hopkins, "with solving a problem, implementing something. You give them guidelines and constraints and say, 'Here's what you need to do.'" Thanks to its experience with TQM, Government Systems was used to teams. Employees were skilled in problem solving and knew how to work in groups. Hopkins, an engineer by training, became the team's first leader. The other ten members came from a variety of positions—and from both of the division's offices, one in Kansas City and the other in Herndon, Virginia, near Washington.

Their mission: Introduce something like the Great Game of Business—open-book management—to their division.

*The process is less than two years old as this book goes to press—too early for definitive results when you're working on a scale this big. But the Sprint team planned its steps with extraordinary care and executed them with remarkable success. If you're trying to get the ball rolling in a big company, you could do worse—much worse—than emulate Sprint.*

# How It Works

Maybe it was Hopkins's engineering background. Maybe it's just the culture in a technologically sophisticated company such as Sprint. Whatever the reason, the team planned and executed its moves systematically.

## Step one: Collect data.

"The first major thing we did was to develop an employee survey," says Mary Hansen, manager of expense budgets and operations analysis, a Challenge Team member who eventually succeeded Hopkins as leader. "I think there were nineteen questions. Everything from 'Do you see financial reports?' to 'If you don't, could you do your job better if you did have them?' and 'Do you base your decisions on financial information?' It was just a variety of questions to see whether people get and use financial information in the division."

Team members passed out copies to everyone and got a response rate of more than 90 percent. They found pretty much what they (and Rooney) had expected.

"People were not getting information," says Hansen. "Or people who were getting information didn't understand it. One of the questions we asked was, essentially, 'Do you see how what you do ties in with the bottom line, with the financial results?' And a majority of the people in the division didn't know."

## Step two: Planning.

"We went off for a couple of days," remembers Rick Smith, a senior federal accounts manager in the Herndon office who also served on the team. "We said, in an ideal world, where would we want this division to go? What do we see as the future?

"It went beyond the financials. We asked ourselves, can this be used to change the culture and make the division a better place to work?" The team brainstormed. They put ideas up on the walls. They decided that their next step had to be "training people to implement this concept."

## Step three: Training.

Working with the consultants, the Challenge Team developed a curriculum. They planned a three-day training session for managers and a one-day session for line employees.

The sessions included basic business literacy. "We started out with just trying to get people comfortable with the fact that we use numbers every day of our lives," says Smith. "People have a tendency to clam up when they hear 'finance,' because they're just turned off by it.

"But people do use numbers that are important to them. So we went around and asked people to write down what was a critical number for them. 'Four' might mean someone had four children. 'Five' might mean five years to retirement. They began to see, yes, I do use those numbers and I do make plans based on them. We said, that's all we're trying to do, to use the numbers that are wrapped up in a P&L and a balance sheet to make good decisions about getting business for GSD.

"From that we went into the mechanics and structures of the various reports. We used simple examples: 'Here's a little construction company building a deck. How much are their nails? How much is their wood? Do they make a profit or a loss?' And from there you just gradually move into the actual P&L and balance sheet of the division."

The session also included discussion on relating the information to the work of the division.

"We had people talk about critical numbers in their departments. That did two things: It helped generate ideas for what we should use as critical numbers [in the implementation stage]; and it helped educate people. For example, I may not know that you're under a gun, under some measurement that makes you act in a certain way. Just being aware of that will make me more sensitive to what you're doing.

"We spent some time saying, 'Here are the ratios that are important to our division.' Revenue per person, for instance, is one way of looking at how well the organization is doing. Then the next obvious step is, how has it changed over time? And how do you use the number to help you manage your part of the business?"

Smith and others believe that four "tricks" helped make the training successful:

• Challenge Team members did the training themselves rather than relying on the company's training department. "We have a highly qualified training department. They were involved as participants. But we wanted the people who were doing the actual development of the program to do the training, the people who have committed the time and effort to make this work."

• The team prepared a manual—a workbook—that employees could take away with them. "It included financial terms. It included our strategic plans. It had the current work chart. It discussed the different budgetary cycles and the programs that go on in our company. That was one way of ensuring that people take away the information rather than just getting it in the class."

• The training session included videotapes of top executives supporting the program. "I think this was very effective. They said, 'Here's our perspective. Here's what we want to get out of the program. And it's something we're going to stay with over the long run.' We want to do everything we can to make sure it isn't just a hit for one year and then fades quietly into the background."

• And the session included practicing "huddles," which would be central to the next step—

## Step four: Implementation.

At the heart of Sprint's system are SRC-style huddles, which the division holds monthly. The huddles are simply meetings with a specific agenda: to go over the financials line by line. Huddle participants compare current performance to budget. They gather opinions on the upcoming months, thereby creating a rolling forecast. They scrutinize variances for problems—or for unforeseen opportunities.

What makes the huddles different from any well-run managerial meeting is that, at some point, they involve everybody. Rick Smith: "Something like this was already being used at the management level. We said, let's push it down. That was part of the message that we wanted everyone to see, that we're all in this together." Departments meet in "prehuddles" to assemble the numbers for which they are responsible. They meet in "posthuddles" to go over and discuss the division's performance and forecasts.

As with any new system, Sprint's huddles took a while to get going. The team got support from top executives such as Don Teague, who had succeeded Chris Rooney as head of GSD. Teague encouraged departments to hold their prehuddles and posthuddles. That helped.

So did the built-in dynamic. In the huddle system, specific individuals "own" line items, which means they are publicly accountable for knowing and understanding those numbers. Carl Hopkins says, "When Jim Steffens, who leads the main huddle, says, 'Rob, why is this variance so high?', you just don't want to say, 'Gee, I don't know' too many times. 'Gee, I don't know' isn't too good an answer."

In short: If the meetings are held—and if they're taken seriously by those at the top of the organization—the participants will make it a point to know the numbers.

Meanwhile, team members continue with financial education and information dissemination. They set up a board listing Sprint's daily stock price in the lobby of both main offices. They compile a "GSD scorecard" with key operational numbers on it (number of proposals going out to prospective customers, win/loss ratio on proposals submitted, etc.). They prepare newsletters that explain significant income-statement or balance-sheet figures. ("People are still real confused about accruals," laments Mary Hansen.) They organize brown-bag lunches to discuss key issues.

Sprint's annual bonus gives Government Systems' employees a *stake in the division's success*. It's tied to certain performance targets, and it was in place before the open-book system was implemented. Today, there's a new attitude toward it.

"In the past," says Hansen with a laugh, "there was this check that showed up in March. It was great! 'I have this check; I don't really know why I got it, but it's here.'

"This year I think, a heck of a lot more people understand why they got it and how they affected that performance."

# The Payoffs

The initial reaction to open-book management among GSD's employees: some enthusiasm, mixed with a healthy degree of skepticism. "Some people were ready to go, to leap in," says Carl Hopkins. "Others said, 'This is our flavor of the month; if I don't do anything it will pass me by.'" But over time, both team members and managers began to notice a difference in the way people in the division thought about their jobs.

Sometimes it was merely a matter of attitude. "People see now if they go out and get everybody in their department a pager," says Hansen, "that's not just coming out of some bank account they don't have to worry about. They're looking at reports, and maybe they're seeing an increase [in a given item], and they're starting to base decisions on what the financial impact is going to be.

"A customer-service representative might say, 'I have no influence on the bottom line, I just answer calls.' But the response is, 'You are an expense. What are those customers calling you about?' Maybe they say, 'My service needs to be turned off.'

"Well, if we were supposed to turn off someone's service and didn't, then that's an extra cost we're incurring. So if you can get it off quickly and find out what happened so it doesn't happen again, that's the impact you can have."

There was evidence, too, of a new approach to *managing* the division's costs and revenues—in effect, seeing the division as a business rather than as a bureaucratic appendage of a giant corporation.

CARL HOPKINS: "We're three hundred people of a large company. Finance tells us what our margin has to be. And we have allocated costs that come to our division. As a result, our access group can say, 'Sorry, we have to give you more costs,' and headquarters can say, 'You need to make more margin,' and neither one of these is very much in our control. It isn't arbitrary, but to us it *feels* arbitrary.

"Now, we're understanding and managing the allocations better. We have people watching what's happening. If the allocations start growing, we think of it as a supplier increasing its prices. We ask, 'Why did you increase your price to us?'"

MARY HANSEN: "People are also understanding what's in those allocations. They know if they go to corporate marketing and ask for a flyer to be done or a piece of advertising or whatever, it doesn't just come out of some giant pocketbook over there. They see that cross-charge now in the allocation, and they know that they had some control there."

CARL HOPKINS: "We're influencing things that had been perceived as unable to be influenced. For example, there was a group that decided to manage how our corporate Information Services Group charges our division back. That was something people said couldn't be done. They'd give you this amount and you'd take it and say thank you that it wasn't any bigger.

"But you use facts and you document your argument and you find out how they're allocating you—'What algorithm are you using?' Maybe you say, 'Oh, boy, that doesn't work for us, and here's why.' We're driving costs out of the division—and not just out of the division, out of the business as a whole. Because if I just shove it to another division that doesn't help my stockholders.

"Take our training budget, which again is allocated from corporate. Mary and I put together a two-page summary of why we shouldn't have this much. . . . Since we now understand how they do it, we can say, well, we have this many people, we need only this much training, here's why. And usually we want less."

Sprint doesn't yet have numbers that demonstrate the effect of open-book management on the bottom line. Those numbers are hard to come by in an industry that is as competitive—and changes so rapidly—as GSD's. Still, that kind of thinking may be just what the number three long-distance company needs over the long haul.

*      *      *

I asked Rick Smith, the federal accounts manager in Herndon, if he wanted to add anything—in particular, if he had anything he'd say to other big-company managers considering open-book management. He had this to say: "I'd say start it. Do it. Because the fundamental way businesses have been set up in the past is changing.

"We talked with a lot of people during the training, and we all felt we were set up in kind of a production line. Go into school in kindergarten, come out in twelve years, and boom, you're an educated person. Put me in the workforce until I'm dead and buried.

"But that doesn't cut it anymore. People need to be more flexible, more adaptive. And this gives you a framework to do that. Because people take ownership. They'll understand what's going on in the business. They can make better decisions for the company.

"It takes time. You really need to start now, because you've got to bring it into the culture. You've got to create those linkages.

"Don't be afraid to do it!"

## CHAPTER 14

# Objections, Costs, Challenges
## Questions and answers about open-book management

Yes, but . . . (I hear you say). Or maybe, *Wait a minute!*

I don't blame you. Open-book management is a new idea. It never hurts to be skeptical of new ideas.

Besides, what I'm proposing in this book is a big change. Change rarely comes easily. It always involves costs and difficulties. Only a fool would leap in without asking how steep those costs are and how serious the difficulties might be.

So this chapter is nothing but questions and answers—not about techniques, which have been pretty well covered elsewhere, but about whether open-book management is right for *your* company.

The questions are ones I've heard over and over. They're the questions the pioneers of open-book management asked themselves when they started out. They're the questions you can hear today at a conference or seminar on the subject.

The answers come from experience.

The nice thing about the open-book approach, after all, is that it isn't fresh off the drawing board. Open-book companies have run into problems. They have learned which problems are avoidable and which aren't. They have learned how long it can take to change a whole culture. They have learned what's essential to the very idea of open-book management and what can be tailored to fit the situation.

So let's start with the most basic objection:

*All this focus on the bottom line—isn't that just what's wrong with American business?*

Strange but true: "Profit" these days is a dirty—or at least a not completely wholesome—word.

It isn't just the antibusiness types who are antiprofit. The skeptics include well-respected business leaders and thinkers.

One school of thought holds that U.S. companies focus too much on quarterly earnings and not enough on the long-term health of the business—as measured by market share, say, or number of new products. It's Wall Street's fault, say these thinkers; investors and fund managers are always looking at the short term, which forces corporate executives to do so, too. Japanese companies, by contrast, are said to be willing to sacrifice short-term profits for long-term gain.

You don't need to take sides in this debate to acknowledge an obvious truth, which is that any company *can* pay too much attention to short-term earnings at the expense of long-term prosperity.

In an open-book situation, the trick is to devise incentives that build in long-term as well as short-term concerns.

It should come as no surprise: You get what you pay for. If a bonus system is pegged only to quarterly earnings, employees will howl if the CEO then decides on a course of aggressive growth at the expense of profits.

But if employees own equity—or if they have a bonus pegged to some measure of share value ("phantom stock," for example)—they'll have as much interest as any long-term owner in building up the company.

There's another sense, too, in which profit has become a dirty word.

When companies write out mission statements, when CEOs give those speeches designed to fire up the troops, they don't usually say, "We want to make as much money as possible." They use highfalutin phrases like *serving the customer, delivering top-quality goods, meeting people's needs.* They pooh-pooh the importance of mere money. Focus on the noble goals, they seem to be saying, and profits will flow.

But profits don't always flow. And don't be misled, anyway. Whatever they may say in the mission statements or the inspirational speeches, believe me: Those CEOs are keeping a hawk's eye on the bottom line.

There's really no contradiction here. Ultimately, delivering goods and services that people need or want *is* a business's social purpose, not to mention the fact that it provides jobs along the way. But businesses can do all that good stuff if and only if they make money.

And if they make a healthy return, they can plan on continuing to provide goods and services in the future. They can offer job security, and opportunities for advancement, and the prospect of a nice nest egg for retirement.

So that's the reason for focusing on the financials. In ordinary circumstances, *profit is no more than the market's way of saying that you're doing things right.* As a company, you're providing something that customers want and are willing to pay for. You're doing your job at least as well as the competition. Sure, anyone can think of situations in which making a lot of money and meeting people's needs are contradictory rather than complementary—think of price gougers after a hurricane. But the exceptions don't disprove the rule.

Samuel Smith, president of Smith & Co. Engineers, once asked his employees what they wanted to see the firm accomplish. Like good engineers they came up with answers such as, "Build good bridges." Smith nodded assent. If an engineering firm doesn't build good bridges it won't be in business long. But then he asked them how many would show up for work if the company couldn't pay them. Nobody raised a hand.

The moral, said Smith: Our objective is first to make money. That's what makes it possible for us to do everything else.

*The open-book system seems to get everyone thinking about costs. But my business is different. Costs aren't really the issue; what matters most is _____ .*

Fill in the blank.

An ad agency or movie studio might say "creativity." A software company might reply, "staying on the cutting edge." A newspaper would say "selling advertising."

Companies talk this way, of course, when they're flying high. When they hit the skids—or when they face a new competitive environment—they suddenly remember that they're businesses after all. Today, even utilities are paying attention to costs.

But the point of open-book management, at any rate, is to get people thinking like businesspeople, not like bean counters. Labor efficiency or the cost of office supplies really isn't as important in some businesses as in others. But you can bet that the CEOs of the ad agencies and the software companies and all the rest know *some* critical numbers as well as they know their ATM codes. Maybe it's the acceptance rate for proposals, or the accuracy of product-development schedules. Maybe it's the "burn rate" for start-up capital, or revenue per inch of advertising.

And make no mistake: The best companies in any industry *always* watch those key numbers, even if the numbers alone don't guarantee success.

Pay a visit, for example, to the stylish San Francisco offices of Macromedia, Inc., a developer of software tools for multimedia programming. Ask Bud Colligan, the president, what will determine his company's success or failure. Instantly Colligan responds, "We've got to stay on the cutting edge of technology. People will use our tools so long as they're the best tools."

Walk around the place, though, and you see nothing but charts, graphs, and tables, all of them tracking one or another aspect of Macromedia's performance as a business. Revenue by product line. Total revenue versus plan. Accuracy of product-delivery dates. Departmental expenses. Average wait time for callers to the service department.

Staying on the technological leading edge, explains Colligan, does no good if Macromedia can't deliver products effectively, can't control its costs, doesn't make good business decisions. "I want people able to make decisions in this company as if they were the general manager. And the only way they can be a general manager is if they understand what goes on in all the departments."

*I work in a nonprofit. Any way of applying open-book management there?*

I heard a hospital administrator speak at a conference on open-book management, and for a while all he could do was shake his head. Call him Ted.

Ted had listened to manufacturers talk about tracking the cost of goods sold. He had heard service companies describe how they got employees focused on saving money. He had heard everybody talking about satisfying the customer. When he rose to speak, his voice was plaintive. "Our situation is a little different," he said.

The hospital, Ted explained, had multiple customers to satisfy. Patients. Patients' families. Doctors. Insurance companies. No mere mortal could satisfy them all at once.

Most of the hospital's resources were allocated according to the decisions of physicians. This patient needed a bed. That one needed a chest X ray. But the doctors weren't even hospital employees. They had little interest in minimizing expenditures.

As for costs, well, the hospital really didn't know its costs. Ted had just ordered cost-accounting software. But he wasn't looking forward to the debates about how to allocate indirect expenses among different departments and units.

A hospital is the clearest example of what you might call double-bottom-line organizations. Schools and universities fit into the category. So do most other nonprofits. As organizations, they have to make sure their revenues exceed their expenses. But their employees generally don't think of themselves as in the business of making money, and a single-minded focus on the financial bottom line is usually inappropriate. Like Ted's hospital, they typically don't know (or can't accurately measure) the cost of any given activity. Traditionally, they spend whatever they can get—and then pressure the fund-raisers to bring in more.

Maybe someone will eventually write the definitive book about applying open-book management in this context. Meanwhile, here's what pioneers like Ted have figured out:

• Any nonprofit has to devote primary attention to its mission—good health care, good education, whatever.

• All nonprofits are accountable to those who pay the bills, whether it's taxpayers, donors, members, or insurance companies. They have a moral and practical obligation to deliver the most bang for the buck.

So that's where open-book management comes in. If people in a hospital or any other institution understand and take responsibility for matters such as costs, revenues, and budgets, they'll run a better business. Running a better business won't necessarily put more money in their pockets—that's often not the point—but it will allow them to do what they do more efficiently, which is really a goal of all businesses.

What can be done? Costs *can* be tracked and allocated, tough though the process may be. Budgets can be decided upon collectively, then posted and tracked. Sometimes modest financial incentives can be paid or other rewards provided (extra vacation, etc.). The trick is to figure out what the organization's key numbers are—the numbers that, if you meet them, indicate that you're doing your job well. Then you can get everybody involved in hitting those targets.

The sad truth is that people who work in nonprofits often assume that, because they're on the side of the angels, they don't need to dirty their hands with financial matters. "You're trying to run this place as if it were a business!" one outraged nurse told Ted.

It might be nice if Ted didn't have to. But he does. These days, nearly every nonprofit faces stiffer competition, tighter budgets, a changing environment. Those who learn to function as businesses while they're pursuing their mission are likely to survive. Those who don't, won't. And those who are most careful about their resources will provide the best service.

*We have TQM; we have work teams; we've reengineered. Isn't that enough?*

Now it's my turn to holler, Wait a minute! If you ran a public company, would you say that to your shareholders?

Not likely. You'd point to some difference all these efforts made—to the stock price, or to earnings, or to some important operational indicator such as gross margins.

Maybe you *can* point to such accomplishments. TQM and other management reforms can accomplish great things in the right circumstances. But over time they inevitably run into two obstacles.

One is that they can become ends in themselves.

Remember the Wallace Co., which won the Malcolm Baldrige Quality Award and then went broke? Or Varian Associates, which plunged into TQM and found itself staring at red ink? You see the same thing on a smaller scale in a lot of TQM companies. "Suppose I have five people working on this problem and solving it is going to save me $20?" says one TQM skeptic. "We're supposed to get better—continuous improvement and all that. But there's no bottom-line accountability." If a management approach doesn't produce results, of course, it's amazing how quickly CEOs lose interest in it.

The other obstacle is even more basic. As Mark Miller of Chick fil-A puts it, *TQM and teams and reengineering may teach people the "how-to." They don't instill the "want-to."*

Think about it: Why should anyone in the rank and file bother doing everything that these new management philosophies ask for? They're imposed from the top. The business logic behind them is rarely explained.

To be sure, employees do typically go along with new programs. Think back to the famous Hawthorne experiments in the 1920s. Researchers turned the factory lighting up and watched productivity rise. Then they turned the lighting down—and productivity rose again. Any change can make a difference for a while. But if the change is only superficial, the enthusiasm wears off and things revert to where they were before.

Open-book management isn't like that. It will fail if a company starts it and then forgets about it (see below). But the logic of open-book management is the logic of business itself. Once people come to understand that they're in business to make money—and that it's the financials that indicate how well they're doing—they need no motivation other than a stake in success.

"Owners, real owners, don't have to be told what to do," writes Jack Stack. "They can figure it out for themselves."

*We pay good wages and good benefits. We have a generous profit-sharing plan and a 401(k). Our employees seem happy. Why do we need open-book management?*

Open-book management isn't about generosity, though the people who have pioneered it often have generous impulses. It isn't about creating a good work environment, though it does that, too. And it isn't just another benefit.

Open-book management is a business strategy, a way of organizing a company to survive in a mercurial new economy. If your company can get along with people who think of themselves as well-paid hired hands, good luck. I hope your happy situation lasts.

*To me, open-book management sounds like all the other tools that are supposed to motivate people to act for the good of the company. You want salespeople to meet quota, you offer them a trip. You want front-line workers to come up with ideas, you pay for suggestions.*

Motivation! It's the manager's most difficult and least appreciated job. Ever since physical coercion went out of style, supervisors and bosses have been faced with the task of getting employees to *want* to do what's best for the company. Hence the vast array of incentives that permeate business organizations. Sales awards. Employee-of-the-month plaques. Recognition awards. Spot bonuses and "freebies." Companies jump through hoops to get employees to do what they're supposed to.

Some of the games and incentives described in this book aren't so different—on the surface.

Get a millimeter below the surface, however, and they're as different as can be.

Most employee incentives are in what I call the M&M category. Here—you did the right thing, have these M&Ms. Don't expect to understand what's going on here; don't expect a piece of the action. Just do as we want you to, and you'll get these M&Ms.

Open-book management, by contrast, makes people partners in an enterprise. They understand the financials. They share in the risk if the company fails and in the rewards if it succeeds. They understand how the company makes money, so they understand *why* certain kinds of behavior are important.

Like any company, open-book companies sometimes hold contests, give awards, single out individuals for exceptional performance. But all those games and incentives supplement the role of partner rather than replacing it. They add a little spice to the day. They help people educate themselves about what's really important in the business. They don't have to carry the whole motivational ball; people *already* know why they're working.

Motivation will always be a problem in a business, just as it is in every other social organization. No one wants to do everything that needs doing every minute of every day. But open-book management gives people a common language for discussing motivation and a common interest in boosting it. People in an open-book company can thus act like human beings rather than like laboratory pigeons scratching for more M&Ms.

*Truly now: Isn't this just another fad—another consultant-spawned, top-down, prepackaged solution to business problems?*

Funny thing about open-book management. Until recently, there were only a couple of consultants who even knew it existed.

Open-book management has been developed by practitioners. By businesspeople. And it's about as un-prepackaged as you can get. There are basic principles, but there are no set rules for implementation. And though the principles have to be introduced from the top of an organization, the practice better involve people at other levels from day one.

Few people know this as well as Joe Jenkins, one of the three brothers who own Jenkins Diesel Power, a truck dealership in Springfield, Missouri.

Jenkins got fired up about open-book management after visiting nearby Springfield ReManufacturing Corp. and hearing Jack Stack speak. He came back and proposed that the company pay no more annual raises. Instead, people would get bonuses for profit improvements. They'd also get an eventual share of the company through an ESOP.

The reaction? "Stone-cold silence," says Jenkins. Then turmoil. "I had a near riot on my hands. It took six months for the company to get back to normal." *Normal,* he adds, meant "people walking around on the floor with about a minus-five reading on their give-a-damn meter."

Then Jenkins started over.

He first gave profit-and-loss statements to his three department heads—the company had never done that before—and taught them about their departments' contribution to profitability.

After a few months, he offered all three a choice: Forgo your raise, and instead share in net profit. Two of the three took him up on it. They made more money that year than they ever had before.

Then he began teaching line employees about the business. He started with simple introductory material, then moved on to explain the company's financials.

He also moved toward empowering people.

In the parts department, for example, he asked each of the ten employees to come up with a list of fifteen suggestions for improvement in return for $50 cash. Next he asked them to rank the suggestions. Together, they boiled the list down to the most important ones. "They taught me how to improve the parts department."

Then, with people beginning to get excited, he posted a target number—how much the department had to bring in to cover its expenses. There would be no raises. But 25 percent of the amount over the target would be divided up among the department's employees.

The next year, parts had a 65 percent profit increase. Employees averaged about a dollar an hour *more* than what they would have made with a raise.

No consultants. Trial and error. From the ground up. That's how open-book management has evolved. With all due respect to consultants, maybe that's why it works so well.

*I run a division of a giant corporation. There's really no relationship between what people in my shop do and the corporate balance sheet.*

Every time I hear this statement I think of a woman—call her Louise—who is vice president and general manager for one of the regional Bell telephone companies. She's in charge of operations for an entire state. She supervises two thousand of the giant company's sixty thousand employees, and contributes about 6 percent of its revenues.

Until recently, Louise's employer was a classic corporate bureaucracy. State operating divisions such as hers didn't even become business units until 1993. When she took over the division, she wanted to move in the direction of open-book management. But she knew she couldn't convert the whole enterprise overnight. It would be hard enough to persuade a union telephone technician that what he or she did tomorrow could somehow affect the corporation's balance sheet.

So Louise did some little things.

She began holding monthly meetings of managers. At those meetings, she would pass out the division's financial reports—"exactly the same reports that I'm accountable to my superiors for." It was the first time most managers had ever seen any such reports.

She asked the managers to go back to their units and figure out which lines of the financial reports their employees had an impact on, then explain that to their people.

She made sure budgets and performance reports for each unit were circulated to every other unit—and that everyone understood how one impacted the other. "If engineering is late with a design for a new system, then installation has to work overtime." No one in either department had any way of knowing or tracking that connection before.

She got her superiors to agree that any performance-related bonus the corporation might give would be tied partly to her unit's numbers, not just to the overall performance of the company.

What's next? Tune in tomorrow—at this writing, Louise has been at it for only a short while. But there are two points to be made here.

One, what's important about open-book management is the mind-set it engenders. Louise is getting her employees to think like businesspeople rather than like hired hands. The techniques aren't the same as they might be at a smaller company. So what?

Two, that mind-set *can* make a difference even to giant corporations. Granted, no one can know whether any of the Baby Bells will be prospering or struggling ten years hence. It will depend on technology and regulations and a dozen other variables.

But it will also depend on how line employees go about their jobs every day. "Competition is coming to local telephone service," says Louise. "If we don't get employees to think like owners we'll lose the business." Of many small victories are large victories made.

One small victory: In the first several months of 1994 the weather in Louise's state was bad. The company's overtime, in the past, would have soared. This year, with people all over the company watching the numbers, it was running 5 percent under budget.

*My company is public. Won't sharing financial information get us in trouble with the Securities and Exchange Commission?*

If you're in a publicly traded company, by all means consult a knowledgeable lawyer about the SEC's rules and regulations.

But do not—repeat, do not—let the lawyer dissuade you from getting into open-book management if you think it will help the business.

You can still share operational numbers and plant-level or departmental budgets and performance figures.

You can still share quarterly financials as soon as they are released to the public.

You can teach employees to understand business. You can empower them to take responsibility for the numbers that they can affect.

Best of all, you can use the public markets to reward employees, as Microsoft, Wal-Mart, and a thousand other companies have done. Pay them partly in stock. Hope that investors bid that stock up. It's the best formula in the world for generating personal wealth. And there's nothing like an equity stake in a public company to help employees think and act like businesspeople.

Patrick Kelly started Physician Sales and Service in 1983. In 1994, with sales in the $200 million range, PSS went public at $11 a share. That event alone created eleven millionaires, three of whom had started with the company as truck drivers. When the stock rose to $18 later in the year, five more people had enough stock to make them millionaires.

Kelly disseminates information throughout his company, every day and every month. He does things like conduct on-the-spot quizzes relating to the P&L, with $50 rewards for people who get the answers right. He has created several different methods through which employees can buy PSS's stock. His personal goal: to create a hundred millionaires.

You think there are many people who view working at PSS as "just a job"?

*What's the most likely source of trouble in the process itself—and how do I avoid it?*

The biggest problem? Inertia.

You start with good intentions. Then the press of business closes in. The meetings don't get held. The financials don't get distributed. Employees get a little training, but it peters out.

Oh, yes—you promise to pay a bonus. Then you decide the company can't really afford it.

It doesn't take long, in other words, for the whole thing to die. As with any management program that crashes and burns, you will have succeeded only in raising the cynicism level at your company.

How to avoid it? Open-book management needs a champion. Someone who watches over it and takes responsibility for making it happen.

Maybe the champion is the boss. Maybe it's a vice president, or the director of quality, or the chief financial officer. Maybe it's a team of employees, a cross-section who understand the concept and are ready to run with it.

*Someone* has to learn the ropes, figure out how to distribute the information, organize the business training, make sure the meetings happen. Someone has to come up with, and cost out, a bonus plan.

Sprint relies on its Challenge Team. Pace Industries has a "Great Game of Business Committee." At The Body Shop, training manager Karen Delahunty has taken the lead, along with Chief Financial Officer Paul Crawley and financial analyst Mia Roth. Your shop needs someone—or a group of someones—too.

*The big picture, please: If I set out to change my company along these lines, what am I letting myself in for?*

Naturally it depends on your company's situation. But here's what people who have plunged in have found:

• You can get started quickly (see chapter 8). And you can realize results quickly. But ultimately what you're trying to do is change people's instinctive ways of thinking and behaving at work. You're trying to create a new culture.

This is a long process, particularly in a big corporation. Jack Callahan of Allstate's Business Insurance group estimates it takes four years to change a company's culture. Tom Corbo of Manco agrees. Small, entrepreneurial companies may do it faster—but not a whole lot.

• One thing that takes time is repetition. People learn from hearing something and doing something over and over again.

So the first time you teach people how to read an income statement or a balance sheet it won't sink in. For the first year, the meetings to review the financials may go slowly. From the average employee's point of view, even the first bonus may seem to materialize out of thin air. Never mind: Keep it up. People have been taught for years—decades—that they can't understand financial matters. They've learned that good employees do no more than what they're told. They're likely to view any new scheme with skepticism, even cynicism. It takes a while to unlearn these lessons. Repeat, repeat, repeat.

• Not everybody will go along with the process.

Steve Wilson of Mid-States Technical lost half his managers when he instituted his open-book system. Bob Frey of Cin-Made lost some, too. They figured the boss was nuts, and they didn't want any part of this new approach to business. Employees, too, may quit. Some people prefer a job in which they don't have to think. Some will fear the new responsibilities and obligations.

Any manager who institutes an open-book system will have plenty of critics. "Change is long, hard work," says Harvard's Rosabeth Moss Kanter, "and everything looks like failure in the middle. That's when the critics surface."

Is it worth it? You may have to take a lesson here from America's manufacturers.

Back in the late 1970s and early 1980s, U.S. manufacturers found themselves up against serious overseas competitors for the first time. Waves of imported goods were washing up on our shores.

The Japanese in particular seemed to best American companies on almost every front. Quality. Price. Rate of innovation. U.S. manufacturers began to discover what was behind the Japanese success—and to see how difficult it would be to catch up. They'd have to learn wholly new quality systems. They'd have to manage inventories differently. They would need to ask more of their frontline employees. Engineering would have to work with manufacturing, manufacturing would have to work with marketing. The factory itself would have to be redesigned, and new technology utilized to the fullest.

It was a monumental task. It meant rebuilding a sizable portion of the U.S. economy from the ground up. It meant training millions of people to work in new ways.

But a lot of American manufacturers did it. Those that did can now compete with any company in the world.

Those who didn't—well, they're no longer with us.

Was it worth it?

In the end, these manufacturers had no real choice. Do you?

# CHAPTER 15

# A Company of Businesspeople

*If you do what you've always done, you're gonna
get what you always got.*

—YOGI BERRA

Sometimes I think you could take all the principles and precepts and practices of open-book management and boil them down into One Big Axiom, which is this: Treat people like adults.

Even after a decade of teams and empowerment and participatory management, most American companies don't.

They treat employees like children. They order them around, punish them for transgressions, spell out in minute detail exactly what will be required of them and when. They assume that employees aren't competent to make decisions, so they don't provide them with the information or training they'd need to make smart ones.

As I write this, for example, the hot issue in a lot of workplaces is forced overtime. Companies don't want to add more people to the payroll, so they're demanding that employees work longer hours every week. Workers are grumbling and even striking because the overtime is so onerous. That gets them into trouble. At General Motors, reports *The Wall Street Journal,* refusing overtime is grounds for being "written up." Seven such write-ups and you're fired. At Delta Air Lines, clerks who refuse overtime get "notes in their permanent personnel files"—unless they bring in an excuse from their doctor.

At Allegheny Ludlum Corp., a steelworker asked to be excused from overtime for one day because he was getting married. The boss finally went along—but only after he telephoned the prospective bride to make sure the guy wasn't lying.

The issue here isn't how much overtime companies need, it's the way overtime requirements get decided and communicated. Management makes the decision and issues the orders. Employees do as they're told. If they don't, they get exactly the kind of reprimand they could once expect in school. Notes in a file. A trip to the boss's office. We're past the time—in most workplaces, anyway—when frontline workers have to ask permission to go to the bathroom. But the mentality lives on. If you're absent, bring an excuse. If you're late, we'll dock your pay.

Know what? It doesn't need to be this way.

Where overtime is concerned, for example, is it really so difficult to say, hey, folks, we've got a problem here? Is it so hard to involve employees in scheduling workplace operations?

And if people had some business training and a stake in the company's success, couldn't they be trusted to make their own judgments as to whether extra overtime or hiring more employees made the most economic sense?

I'm reminded of an episode at Sandstrom Products, the specialty-coatings company that developed a homegrown form of open-book management. Sandstrom not long ago got a big new contract from a customer— more, so it seemed, than it could possibly produce.

Plant employees came to Jim Sandstrom, the owner. We need half a million dollars' worth of new equipment if we're going to fulfill this contract, they said.

Gee, said Sandstrom, I don't have half a million dollars.

Furthermore, he added, I don't think we want to borrow it, because we don't know if this increase in business is permanent or temporary. He walked the employees through the financial analysis. He asked them if they had any other ideas what to do.

The workers got together and came up with the idea of dividing up into three shifts rather than two, thereby maximizing production from the company's existing equipment. They negotiated who would work which shifts. They agreed there would be no shift differential and that they didn't need any extra people. They put the plan into effect immediately.

Sandstrom thought he was used to the effects of open-book management, but even he was amazed. "If management had come down and said, there's only one answer, we're gonna work three shifts, there'd have been pandemonium. Everybody would have been screaming, I'm not working another shift! I want differential pay!

"As it was, we completed the entire contract in thirteen weeks. Productivity in that quarter was up 86 percent." The whole thing went smoothly, and Sandstrom racked up record profits.

Thanks to the company's gain-sharing plan, workers each took home roughly $700 a month during this period, over and above what they made in regular wages. "The guys paid themselves a nice bonus," says one of Sandstrom's managers with a smile. "If they'd bought the equipment, there wouldn't have been a penny."

Any workplace needs rules, policies, and procedures. Any workplace needs to establish its business priorities and deploy its resources and solve its problems. General Motors may need all that overtime. Sandstrom certainly did. A company isn't a democracy, so the ultimate responsibility for all those decisions lies with its executives.

But too many companies are hung up on that "ultimate." Their executives and managers start issuing orders and directives that workers are expected to follow without question. That sets off a vicious cycle. Employees—who can see they're being treated like children—grow cynical and resentful. If they're unionized, maybe they file a grievance, or go out on strike. If they aren't, maybe they decide the game is to outsmart management and get away with as much as possible. Managers then decide they can't trust anyone. That leads to inanities like requiring a doctor's note—or calling someone's fiancée to find out if he's really getting married.

Treating people like adults, by contrast, means trusting them to take part in the decisions that affect them. Start from that notion and all the principles of open-book management follow. People *can't* make good decisions unless they have information, and the ability to understand it. They *won't* make decisions in the best interests of the business unless they have a stake in the company's success, as Sandstrom's employees did.

Funny thing: When treated like adults, people act like adults.

Goethe, the poet, said, "Treat a man as he is and he will remain as he is. Treat a man as he can and should be and he will become as he can and should be."

Barry Posner, a professor at Santa Clara University, made a similar point in a speech not long ago.

We've always assumed, said Posner, that power corrupts, and absolute power corrupts absolutely.

But in a workplace, it's powerlessness that corrupts—and absolute powerlessness that corrupts absolutely. "When people don't *feel* powerful or responsible they don't *act* powerfully or responsibly."

Now, there's a little problem here, which is that you can't very well put "a company of adults" up on the wall next to your mission statement, at least not without generating a few quizzical stares (or raised eyebrows). So if you want a short phrase for the kind of company open-book management seeks to create, a phrase appropriate for the lobby wall or the annual report, I'd propose this: *a company of businesspeople.*

What we have, of course, are companies of employees. I don't mean just hourly workers. I mean everyone, whatever their job, who assumes that it's somebody else's concern whether their company succeeds in the marketplace.

Employees, like kids, do as they're told. Businesspeople, like adults, figure out what needs to be done and do that.

Employees, like kids, don't bear full responsibility for their actions. Businesspeople do. They know they're accountable to the marketplace, and to each other.

Employees, like kids, aren't expected to see or understand the big picture. Businesspeople know they have to.

It's really pretty amazing when you stop to think about it. We live in a democracy. We're free, independent, responsible citizens. We raise families, manage our finances, and elect the people who govern us. We're *grown-ups.*

And yet, when it comes to the workplace, most of us assume that our obligation is to look for a job, hope that some company "gives" us one, and then do whatever the boss tells us to. Our obligation is to be a good employee. That's the lesson we have learned from the first hundred years of industrial capitalism, and we have learned it well.

Now, maybe for the second hundred years, we have to learn a new lesson. We have to learn how organizations survive and prosper—how they make money—and how we as individuals contribute to that.

We have to become entrepreneurially minded—not so we can all start businesses, but so that we can maximize our chances of success in the businesses we work for.

Open-book management is a training ground for this approach to life. It teaches us how the system works. It teaches us how we can compete. It teaches us to take responsibility for our livelihoods.

It teaches us to be businesspeople, not employees. To be capitalists, not hired hands. To be economic grown-ups, not economic children. That's the only way we can survive and thrive in today's new economy.

Maybe in the future we'll all approach work a little more the way Charlotte Eckley does.

Eckley is a young woman who graduated from Southwest Missouri State University in 1988. Her first job out of college was with Springfield ReManufacturing Corp. She worked in customer service and marketing. She learned the Great Game of Business, SRC's system of open-book management. Along the way she got married.

When the Gulf War came along, her husband was commissioned from the Marine Corps reserve into active duty and stationed in North Carolina. She went with him, and the couple ended up living there for a couple of years. Looking for a job, she got an interview with an automotive and industrial aftermarket parts company. They liked her experience and skills and offered her a position on the spot.

Schooled in open-book management, she asked them a question. Before I take this job, would you mind if I look over your financials?

The owner and two others who were interviewing her burst out laughing.

Sorry, they said, we don't let *anybody* see our financials.

Pity, thought Eckley, who was all of twenty-four. Without seeing them, she wouldn't have any idea what shape the company was in. Nor would she have much of an idea how to help it do better.

As it happened, she took the job anyway. Finding work as a military wife is difficult, and the company seemed like an OK place.

Once on the payroll, she did get to see some sales numbers—and discovered that revenues had dropped by several percent over the previous year. None of the employees had had a raise. Morale was poor.

Eckley asked the company's sales-and-service reps what the sales goal for this year was. There wasn't one. How did they track their performance? she wanted to know. Well, they said, we put a slash mark up on the wall there when one of us takes a call.

She wondered if there was any way of applying what she had learned at SRC to her new situation.

Hmm, she thought, even if the owner won't share all the financials, maybe he'll let us see sales and cost-of-goods data. That will let us calculate gross margin. Then we can set a goal for both sales and margin.

She put together an incentive package for the sales employees: sales targets, margin targets, modest financial rewards if they hit them. She proposed her plan to the owner, who approved it.

She next prepared a daily scorecard on how the company was doing. She sent a copy of the scorecard throughout the company, whose thirteen employees had never had any idea how sales were shaping up. The owner wouldn't give employees any cash rewards, but he agreed to give them extra time off if the company reached its goal.

Within two years after her arrival, Charlotte Eckley's new company had increased its sales more than 35 percent. Margins had held steady. Amazingly, the owner never did open the books completely. But just the little information Eckley was able to assemble made a huge difference in how the parts company's employees viewed their work.

Today, Eckley is back working at SRC.

But the fact is, she could work anywhere in today's new economy, particularly as more and more companies discover the astonishing power of open-book management and of people—grown-ups!—like Charlotte Eckley, who understand what it is to be in business.

# Next Steps . . .

Open-book management is a fast-growing and rapidly changing field. To learn more about how to implement it in your company, send for a free list of resources compiled by the author of this book. The list includes information on:

- the biweekly newsletter *Open-Book Management BULLETIN*
- consulting services and seminars in open-book management
- videos, workbooks, board games, and other training materials that open-book companies have found useful.

The list is available from:

John Case
37A Prentiss Street.
Cambridge, MA 02140
USA

24-hour voicemail: (617) 248-8457
Fax: (617) 492-3607
Internet: john_case@incmag.com

# References

The factual material in this book is mostly derived from interviews conducted by me or by Brendan Case in 1994 (see Acknowledgments). I also drew on work previously published in *Inc.* magazine, especially my article "Emancipation Capitalism" in the April 1993 issue.

Finally, I took some information from the following published sources, listed in roughly sequential order:

## Foreword

Chris Lee, "Open-Book Management," *Training,* July 1994.

## Introduction

Robert Frey, "Empowerment or Else," *Harvard Business Review,* September–October 1993 (including a contribution by Ocelia Williams, the former union shop steward); also Robert Frey, "The Empowered and the Glory," *Washington Post,* December 26, 1993.

## Chapter 1

Paul Krugman, *Peddling Prosperity* (New York and London: W.W. Norton & Co., 1994), pp. 257–59.

John Huey, "Waking Up to the New Economy," *Fortune,* June 27, 1994, p. 36 ff.

U.S. Bureau of the Census, *Statistical Abstract of the United States* (Washington, D.C.: U.S. Government Printing Office, 1992 and 1993 editions); also *Historical Statistics of the United States: Colonial Times to 1970* (Washington, D.C.: U.S. Government Printing Office, 1975).

Barbara Garson, *All the Livelong Day: The Meaning and Demeaning of Routine Work* (New York: Doubleday, 1975; paperback reissued by Penguin Books, 1994).

Neal Templin, "Team Spirit: A Decisive Response to Crisis Brought Ford Enhanced Productivity," *The Wall Street Journal,* December 15, 1992, p. 1.

Bridget O'Brian, "Southwest Airlines Is a Rare Air Carrier: It Still Makes Money," *The Wall Street Journal,* October 26, 1992, p. 1.

## Chapter 2

David Montgomery, *The Fall of the House of Labor* (Cambridge, England: Cambridge University Press, 1987).

Thomas J. Schlereth, *Victorian America: Transformations in Everyday Life* (New York: HarperCollins, 1991).

Tamara K. Hareven, *Family Time and Industrial Time* (Cambridge, England: Cambridge University Press, 1982).

Sanford M. Jacoby, *Employing Bureaucracy: Managers, Unions, and the Transformation of Work in American Industry, 1900–1945* (New York: Columbia University Press, 1985).

David A. Hounshell, *From the American System to Mass Production, 1800–1932* (Baltimore and London: The Johns Hopkins University Press, 1984).

Alfred D. Chander, Jr., *The Visible Hand: The Managerial Revolution in American Business* (Cambridge, Mass. and London: The Belknap Press of Harvard University Press, 1977).

Stuart D. Brandes, *American Welfare Capitalism, 1880–1940* (Chicago: University of Chicago Press, 1976).

Daniel Nelson, *Managers and Workers: Origins of the Factory System in the United States, 1880–1920* (Madison, Wisc.: University of Wisconsin Press, 1975).

Daniel Bell, *The End of Ideology* (New York: Collier Books, 1962).

Charles D. Wrege and Ronald G. Greenwood, *Frederick W. Taylor, The Father of Scientific Management: Myth and Reality* (Homewood, Ill.: Business One Irwin, 1991).

Barbara Garson, *All the Livelong Day: The Meaning and Demeaning of Routine Work.*

John Hoerr, *And the Wolf Finally Came: The Decline of the American Steel Industry* (Pittsburgh: University of Pittsburgh Press, 1988).

Michael Hammer and James Champy, *Reengineering the Corporation* (New York: HarperBusiness, 1993).

Thomas J. Peters and Robert H. Waterman, Jr., *In Search of Excellence* (New York: Warner Books, 1982).

Tom Peters, *Thriving on Chaos* (New York: Harper & Row, 1987).

Tom Peters, *Liberation Management* (New York: Alfred A. Knopf, 1992).

Philip B. Crosby, *Quality is Free* (New York: Mentor, 1980).

Rosabeth Moss Kanter, *When Giants Learn to Dance* (New York: Simon & Schuster, 1989).

John A. Byrne, "The Craze for Consultants," *Business Week,* July 25, 1994.

Jay Mathews, "Totaled Quality Management," *Washington Post,* June 6, 1993.

"The Big Picture" [chart], *Business Week,* November 7, 1994.

"Re-engineering Reviewed," *Economist,* July 2, 1994.

Brian Dumaine, "The Trouble with Teams," *Fortune,* September 5, 1994.

David H. Freedman, "Is Management Still a Science?" *Harvard Business Review,* November–December, 1992.

Jack Stack, with Bo Burlingham, *The Great Game of Business* (New York: Doubleday/Currency 1992; paperback 1994).

"Top Negotiators Ponder the Baseball Impasse," *The Wall Street Journal,* August 12, 1994.

Deirdre Carmody, "Retraining but No Layoffs, Fortune Editor Tells Staff," *New York Times,* June 9, 1994.

## Chapter 3

John Holusha, "LTV's Weld of Worker and Manager," *New York Times,* August 2, 1994.

David Greising, "Quality, How to Make It Pay," *Business Week,* August 8, 1994.

Chris Lee, "Open-Book Management."

## Chapter 4

Peter Drucker, *The Practice of Management* (New York: Harper & Row, 1954).

Charles A. Coonradt, with Lee Nelson, *The Game of Work* (Salt Lake City: Shadow Mountain, 1984).

Laurie Hays, "Blue Blood: IBM's Finance Chief, Ax in Hand, Scours Empire for Costs to Cut," *The Wall Street Journal,* January 26, 1994.

## Chapter 5

Ralph H. Saunders, "Behind the Labor Statistics," *Boston Globe,* March 1, 1994.

Lee Berton, "College Courses on Accounting Get Poor Grade," *The Wall Street Journal,* August 12, 1994.

## Chapter 6

Saul Hansell, "An End to the 'Nightmare' of Cash?" *New York Times,* September 6, 1994.

John Simmons and William Mares, *Working Together: Employee Participation in Action* (New York and London: New York University Press, 1985 paperback).

Judson Gooding, "It Pays to Wake Up the Blue-Collar Worker," *Fortune,* September 1970.

The Editors of Fortune, *Working Smarter* (New York: The Viking Press, 1982).

Brian Dumaine, "The Trouble with Teams."

Commission on the Future of Worker/Management Relations, "Mission Statement," mimeograph, 1993.

"Now Hear This" [Rich Teerlink quote], *Fortune,* August 22, 1994.

Jack Stack, with Bo Burlingham, *The Great Game of Business.*

Tom Peters, *Liberation Management.*

**Chapter 7**

Jack Stack, with Bo Burlingham, *The Great Game of Business*.
Robert Frey, "Empowerment or Else."
Edward O. Welles, "Bootstrapping for Billions," *Inc.,* September 1994.

**Chapter 8**

Bob Filipczak, "Why No One Likes Your Incentive Program," *Training,* August 1993.

**Chapter 9**

Tom Peters, *Liberation Management*.

**Chapter 14**

David Greising, "Quality, How to Make It Pay."

# Acknowledgments

This book owes its existence to all the people who are inventing and developing open-book management in their companies, and who took the time to share their experiences with me. Before I list some of their names, I want to single out a few other people who helped make the book possible.

Bo Burlingham and George Gendron, my friends and colleagues at *Inc.* magazine, have been helping to spread the word about open-book management for some time now. Bo—writer, consultant, coauthor of *The Great Game of Business,* author of a forthcoming book about the people of Springfield ReManufacturing Corp.—read this book in manuscript and offered many helpful comments. George, editor in chief of *Inc.,* has opened the magazine's pages to the experiences of open-book companies, has encouraged me and others to write about them, and has himself given numerous speeches on the subject. I have learned enormous amounts from both.

I owe a substantial debt to other colleagues as well.

At *Inc.,* Jeff Seglin read this book in manuscript and offered helpful suggestions. Nancy Lyons and Michael Hopkins edited the articles that eventually led to the book; Michael arranged for me to take time off to write it. Nancy Cardwell did a great job editing it.

My older son, Brendan Case, who worked as my research assistant, showed himself to be a skilled and savvy interviewer, thereby demonstrating that a little nepotism isn't necessarily a bad thing. I couldn't have covered nearly as much ground without his help. On the home front, Liam Case and Gina Grant listened to me ramble on about open-book management over many dinners—and didn't yawn more than once or twice.

My wife, Quaker Case, somehow found time to read this book, as she reads everything I write, and to help me make it better. How she does this in the midst of her own exacting career as a psychotherapist is beyond me.

Now for the open-book management folks. I wish I could list by name everyone Brendan or I spoke with, but I'll have to limit myself to the people we spent the most time with.

Jack Stack, president of Springfield ReManufacturing Corp. and the grandfather of open-book management, is in a class by himself. A visionary and teacher as well as a business leader, he not only has transformed SRC but has inspired hundreds of other companies to explore these ideas. Jack says in his book, *The*

*Great Game of Business,* that he wants to leave the world a better place. By my lights, he already has.

Special thanks to the people who invited us into their companies and took time from a busy workday to talk with us:

Gary Brown, Dan Rourke, Tom Samsel, Dennis Sheppard, Charlotte Eckley, and Denise Bredfeldt of SRC; Andy Crowder and many other employees of Pace Industries Cast-Tech Division; Bob Argabright, Yong Kim, David Shanahan, the members of Boxbusters, and other employees at Chesapeake Packaging Co.'s Baltimore plant; Steve Wilson and David McCracken of Mid-States Technical Staffing Services; Jack Kahl, Tom Corbo, Diego Perez-Stable, and Charlie MacMillan at Manco Inc.; Emma Lou Brent and many other employee-owners of Phelps County Bank; Rick Smith, Carl Hopkins, and Mary Hansen of Sprint's Government Systems Division; Richard Bohnet, Barry Fishman, and others at Acumen International; Bill Palmer of Commercial Casework; Mike Chiles and Dan Chiles of Heatway; Eric Gershman, Nancy Cohen, and the "Quality Matters" team of Published Image; Jim Sandstrom and others at Sandstrom Products; Evan Grossman of Share Systems; Eric Paulsen of Engines Plus; Terry Meek and Tom Buckner of Meeks Building Centers; Lynn Thompson of Thompson Pontiac and Cadillac; John (Bud) Colligan of Macromedia; Rick Surpin of Cooperative Home Care Associates; Gary Hershberg, Ed Souza, and John Horan of Stonyfield Farm; and Andrew Morris of Warner, Bicking, Morris & Partners.

And thanks to the many people who collectively spent hundreds of hours with us on the telephone or in face-to-face interviews in airports or at conferences. We learned from all of them:

Roger Wilhoit, Dean Krieter, and John McGrail of Allstate Business Insurance division; Ken Anderson of Anderson & Associates; Peter Metcalf and Clarke Kawakami of Black Diamond Equipment; Karen Delahunty of The Body Shop USA; Don Barkman of The Business Center; Deighton Brunson of Brunson Instrument Co.; John Schuster of Capital Connections; Kate Walters of Caring Home Support Services; Dennis Beach of Chaparral Steel; Mark Miller of Chick fil-A; Bob Frey of Cin-Made; Ed Zimmer of ECCO; Becky Cannon of Family Clubhouse; Chuck Mayhew of Foldcraft; Jim Schreiber of Herman Miller; Jeannette Hendrych of the Embedded Microcontroller Division, Intel; Jim Jenkins and Joe Jenkins of Jenkins Diesel Power; Leslie Fishbein of Kacey Fine Furniture; Craig Taylor and Mimi Taylor of Marketing Services by Vectra; Margaret Cossette of Missouri Home Health Care; Roger McDivitt and Alison May of Patagonia; Patrick Kelly of Physician Sales and Service; Ted Castle of Rhino Foods; Ann Rhoades of Southwest Airlines; Capt. Randy Clutter of the Springfield, Missouri, Police Department; David Lough of Towers Perrin; Neil Schmid of Viking Glass; Jerry Ehrlich and Chuck Fish of Wabash National; Charles Edmunson and Rob Zicaro of Web Industries; Chris Kowal and Teri Cassady of YSI; Ari Weinzweig and Paul Saginaw of Zingerman's Delicatessen; Jerry Hatcher of Zion, Inc.; and David Zapatka of Z-Tech Cos.

Thanks, too, to Steve Ashton and Cora Gangware of Ashton Photo; Jack Round of AMCI; Pam Haack of Carlson Travel Network; Dave Mileski of Cloverland Engines; Dave Wetmore of Crop Quest; Robin Richey of Darling Industries; Bill Wheeler of Dowty Aerospace; David Dwinell of Dwinell's Visual Systems; Keith Reynolds of Image National; Mike Mobey of Isabella County, Michigan, Transportation Commission; Liza Webb of Kaiser Permanente; Steve Voigt of King Arthur Flour; Don Critten of Landmark Manufacturing; Ed Peterlinz of L. Karp & Sons; Bill Main of Landscape Forms; Bill Lytle; Jack McDonnell of McData Inc.; Tony Castaldo of MicroScope; Brad Brunts of Prudential Home Mortgage; Michael Cross of QED Environmental Systems; Ron Fendrick of Quaker Chemical; Shep Beyland of Rome Cable Corp.; Mary Wendt of Scot Forge; Rick McCloskey of System Connection; David Hobba of Tyler Mountain Water; Chuck Nason of Worzalla Publishing Co.; Dean Bodem of Viking Engineering and Development.

Finally, a word of thanks to a few pioneers of employee ownership. Their names may not appear in the book, but they're among the people who first got me thinking about different ways to run a company:

Corey Rosen of the National Center for Employee Ownership; Michael Quarrey and Robert Sloss of Connor Formed Metal Products; Cecil Ursprung and David Edgar of Reflexite Inc.; and Malte von Matthiessen of YSI.

# Index

Accountability, employee, 89–92
  huddle system, 90–92
Accounting Game, The, 80
Acme Parts Inc., 5
Acumen International, xiv, 64–67
  ESOP of, 118–19
  Kellow principle and, 64–66
Agricultural work, 10–12
Airline industry, 102, 175. See also
        Southwest Airlines
Allegheny Ludlum Corp., 175
Allstate Business Insurance, xi, 34, 173
  business literacy and, 82
All the Livelong Day (Garson), 12
American Management Association, 22
Amoskeag textile mills, 19, 22
Anchor Steam beer, 7
Anderson, Ken, 47, 93
Anderson & Associates, 47, 70
And the Wolf Finally Came (Hoerr), 24
Anheuser-Busch, 7
Ansara, Mike, 116
Argabright, Bob, 34, 123–26, 128–29
Armour & Co., 22
Ashton, Steve, 116
Ashton Photo, 34, 116
Assembly lines, 12–13
Automobile industry, 5
Avis, 108

Baer, Tom, 7
Baltimore & Ohio Railroad (B&O), 86

Barkman, Don, 83
Beach, Dennis, 32
Beer industry, 7
Berra, Yogi, 175
Bethlehem Steel, 23
B.F. Goodrich tire factory, 24
Biz Wiz, 83
Black Diamond Equipment, 75
Blue-collar workers, 22–23
Bob's Big Boys, 125, 126
Body Shop, The, 9–10, 79, 80, 173
Bohnet, Richard (Dick), xiv, 118–19
Bonuses, 105–8, 115
  amount of, 105–6
  division of pool of, 106–7
  information distributed with, 115–16
  at Mid-States Technical Staffing
        Services, Inc., 134–35
  pitfalls of, 97–101
    discretionary plans, 98–99
    incomprehensible plans, 99
    invisible plans, 99–100
    same payment, 99
  at Sprint Government Systems Division,
        159
  timing of, 107–8
Boston Globe, 74
Bottom line, focus on, 162–64
Boxbusters, 125, 127
Boyda, Melanie, 151–53
Brandeis, Louis D., xxiii
Brandes, Stuart D., 19

Bredfeldt, Denise, 32–33, 80, 120

Brent, Emma Lou, xii, 106, 146–49, 151, 152

Bucket plan, 107, 130–36

Budget, information about, 64

Bunning, Jim, 35

Bureaucracy, 22, 25, 26

Burlingham, Bo, 33

Business
    definition of, xvii
    metaphors for, 51–53

Business center idea, 93–95

Business illiteracy, prevalence of, 74–75

Business literacy, 73–84
    at Chesapeake Packaging Corp., 125–26
    decision making and, 77
    education and
        classroom instruction, 78–80
        reinforcement, 81–84
    labor unions and, 76
    at Manco, Inc., 142
    at Mid-States Technical Staffing Services, Inc., 135
    at Phelps County Bank (PCB), 148–49
    power of, 75–78
    waste curtailment and, 76–77

Businesspeople, companies of, 175–80

*Business Weekly* (magazine), 48

Byrne, John A., 28


Callahan, Jack, 173

Capital Connections, 82, 154

Carpenter, Jill, 155

Carter, Craig, 155

Carter, Jimmy, 124

Cashless society, 85–86

Castle, Ted, 34, 69

Castleman, Don, 147

Challenge, The, 116–17

Challenge Team, 155–59, 173

Champy, James, 25–27

Chandler, Alfred D., Jr., 22

Chaparral Steel, 32

Chesapeake Maintenance Services, 125

Chesapeake Packaging Corp., 34, 45, 108, 123–29
    internal companies of
        background, 123–24
        how it works, 124–26

    payoffs, 127–29
    profit sharing at, 126

Chiles, Dan, 112

Chiles, Mike, 50, 112, 120

Cin-Made, xv–xviii, 45, 76, 173
    profit sharing at, xvi–xvii, 99

Clinton, Bill, 34, 87

Clutter, Randy, 35–36

Colgate-Palmolive, 14

Colligan, Bud, 165

Commercial Casework, xii, 64
    business literacy and, 80

Commission on the Future of Worker/Management Relations, 87

Companies. *See also specific companies*
    of businesspeople, 175–80
    change in, 57–60. *See also specific topics*
        business situation, 57–58
        downsizing, 59
        perseverance, 59–60
    nonprofit, 165–66
    publicly traded, 171–72
    size of, xxii
    as social organizations, 46
    success of. *See* Success, company

Competition, 3–10
    business planning and, 15
    entrepreneurialization and, 7–10
    execution of business strategy and, 15–17
    globalization and, 4–5
    information revolution and, 5–7

Computers (computer industry), 5–6, 13
    Kellow principle and, 64–66
    staff meetings and, 62–63

Congress, U.S., 108

Connell, David, 148

Construction-related business, 64

Continuous learning, 49–50

Coondradt, Charles, 63–64

Coopers & Lybrand, 34–35

Corbo, Tom, xiii, 106, 140, 142, 144, 173

Corrugator Specialties Unlimited, 125

Cotton mills, 19

Craig, Angel, 127

Crawley, Paul, 173

Crop Quest, 70

Crosby, Phil, 27

Cross-functional team, 87–88
Crowder, Andy, 39–42, 44, 48, 106
CSC/Index, 29

Davey, Martin L., 23
Decision making, 77, 121–22
Delahunty, Karen, 80, 173
Delta Air Lines, 175
Department stores, 49
Diapers, disposable, 14–15
Dodd, Donna, 42
Douglas, Patti, 146, 149–52, 150
Downsizing, 59
Drucker, Peter, 11, 61–63
Drugstores, 9–10
Drypers Corp., 14–15
Dwinell, David R., xii, 68
Dwinell's Visual Systems, xii, 68

Eaton Corp., 13, 69
ECCO (Electronic Controls Co.), xii, 114
    goals of, 104–5
Eckley, Charlotte, 178–79
Economy
    global, 4–5
    service, emergence of, 10–11
Edmunson, Charles, 81, 109
Education, business, 22, 27
    business literacy and, 78–84
        classroom instruction, 78–80
        reinforcement, 81–84
    continuous learning and, 49–50
    Great Game of Business seminars and,
        34, 40
    at Phelps County Bank (PCB), 148–49
    at Sprint Government Systems Division,
        156–58
Educational Discoveries, Inc., 80
Ehrlich, Jerry, 31, 78
Employee involvement. *See* Empowerment
Employees. *See* Labor force
Employee stock ownership plan (ESOP),
        108–9, 118–19, 143
    at Phelps County Bank (PCB), 147,
        150–52
Empowerment (participatory manage-
        ment), 26, 28, 30, 85–96
    accountability and, 89–92
    with brains, 87–90

business transparency and, 89
    at Chesapeake Packaging Corp., 126
    final advice on, 95–96
    implementation of, 90–95
        collection of smaller-but-identical
            companies, 92–93
        company within a company (business
            center idea), 93–95
        huddle system, 90–92
    at Manco, Inc., 142
    at Mid-States Technical Staffing
        Services, Inc., 133–34
    at Phelps County Bank (PCB), 149–51
    teamwork and, 87–88, 93
    as trend that never happened, 86–87
Engineering, rise of, 20–21
Engines Plus, xii, 102, 115–16
Entrepreneurialization, 7–10
Equity. *See* Stock ownership
Ernst & Young, 28–29
ESOP. *See* Employee stock ownership
        plan
Execution of business strategy, 15–17
Executive Training Institute, 34, 40
Exports, 4

Factory work, 12–14
Farming, 10–12
Feedback, information as, 63–64
Fidelity Investments, 4
Financial goals, 102–5
    focus on, 162–64
Fishbein, Leslie, xi, 45–46, 71–72, 111,
        116
Flanders, Sherry, 94
Flexo department, 125, 127
Foldcraft Inc., xiii, 94, 104, 114–15
    business literacy and, 79–80
Ford, Henry, 20
Ford Motor Company
    Highland Park plant of, 18, 19
    Walton Hills metal stamping plant of, 13
Foreman's empire, 20, 21
*Fortune* (magazine), 6, 29, 35, 87
Fotsch, Bill, 82–83
Freedman, David H., 29
Freeman, Barbara, 148
Frey, Bob, xv–xviii, 76, 99, 115, 173
Fulwiler, Terry, xiii, 81–82

Gaines dog-food plant, 87
Game metaphor. *See* Great Game of
    Business
*Game of Work, The* (Coonradt), 63–64
Games
    business education and, 80, 82
    learning and, 120–21
    starting open-book management and,
        116–18
Garson, Barbara, 12
Gates, Bill, 138
General Motors, xxiii, 24, 175, 177
Generosity, 168
Gershman, Eric, 92–93, 111, 115
Globalization, competition and, 4–5
Goals, business
    affecting the outcome of, 104
    ambitious but attainable, 104–5
    financial, 102–5, 162–64
    fiscally responsible, 104
    importance of, 103
    operational, 102
    public tracking of, 103–4
    setting of, 103
Goethe, Johann Wolfgang von, 177
Gompers, Samuel, 47
Goodyear Tire & Rubber, 95
Graham, Ruth, 125
Granite Rock Co., 4–5, 12
Great Game of Business, xxiii, 33–36, 52,
        90, 154, 155
    seminars on, 34, 40
*Great Game of Business, The* (Stack, with
        Burlingham), xxiii, 33, 34, 95
Green, Tim, 127
Greising, David, 48
Gross domestic product (GDP), 4
Grossman, Evan, 116–17

Hall, Bill, 144
Hammer, Michael, 25–27
Hansen, Mary, xiv, 156, 159, 160
Hardcastle, Danny, 41
*Harvard Business Review,* 29
Hatcher, Jerry, 83
Hawthorne experiments, 167
Health maintenance organizations
        (HMOs), xviii–xix, 9, 66
    Meaningless Bonus and, 100–101

Heatway, 102, 112, 120
Helena Rubenstein, 12
Hendrych, Jeannette, 82
Henkelman, Leo, 122
Herman Miller, xi, 31–32, 70, 87
Hoerr, John, 24
Holiday Inn, xxiv
Homely truths, 43–45
Homestead (PA), U.S. Steel complex in,
        18, 19
Hopkins, Carl, 155, 156, 158–60
Hotel business, xxiv, 16
Huddle system, 90–92

IBM, xxiii, 67, 77
Imports, 4
*Inc.* (magazine), 6, 33, 35, 69
*Industry Week,* 138
Information, 61–72
    bonuses attached to distribution of,
        115–16
    at Chesapeake Packaging Corp., 125
    confronting the great fear about,
        70–72
    financial, 62–72, 75–76
        budget, 64
        Kellow principle, 64–67
        right, 66–68
        scoreboards, 68–69
    Kellow principle and, 64–67
    at Manco, Inc., 139–42
    meetings and, 62–63, 69–70
    at Mid-States Technical Staffing
        Services, Inc., 132–33
    at Phelps County Bank (PCB), 148
    power of, 63–66
    at Sprint Government Systems Division,
        156
    understanding. *See* Business literacy
Information revolution, 5–7
Innovation, 49
    at Manco, Inc., 138
*In Search of Excellence* (Peters and
        Waterman), 26
Insurance, 25
Insurance companies, 49
Intel Corp., Embedded Microcontroller
        Division (EMD) of, 82, 120–21
Internal Revenue Service (IRS), 8

International Harvester (now Navistar), xxiii, 32

Inventory accuracy at Pace Industries, 41–42, 48

Japan, 4, 174
  auto industry in, 5
Jenkins, Jim, 81, 114
Jenkins, Joe E., xiii, 169
Jenkins Diesel Power, xiii, 81, 114, 169
J.I. Case, 82–83
Jobs
  manual, 11–12
  narrowly defined, 20

Kacey Fine Furniture, xi, 45–46, 71–72, 75, 102, 111, 116
Kahl, Jack, 137–40
Kanter, Rosabeth Moss, 27–28, 29, 174
Kawakami, Clark, 75
Keane-Fowler, Ornaith, 65, 67
Kelleher, Herb, 30
Kellow, Rob, 64–66, 119
Kellow principle, 64–67
Kelly, Patrick C., xiii, 172
Kiechel, Walter, III, 35
Kieffer, Jim, 130, 131, 133
Kim, Yong, 125–26, 128
Kimberly-Clark, 14
K mart, xxiii
Knowledge work, manual jobs and, 11–14
Kohl, Jerry, 6–8
Krueger, Kevin, 140
Krugman, Paul, 4

Labor force (workers)
  blue-collar (industrial), 19, 22–23
  close, direct supervision of, 20
  white-collar, 11, 21–23
    business illiteracy, 74–75
Labor unions, 47–48
  business literacy and, 76
  Cin-Made and, xv–xvii
  rise of, 23–24
  strikes and, xvi, 19, 23
Landers, Ann, 57
Learning
  continuous, 49–50
  as game, 120–21

Leather belts, 6–7
Lee, Chris, xiv, 50, 89
Leegin Creative Leather Products Inc., 6–7
*Liberation Management* (Peters), 26, 93
Little Steel strike (1937), 23

McCormick reaper plant, 18
McCracken, Dave, 130, 131, 136
McDivitt, Roger, 97
McDonnell Douglas, 28
MacMillan, Charlie, 107, 139–42
Macromedia, Inc., 68, 94, 165
MacTemps Inc., 6
Management
  adversarial unions and, 23–24
  open-book. *See* Open-book management
  paradigm for, 20
  participatory. *See* Empowerment
  professionalization of, 21–23
  scientific, 20–23
Manco, Inc., xiii, xxiii, 45, 58, 68–69
  bonuses of, 106
  Wal-Mart model of, 137–44
    background, 137–39
    how it works, 139–43
    payoffs, 143–44
Mantooth, Teri, 13
Manual jobs, knowledge work and, 11–14
Marketplace demands
  competition and, 3–10
    entrepreneurialization, 7–10
    globalization, 4–5
    information revolution, 5–7
  new workplace and, 10–14
Marshall, Bill, 148
Martin, Estel, 127
Martin, Tom, 66
Mayhew, Chuck, xiii, 79–80, 94, 104, 114–15
Maytag, Fritz, 7
Meat-packing plants, 19
Medco Containment Services, 9
Medical-technology businesses, 49
Meetings, 69–70, 170–71
  at Springfield ReManufacturing Corp. (SRC), 62–63, 69–70
Melvin A. Andersen, 137
Metal-bending manufacturers, 49
Metaphor, power of, 51–53

Microsoft, 172
Mid-States Technical Staffing Services,
    Inc., xiv, 72, 108, 173
  bonuses of, 106, 107
  bucket plan of, 130–36
    background, 130–31
    how it works, 131–35
    payoffs, 135–36
  business literacy and, 80
Miller, Mark, 167
Miller, Ronnie, xxii, 42
Mills, textile, 19, 22
Mills, Wally, 16
Mistrust, employee, 46–47
Monroe City Chamber of Commerce, 42
Montgomery, David, 21
Moore, Sydney, 62–63
Motivation, 168–69
Mueller, Adolph, 146

National Labor Relations Act (Wagner Act,
    1935), 23
Navistar. *See* International Harvester
Nelson, Daniel, 20
"Net Results," 34
New economy
  characteristics of, xix–xx
  old-style management and, 24–29
*New York Times,* 35, 86
No-excuses management, 89–92
Nonprofit companies, 165–66
Nucor, 102

Objectives, business, xx, 15
Old-style management
  new economy and, 24–29
  origin of, 18–24
Open-book management
  basics of, 37–38
  birth of, xix–xx, 29–36
  coining of phrase, 33–34
  components of, xx
  getting started with, 111–22
    among the managers, 113–15
    announce the end of annual raises,
      115
    ask people to show how they make
      money for the company, 119–20
    business games, 116–18

decision making, 121–22
    ESOP, 118–19
    "guess the gross" or "guess the
      costs," 112–13
    information distribution with a bonus
      attached, 115–16
    learning as game, 120–21
  homely truths of, 43–45
  implementation of, 55–180. *See also*
      Business literacy; Empowerment;
      Information; *and specific compa-
      nies*
    case studies, 123–61
    getting started, 111–22
  information sources for, 181
  as no-excuses management, 89–92
  questions and answers about, 162–74
  what it is not, xxi–xxii
  why it works, 45–51
Operational goals, 102
OTR Express (OTRX), 8
Owners, thinking and acting like, 30–32,
    108, 168

Pace Industries, 38–45, 50, 69, 108, 173
  bonuses of, 106
  Cast-Tech Division of, 39–45, 102
  inventory accuracy at, 41–42, 48
  scrap reduction at, 42, 48
  turnaround at, 38–43, 45
Palmer, Bill, xii, 64, 67, 80
Palmer, Tom, 70
Paradigm, management, 20
Participatory management. *See*
    Empowerment
Partnership, business as, 30
Paulsen, Eric, xii, 115–16
PCS Health Systems, 9
Perez-Stable, Diego, 141–42
Perkins, Orie, 42
Perseverance, 59–60
Peters, Tom, 26–27, 93, 95, 127
Phelps County Bank (PCB), xii, 45, 58,
    108
  bonuses of, 106
  employee takeover at, 145–53
    background, 145–47
    how it works, 147–51
    payoffs, 151–53

Physician Sales and Services, xiii, 172
Pitney-Bowes Management Services, 29
Plan, business, 15
Planning, at Sprint Government Systems
    Division, 156
Polaroid, 108
Posner, Barry, 177
Poyfair, Will, Jr., 21
*Practice of Management, The* (Drucker),
    61
Prock, Bonita, 150
Procter & Gamble (P&G), 14–15, 87, 108
Professionalization of management, 21–23
Profit and Cash (game), 82, 120–21
Profit and loss (P&L) responsibility,
    xvii–xviii, 94, 95, 157
Profit sharing, 30
    amount of, 105–6
    at Chesapeake Packaging Corp., 126
    at Cin-Made, xvi–xvii, 99
    pitfalls of, 97–101
        discretionary plans, 98–99
        incomprehensible plans, 99
        invisible plans, 99–100
        same payment, 99
Publicly traded companies, 171–72
Published Image, Inc., 92–93, 111, 115
Publix Supermarkets, 108

Quality College, 27
Quality (quality systems), 27–29, 67. *See
    also* Total Quality Management
    assessment of, 28–29

Raglin, Marlene, 127
Raises, annual, 115
Reengineering, xxi–xxii, 27–29, 167
    assessment of, 29
*Reengineering the Corporation* (Hammer
    and Champy), 25–27
Reflexite Inc., 118
Renew Center, 32
Republic Engineered Steel, 108
Resentment, employee, 46–47
Responsibility
    empowerment and, 89–90
    fiscal, of payout, 104
    P&L. *See* Profit and loss (P&L) respon-
        sibility

Rhino Foods, xiii, 34, 69
Rhoades, Ann, 31
Rooney, Chris, 154, 158
Roth, Mia, 173
Ryan, Steve, 41, 43, 45, 106

Saginaw, Paul, 94
Sales departments, 48
Sanders, Jody, 146
Sandstrom, Jim, 58, 71, 115, 121–22, 176
Sandstrom Products, Inc., 115, 121–22,
    176–77
Scanlon, Joseph, 31, 87
Scanlon Plan, 31, 87
Schmid, Neil, xiv, 111
Schreiber, Jim, xi, 31–32
Schuster, John, 89, 154, 155
Scientific management, 20–23
Scoreboards, 68–69
Scrap reduction at Pace Industries, 42,
    48
Sears Auto Centers, 117–18
Security and Exchange Commission
    (SEC), 171
Self-managing work team, 88
Service economy, emergence of, 10–11
Shanahan, Dave, 125, 127, 128
Share Systems Inc., 116–17
Smith, Rick, 68, 156–58
Smith, Samuel H., xiii, 117, 164
Smith, Winston, 125–27
Smith & Company, Engineers, xiii, 117,
    118, 164
Social organizations, companies as, 46
Software industry, 49
Sole proprietorships, 8
Southwest Airlines, 15–16, 30–31, 112
Specialization, 20, 28
Springfield Police Department, 35–36
Springfield ReManufacturing Corp.
    (SRC), xix, xxii, xxiii, 32–34, 40,
    43, 52, 60, 154, 169
    bonuses at, 107
    Eckley at, 178–80
    Executive Training Institute of, 34, 40
    Fotsch's visit to, 82–83
    huddle system and, 90–92
    staff meetings at, 62–63, 69
    10-20-30-40 system of, 107

Sprint Government Systems Division, xiv,
    57–58, 68, 154–61, 173
  background of, 154–55
  business illiteracy and, 74–75
  business literacy at, 79
  how it works, 155–59
  payoffs at, 159–61
Stack, Jack, xxiii–xxiv, 32–36, 40, 41, 60,
    95, 107, 109–10, 120, 131, 154,
    168, 169
  huddle system and, 90–91
Staples, 7
STATS Inc., 6
Steel industry, 23–25, 102, 175
  labor unions and, 23, 24
Steffens, Jim, 158
Stock ownership, 30, 32, 78, 108–10
  ESOP (employee stock ownership plan),
    108–9, 118–19, 143, 147, 150–51
  at Phelps County Bank (PCB), 147,
    150–52
Stonyfield Farm, 34
Strategy, business, 15, 168
Strikes, xvi, 19, 23
Success, company, employee stake in, 38,
    46–47, 97–110. *See also* Profit
    sharing; Stock ownership
  Chesapeake Packaging Corp., 126
  financial goals, 102–5
  Manco, Inc., 142–43
  Mid-States Technical Staffing Services,
    Inc., 134–35
  open-book approach, 101–2
  Phelps County Bank (PCB), 150–51
Supervisors, 12–14, 21, 77

Taxes, 8
Taylor, Craig, xiv, 105
Taylor, Frederick W., 21
Teague, Linda, 43
Teamwork, 28, 167
  assessment of, 29
  cross-functional, 87–88
  empowerment and, 87–88, 93
  self-managing, 88
  at Sprint Government Systems Division,
    155–61, 173
Technology, 13
  information revolution and, 5–7

  specialization and, 20
  wage cuts and, 19
Teerlink, Richard, 88
Telecommunications industry, 9, 49
10-20-30-40 system, 107
360-degree personal-assessment systems,
    64–66
3M Corp., 138
*Thriving on Chaos* (Peters), 26
Total Quality Management (TQM), xxi, 5,
    12, 27, 48, 167
TQM. *See* Total Quality Management
Training. *See* Education, business
Trucking companies, 8
Truck-trailer manufacturing, 31
Trust, employee, 47

Understanding business, 30, 37, 50. *See
    also* Business literacy
Undertaker, use of term, 7
Unemployment, 19
Unions. *See* Labor unions
United Auto Workers, 24
United Rubber Workers, 24
United States Steel (U.S. Steel), 18, 19
  labor unions and, 24
  management of, 25
United Steel Workers of America, 24
University of Southern California, 87

Varian Associates Inc., 48, 167
Vectra, xiv, 108
  bonuses of, 106–7
  goals of, 102–3, 105
Viking Glass, xiv, 111
*Visible Hand, The* (Chandler), 22

Wabash National, 31, 78
Wages, xvii
  cuts in, xv–xvi
Wallace Co., 28, 167
*Wall Street Journal,* 13, 15–16, 28, 33, 75,
    175
Wal-Mart, 108, 137–39, 172. *See also*
    Manco, Inc., Wal-Mart model of
Walpole, Dick, 8
Ward, Bill, 8
Ward, Kathy, 8
Waste, discouraging, 76–77

Waterman, Robert, 26
Watertown (MA), arsenal of, 23
Wealth, 78
Web Industries, 81, 109
Weinzweig, Ari, 94
Welch, Jack, 138
Whitcomb, Connie, 133
White-collar workers, 11, 21–23
  business illiteracy of, 74–75
Williams, Ocelia, xvii
Williamson, Leona, 146
Wilson, Steve, xiv, 72, 80, 173
  bucket plan of, 107, 130–36
Wisconsin Label Group, xiii, 81–82
Woblesky, Robert, xii
Workdays, length of, 19
Workplace, new, 10–14

Workplace participation. *See*
  Empowerment

XEL Communications Inc., 13

York, Jerome, 67, 77
"You Bet We Can Can-Can" campaign,
  146
Young, Todd, 41
*Yo Yo Company, The,* 80
YSI, 94

Zapatka, David, xii, 35, 113–14
Zicaro, Rob, 93
Zimmer, Ed, xii, 105, 114
Zingerman's, 94
Z-Tech Companies, Inc., xii, 35, 113–14